Ditch the Flip-Flops

Ditch the Flip-Flops

Ace Your Job Interview
Fresh Out of College

Sylvia I. Landy

Keystone Three LLC • Winnetka, Illinois

Ditch the Flip-Flops
Ace Your Job Interview Fresh Out of College
Copyright © 2007 by Sylvia I. Landy

For more information about this book, go to
www.keystonethree.com or www.ditchtheflipflops.com.

Library of Congress Control Number: 2006909229

ISBN-10: 0-9790265-0-4
ISBN-13: 978-0-9790265-0-8

**Library of Congress Cataloging-in-Publication Data
available from the publisher.**

Published by Keystone Three LLC • Winnetka, Illinois

For the boys, who keep me hungry and foolish:

Jimmie, Jamie, Andy and Michael

Contents

Plug In

Connect

Power Up

Introduction

THIS BOOK IS PAYBACK. Yes, I owe you. I put as much head and heart into these pages as I've had the good fortune to reap from your earnest peer group throughout the years. As a result, my advice is as sincere as it is relevant.

I equip soon-to-be degree holders and recent college grads with the skills to ace their toughest test yet: the job interview. Nothing in school has prepared you for the brutal scrutiny of HR managers and the fierce competition you will encounter while trying to land your dream job.

Each year, over 2.5 million graduates vie with one another—and a pool of polished, older applicants—for attractive perks and salaries. Despite a fervent desire to leverage a rigorous and costly education, several hundred thousand students fresh from hallowed halls are left high and dry, because there aren't enough jobs to go around. This predicament will continue throughout the next decade as the number of degree holders outstrips career opportunities across many industries.

While there is an obvious need for savvy interviewing advice, only a handful of resources address the very specific needs of the new grad recruit. Our bookshelves and experts augment a more experienced candidate—one who has been around the job-hunting block a time or two. Or one who is easily lured into believing the erroneous notion touted by far too many titles these days: it's possible to negotiate the treacherous interview learning curve in twenty-four hours, in mere seconds, or even via smoke and mirrors.

On the other hand, campus career-counseling offices provide invaluable interviewing support with hardworking, dedicated staff members at the helm. With personnel stretched to the max and too few hours in the day, however, these professionals sometimes fail to deliver critical details or build necessary momentum for twentysomethings. There simply isn't enough time to fully prepare you, and everyone else, for what lies ahead as you face recruiter after recruiter.

Ditch the Flip-Flops changes all this by teaching new graduates the keys to interviewing success: plug in through A-to-Z preparation; forge meaningful connections via a thoughtful, concerted effort; and power up in the homestretch with initiative and perseverance. I distill two decades of pertinent experiences into manageable strategies to accomplish these objectives.

In the twenty years since I graduated from Northwestern University's Kellogg School of Management with an MBA, I've recruited, hired, and worked side by side with scores of young adults. Early on, I launched a healthcare products start-up from my basement and later sold the nationwide concern to a Fortune 500 giant. I then partnered with another Kellogg grad to spearhead two additional initiatives—one was a for-profit company and the other a nonprofit organization. As a result, I routinely interfaced with managers from a broad range of industries across the country. I had the unique opportunity to see and learn a lot.

From the beginning, my hiring efforts focused on recent degree holders as a calculated cost-cutting measure. However, these recruits quickly became the cream of the crop. I noted how inexperience was supplanted by an unstoppable drive when expectations were clear and goals were well defined. Virtually since day one, new college grads have fortified my rank and file, and I've never looked back.

While my advice is based on these hands-on experiences and positive outcomes, I've also tapped into the trenches for additional wisdom. I enthusiastically share the down and dirty from recently employed college grads and keen insights from seasoned Human-Resources professionals. You can be sure that the opinions cited on the following pages represent a clear-cut consensus of those who are in the know. I gathered this tried-and-true input from conversations conducted over many years, where I made a point to collect both quantity and quality.

As a result, *Ditch the Flip-Flops* expertly arms interviewees with essential fundamentals and cutting-edge tools that are applicable to a majority of job interviewing situations. Included are innovative PR strategies to get you noticed, a fail-safe formula for answering both predictable and curveball questions, and timely cyberspace shortcuts and showstoppers. I also equip you to put your best foot forward when interviews take an uncomfortable turn. A round of rapid-fire interrogation from a roomful of no-nonsense head honchos, an eleventh-hour attack of nerves, or an illicit line of questioning are all nail-biters you can master. All in all, this book is Interviewing 101 at its guts-and-glory best.

Most of you will use this comprehensive guide as a reference manual after thumbing through from cover to cover. You'll pick up *Ditch* frequently, but sporadically, to seek guidance as you encounter one interviewing challenge after another. This is because focusing on the demands of the hour often yields the most effective plan of attack. When it's time to plunk down a tidy sum for that pristine business suit, chapter 5 carefully maps out the head-to-toe standard recruiters expect. Weeks later, after you leave the building the day of your interview, you can consult chapter 12 for a blueprint proven to solidify your fit with a particular organization.

Several basic themes are emphasized repeatedly in this book since they are applicable across a number of critical interviewing moments. Recent college grads confirm that the repetition of key ideas actually bolsters rather than bores when it comes to such high stakes. After all, you're being asked to step up in ways you've never experienced. This transition is a tough pill to swallow in one big gulp.

I'm very sensitive to what you're going through right now. There will be times when you greet important people by the wrong name, reference incorrect facts, arrive a few minutes late, or use a salad fork to cut into your entrée. These shoot-me-now moments happen to all of us, all the time. While these blunders gnaw away at you as being larger than life, they aren't defining moments if you proceed diligently.

It is your sincere effort, rather than robotic perfection, that will carry the day. Recruiters unanimously confirm that informed and enthusiastic candidates who give it their all create a hire-me imprint at every turn.

I connect the dots to instill you with "give it your all" purpose and substance. I go back to square one where we launched our first successful venture together and I realized that straightforward advice and well-defined goals were the ticket to your success. Using this same approach, I help you to own the responsibility and the opportunity of each interviewing challenge you will encounter.

Suddenly, you become the candidate to beat. You have the best chance to defy the sign of our times with newly acquired confidence and a paycheck-worthy style. There's no other way for anyone with a pricey diploma hot off the press to ace the interview test and clinch that dream job.

I wouldn't steer you wrong; I owe you as much.

PLUG IN

PLUG IN

COLLEGE SOLIDIFIES A BRUTAL reality: preparation is the difference between pass or flunk, win or lose, and feast or famine. The lack thereof is the universal deal breaker.

Even something as mundane as painting a room drives home the point; scraping, sanding, and taping are the most noteworthy, salable details of this bright idea. Benjamin Moore is almost an afterthought.

The interview process after a soup-to-nuts prep may not be as sweatfree as a bucket of Dove Gray latex and a drop cloth. But you're definitely headed toward a smooth finish when you make a concerted effort on the front end. And like that freshly painted room gleaming with high gloss possibilities, this is what you're aiming for as you face recruiter after recruiter.

Chapter 1

Stay Hungry. Stay Foolish.

*"Did that commencement address just advise us to rest on our laurels
and not let any grass grow under our feet?"*
*—Recent Graduate, Finance Major and International
Development Minor, University of Michigan*

*His goal: "New York; making enough money
to live on the non-funky side of town."*

THE STRATEGY THAT PAVES the way to clinching a job centers on the counsel offered by our first search engine, which happened to be offline. In the 1970s, the *Whole Earth Catalog* astutely insinuated that satisfaction and success are best accomplished by adhering to this credo: "Stay hungry. Stay foolish." Packaged around "purpose" and "effective" today, the advice still rings true and is the impetus upon which your interview process—and ultimately much more—will flourish.

This chapter focuses on fortifying your hunger and foolishness, your purpose and effectiveness. Some of the suggestions address attitude and creativity, while other recommendations zero in on mechanics and hard copy. You establish a rock-solid foundation for your interviewing process when you adhere to these insights. With this bedrock intact, you will have the best chance to maximize your efforts and realize life-changing outcomes in the pages and days ahead.

A Positive, Urgent Verve

For a variety of reasons, you need both an upbeat attitude and an action-oriented approach as you launch your interview process and tackle the numerous challenges along the way. Job applicants, particularly inexperienced ones, radiate an aura that is deftly picked up by most interviewers' well-calibrated antennae. Additionally, an enthusiastic, get-it-done style is simply self-preservation during recruiting season.

There's no better way to accomplish this positive, urgent verve than buying into the facts. For starters, wrap your arms around these two givens:

1. Among millions of recent college grads competing for the same jobs each year, most need suitable employment sooner rather than later.
2. An optimistic, earnest demeanor beats out a pout and blasé manner each and every time.

Then take the time to gauge your own need for employment. An honest assessment of this personal reality should stoke the fire in your belly.

Next, concentrate on the smile in your head and on your face. Recognize the advantageous position you're in as a degree holder and as someone who did a lot to get where you are. All in all, you have a lot to be happy about, and it's important to personally accept your stature as legitimate.

Now, step back to survey the lay of the land. If you own this moment in all its guts and glory, casual indifference (and an ineffective interview process) won't have a prayer. Basically, this is mojo at its best.

Own Your A-to-Z Reality

The following questionnaire encourages you to think hard about details that are meaningful to your life—and meaningful to the process unfolding at your feet. When you go into interviews with your eyes wide open, fully cognizant of your personal circumstances, you are more apt to be focused and results-oriented. Without a doubt, knowledgeable and hungry sales people strike more bargains than clueless, reluctant bystanders.

My five greatest financial obligations (such as loan repayment, health/
car insurance, rent/mortgage, food, transportation, telephone,
clothing, and so on) during the twelve months following graduation
are:

1. _____

2. _____

3. _____

4. _____

5. _____

The approximate monthly cost of each of these five financial
obligations is:

1. _____

2. _____

3. _____

4. _____

5. _____

My five greatest financial obligations over the next five years are:

1. _____

2. _____

3. _____

4. _____

5. _____

The approximate annual cost of each of these five financial obligations is:

1. _____
_____

2. _____
_____

3. _____
_____

4. _____
_____

5. _____
_____

I understand the difference between gross and net pay and appreciate that there is a material difference, impacting the amount of money available for spending purposes.

YES   NO (circle one)

Provide a brief definition of both net pay and gross pay:
_____
_____
_____
_____

Convert $42,000 gross to net pay (for an exact calculation, go online to a search engine and enter "net pay calculation"):
_____
_____
_____

This net annual amount equals (approximately) how much income on a monthly basis?
_____
_____
_____

I understand that benefits (including vacation time, health/dental insurance, sick days, personal days, pension, tuition, travel, and so on) vary between employers.

YES   NO (circle one)

I understand it is my financial responsibility to fill in any coverage gaps.

YES   NO (circle one)

Three reasons I went to college are:

1. _____

2. _____

3. _____

Three reasons I stayed in college and graduated are:

1. _____

2. _____

3. _____

Three experiences I most enjoyed in college are:

1. _____

2. _____

3. _____

Three personal attributes that were beneficial to my college academic experience are:

1. _____

2. _____

3. _____

_____

Three personal attributes that were beneficial to my college social experience are:

1. _____

2. _____

3. _____

_____

Three experiences I most look forward to in my life after school are:

1. _____

2. _____

3. _____

_____

It would cause me great pain if I had to do without any one of these over the next few years:

1. _____

2. _____

3. _____

_____

Three circumstances I worry about as I approach interviewing for a job are:

1. _____

2. _____

3. _____

_____

Three reasons I'm anxious to get a job are:

1. _____

_____

2. _____

_____

3. _____

_____

Three reasons I'm ready to get a job are:

1. _____

_____

2. _____

_____

3. _____

_____

The following is a meaningful instance in my life where I persevered, dotted the *is*, crossed the *ts*, and came out on top as a result of my sincere hard work and efforts:

_____

_____

_____

_____

I employed these hard-work tactics:

1. _____

_____

2. _____

_____

3. _____

_____

These efforts resulted in the following favorable outcome:

_____

_____

_____

_____

The attributes most often sought by recruiters are:

1. _____

2. _____

3. _____

The number-one reason candidates fail to impress recruiters is:

_____

Three reasons another candidate might be better positioned than me to get a job are:

1. _____

2. _____

3. _____

Three reasons another candidate might interview for a job more effectively than me are:

1. _____

2. _____

3. _____

Three reasons I'm better positioned than another candidate to get a job are:

1. _____

2. _____

3. _____

Three reasons I'll interview more effectively for a job than another candidate are:

1. _____

_____

2. _____

_____

3. _____

_____

Three particulars I love about my life right now are:

1. _____

_____

2. _____

_____

3. _____

_____

The most valuable insights I gained from this brief questionnaire are:

_____

_____

_____

Any value derived from this questionnaire comes from within. Your primary goal is to understand more about yourself as "Pomp and Circumstance" establishes the new beat in your life. Appreciate that you are vulnerable and have more to learn, but understand that you are entitled to confidence. Let this exercise help you own this snapshot in time, with all the opportunities and responsibilities it presents.

Own Your Smile

As a college grad, you belong to an elite group of bona fide equity holders. You've invested your time and tuition dollars wisely, and as a result, you have employment capital for life in the form of your diploma. Make no mistake: you've got what it takes to clinch your dream job. Employers repeatedly emphasize that interviews focus on siphoning out those who are the most:

- Able
- Suitable
- Willing
- Professional
- Team-oriented
- Capable problem-solvers

Since you just emerged victorious from a pulsing think tank that demanded results on a tight schedule, involved intense communications, and necessitated sensitivity among a diverse group of individuals, you fit the bill in spades. You have good reason to trust your instincts, which you will be called upon to do with regularity in the days ahead.

Additionally, as you gleefully watch the union café fade into the sunset, understand that you belong to a club that boasts a well-respected membership. Since your Generation Y cohorts have already proven themselves in many noteworthy ways, you will be similarly categorized until you prove otherwise. Common perceptions in the workplace about Gen Y employees include these:

- Tend to work faster and better than other employees
- Seek out creative challenges and view colleagues as vast resources from whom to gain knowledge
- Intent on making an important impact from day one
- Goal- and deadline-oriented
- Keenly interested in building up ownership of tasks
- Speak their mind and do not have hidden agendas
- Embody multitasking as routine
- Embrace diversity
- Exhibit extreme flexibility
- Learn quickly

As you justifiably ride these coattails into your interviews, closely examine these recent grads who are employed and making ends meet. Also survey your (and your family's) backyard and identify successful professionals of all ages. If you have an opportunity, probe into particulars to better understand how these individuals put the pieces together. You'll quickly recognize a number of similarities between their beginnings and where you sit right now. Your future clearly has the potential to be very bright.

For good measure, explore the time-honored advice of the icons noted below. Recognize that you've got what it takes, according to the best of the best; you couldn't have gotten through college without embracing these tenets. The key is to continue operating in this fashion.

"The dictionary is the only place where success comes before work." —Mark Twain

"Genius is one percent inspiration and ninety-nine percent perspiration. Accordingly, a genius is often merely a talented person who has done all of his or her homework." —Thomas Edison

"People who are unable to motivate themselves must be content with mediocrity, no matter how impressive their other talents." —Andrew Carnegie

"Enthusiasm is the mother of effort, and without it nothing great was ever achieved." —Ralph Waldo Emerson

"Success is connected to action. Successful people keep moving. They make mistakes, but they don't quit." —Conrad Hilton

What Makes You Tick

"Success is not the key to happiness. Happiness is the key to success. If you love what you are doing, you will be successful." —Albert Schweitzer

It might seem hard to get gung ho about brand managing dog food ... or calculating fixed-rate annuities or corralling a bunch of recess-happy first graders. But is it? After all, one person's poison is another's passion. Fido's bowl of chow just might be your dream job come true.

Chances are, you didn't think too long and hard about employment particulars before emerging from your school's hallowed halls. After all, liberal-arts degrees offer up the world as your oyster when it comes to jobs. Conversations with new grads reveal that a clear majority chose a major without pinpointing an exact career choice. Many students further admit writing a half dozen crackerjack résumé objectives to throw against numerous walls in the hopes one would stick like Super Glue.

But even though the economy and your personal finances insinuate that beggars can't be choosers, it's worth your time to take a small step backward. Engage in what should become a lifelong habit: digging deep to identify enjoyable job tasks in which you excel. Figure out what makes you tick.

When you pinpoint your passion, you'll sell from the heart. Candidates who do this consistently outshine others in job interviews and beyond.

Get Married

Many new grads wonder why a prospective boss would be interested enough to listen to a candidate with little or no work experience. But as a recent degree holder, you're a breath of fresh air, and you travel light—without weighty baggage. Your relatively blank canvas is poetic and seductive. The combination of a clean slate and promise packs a universally appealing one-two punch.

This is a time when you can sell hard and strong on factors that form the nucleus of success for every walk of life. As you learned above, employers are first and foremost looking for essentials that can't be taught on the job. Whiz kids who know their way around a balance sheet and income statement are one thing. Whiz kids who are able, suitable, willing, professional and team-oriented problem solvers are jackpot material.

You clearly have a core of salable essentials. These got you into college and through the past several years on the social front, academically, and in your extracurricular pursuits. This set of traits makes you tick.

To create interviewing advantage (and ultimate job satisfaction and success), marry what makes you tick with what makes employers salivate. Isolate essentials that overlap. Interview talk—the sell—primarily focuses on the value you bring to the job, not on what you find particularly enjoyable in life. If you unearth common ground between what you like to do and what employers value, these become one and the same, and there's little stopping you from that point on.

Here are some examples of what might make you tick and also make today's employers salivate:

- **Team building.** Employees who promote "one for all and all for one" foster a congenial and supportive atmosphere that is inviting and productive in tackling the demands of the day.
- **Cheerleading.** Dynamos who rally the troops create enthusiasm and inject a can-do attitude that sets positive momentum into action.
- **Crossing the finish line.** Employees who don't accept any outcome but victory are necessary in a world of stiff competition and stringent customer mandates.
- **Loyalty.** True-blue individuals engender a foundation of trust and strength that supports all-important long-term objectives.
- **Bookworming.** Workers who thrive on page after page of black and white are purposeful and intelligent contributors who tackle the many mundane, but critical, aspects of the workplace.
- **Baptism by fire.** A roll-with-the-punches style is valued for its flexibility and adaptability, which are necessary in today's leaner organizations and fast-paced markets.
- **Psychology.** An astute ability to manage highly charged, emotional circumstances in an even-keeled fashion yields payola of the first order, with customer satisfaction and employee dynamics as key areas of focus.
- **People!** Personalities that ooze approachability and likability are valuable commodities, since warm bodies clamoring for attention reside in the nooks and crannies of most jobs.
- **Organization skills.** Time and mistakes are spared when a razor-sharp focus and executive efficiency are evident.
- **Details.** Unique individuals who enjoy picking and poking spy all kinds of needles in a variety of haystacks. These employees discover the fifty-thousand-dollar loophole in a contract and astutely calculate the reason deliveries routinely arrive two hours late.

- **The big picture.** Strong leaders have an uncanny ability to sort through the vast landscape and zero in on opportunities, challenges and threats. These employees define workplace culture and momentum.
- **Creative license.** Without original strategies, most enterprises couldn't last long these days. Individuals with outside-the-box imaginations make opportunities more probable and profitable.
- **Cyberspace.** Facility with a keyboard and a mouse is appealing, and necessary, just about everywhere. Employees who have technological acumen in any shape or form are pegged as movers and shakers.

As you try on these various attributes for size, it's worth remembering that you'll have to live up to your publicity. Representing yourself as "what you see is what you get" prevents you from being a flash in the pan. You're aiming for a longer shelf life than a latte.

Create the "You" Brand

Once you've pinpointed what makes you tick, select no more than two attributes to build upon. Use this information as a common theme throughout points of contact with a prospective employer. Pretty soon, you'll be linked with these characteristics and they will roll off tongues in tandem with your name. If you choose your message well and thoughtfully incorporate it into your candidacy, you create a branding advantage.

While it takes some skill to accomplish this imprint, you can employ a very natural tactic—beyond repetition—to get your message across. You can take your theme, along with the job on the table, and astutely bring this union back full circle to your résumé in story form. Read on.

Between the Lines of Your Résumé

Résumés among new college grads don't smack of differentiation. There are certainly subtle variations that are irresistible, and statistical outliers who've stolen the show since kindergarten. But the résumés of most recent graduates fall solidly in the range of typical. Computers and desktop publishing have equalized document appearance—and therefore the playing field—even more.

This doesn't mean you should assume that your résumé and cover letter aren't worth your utmost diligence. After all, you're far better off earning points by raising the bar than getting noticed for lowering the benchmark. Do your best to craft a killer résumé, and maybe you will even lead the pack.

As you take the next step in your interview process, it's smart to add luster and depth to this killer résumé. Fill in the blanks, write between the lines. Your best chance to accomplish this comes when you're face-to-face with a recruiter. What's difficult to convey in punctuated form on a piece of ivory-colored paper is just the opposite in spoken conversation, whether over the phone or in the flesh.

Weave a Story

A brief tale dripping with conviction, personality, and plot is far more interesting and memorable than a bulleted list of facts and figures any day. Your competition is using this tactic to spellbind recruiters and you should as well.

Recall actual stories from your experiences to put you on the interviewer's bestseller list. Include details that portray you as a team-oriented problem solver who is able, suitable, willing, and professional. Additionally, be sure to do the following:

- Incorporate your theme.
- Keep the rendition concise.
- Share pertinent, professional information.
- Quantify your accomplishments, if impressive, as much as possible.
- Create a link with the specific job/organization.
- Inject passion into the telling.

While you may have reigned undefeated in one robust game of beer pong after another on campus, look to more appropriate and meaningful instances for material. Consider these circumstances from your most recent years:

- Extracurricular involvement
- Independent study
- Study abroad

- Internships
- Experiences related to your major (such as student teaching, research assistance, club participation, and so on)
- Awards, distinctions, and leadership moments
- Employment

The examples below demonstrate how you can create advantage during your interviews using this advice. These real-life excerpts clearly lean toward a more formal style that is sometimes difficult for young job applicants to embrace. While the stories may not be of the variety you are used to hearing, the renditions are appropriate and get the message across in an all-important professional manner. Your enthusiasm and a conversational style will remove the dry tone you might worry about as you review these samples.

Robert's Between-the-Lines Story

"Yes, I've had a chance to focus on customer service and its critical importance to business. Last summer, when I worked at Lehigh's Grocery, I found myself surrounded by signs we were told to read and understand as if our lives depended on it. I admit that at first, I thought it was a bit of overkill and perhaps just an advertising gimmick. The signs read, 'Rule number one: The customer is always right. Rule number two: If the customer isn't right, reread rule number one.'

"I quickly learned that Lehigh's meant business when it came to service. We went out of our way to assist patrons, answer questions, deal with complaints, and listen to suggestions. I remember delivering a catering order at midnight for a customer's welcome-home party so the food would be at its freshest. I even got invited to stay and ended up booking an additional catering order for another guest. This type of service defined our workplace culture—and, as a result, kept people coming back, despite the fact that our prices were higher than the larger chain operation across the street.

"I learned first-hand to be responsive immediately, sincerely, and proactively. Because I'm someone who values loyalty and typically goes the extra mile in my undertakings, I'm very willing to embrace a high customer-service mandate. Because I'm also very detail-oriented, I find it relatively easy to cover a lot of ground where customer needs are concerned. I would apply this same energy and attention working for you."

Shawna's Between-the-Lines Story

"No, I'm not put off by the need to carefully review a great number of documents. I come by my college nickname, 'Editor in Chief,' naturally, since I ruthlessly tackle paperwork head-on. My courseload throughout the four years shows that I generally opted for classes involving an inordinate amount of reading and writing. My work in the student writing center, where my peers specifically sought me out for assistance, attests to my eagle eye when it comes to the written word. You can definitely count on me to be meticulous and tireless when it comes to document review."

Brad's Between-the-Lines Story

"I've always found that my organizational skills coupled with my creativity strike a balance that fosters opportunities. I saw during my student-teaching experience how valuable this combination is in a classroom with diverse personalities and learning styles.

"One of our fourth-grade students had recently been diagnosed as having dyslexia. The rest of this class was really advanced academically—unusually so. While I knew we were able to service Henry's educational needs appropriately, I worried he would feel left out with this hard-charging group.

"I asked Mrs. Cummings, the classroom teacher, if it would be all right for me to work on a plan to help Henry feel comfortable with his fellow students. Under her supervision, Mrs. Cummings let me run with the idea. I used both my organizational skills and my creativity to come up with a program that was very positive for all of the students in the class.

"Because Henry had to leave the room on a regular basis to receive support services, I had to factor in a lot of movement for him. Helping Henry to exit and reenter in a quiet and easy manner, so that he wouldn't be obvious and disruptive, was a detail important to everyone in the classroom. I made sure that Henry's seat was close to the door, and that he had an assigned buddy who took responsibility for welcoming him back into a small-group setting.

"My creative side led me to discover that Henry has a talent for jamming on the piano. We put Henry in charge of classroom birthdays, and we gave him the spotlight in these instances. Henry was associated with fun and good times, and he developed friendships in this classroom.

"I also kept in close contact with Henry's parents, and they frequently commented on how helpful the link between home and school was in getting their son more invested and happier. Since we were all on the same page, Henry focused on his work, as opposed to worrying about what he was supposed to be doing or how he looked relative to the rest of the class. Henry and I still e-mail each other and I think this connection will continue for a long time.

"I'd really like to bring my creativity and focus to a classroom setting here."

Shun Writer's Block

Writer's block: you know what this lackluster instance is all about. Basically, you've got a sinking feeling that your life is without bells and whistles. Conjuring up a meaty story seems impossible.

There's probably a good explanation for this circumstance. Perhaps you didn't do much beyond the toga party scene and only attended enough of class to squeak by. Or maybe you studied insanely hard and didn't see the light of day for four years.

Either way, adding personality and vitality to your background—and therefore your candidacy—is simply critical when you have a lot of white space on your résumé. Telling a showstopping story is to the underdog's advantage. By hook or by crook, you've got to strut some stuff.

You may not have been to India delivering critically needed medical supplies or off erecting walls for Habitat for Humanity, but you've been doing something worth talking about to recruiters. While lying isn't an option, leaving out certain facts and slightly embellishing others are fair game when the rewrite doesn't misrepresent you.

As an example, you don't have to reveal that it was your father's brother who got you out of the basement poker games, hiring you to be a gopher in his office. After all, this happened to be where you first learned about stock trades, buying on margin, and shorting commodities. Which, by the way, you've been doing rather successfully online in your dorm room ever since. Your résumé doesn't need to say, "Professional experience began with job placement resulting from Uncle Frank's nepotism"; it can say, "Internship for leading fund manager evolved into successful personal portfolio creation and management."

So what if your godmother was the one who launched your dog-walking business for you? So what if the venture only included two other customers? You were the point person, getting up every morning at the crack of dawn with pooper-scooper in hand. You learned the value of pounding the pavement to make a buck, and you got those additional pooches by cold-calling. No apologies necessary—just lessons learned and nose-to-the-grindstone moments worth highlighting. "Unique, demanding pet-care business launched and expanded through grassroots marketing and cold-calling."

For one brief semester, you were a shining star. Remember that group project the professor still mentions in his intro classes? Such references aren't just idle praise, and these accomplishments are assuredly worth mentioning in your interviews. "Spearheaded Anthropology 212's semesterlong project where group dynamics were cultivated and information was crafted to deliver a top-of-the-class outcome."

Unquestionably, you have a story between the lines of your résumé that will infuse your interview with a warm, fuzzy, employable edge. Think hard and with an eye toward embellishment that stays within the bounds of truthfulness.

GEAKE and KISS

Candidates are often advised to envision their job interviews taking place in an elevator with a potential employer. The suggestion is meant to encourage a crisp and mesmerizing sales pitch.

While it's unlikely you'll be interviewed between floors six and nineteen, you will be confronted with similar circumstances in terms of privacy, time constraints, and competition as insidious as Muzak. Thus, it's wise to package the highlights of your candidacy to fit these realities. This serves to keep you in the running as a strong contender at every turn.

There are two components to this package approach, both of which should be at the ready and polished to a high gloss early on: GEAKE and KISS.

Front and Center with GEAKE

GEAKE, otherwise known as your "grab 'em and keep 'em" pitch, is a minute-and-a-half-long bio that quickly tells the employer who you are and what you can do. You might use it over the phone, face-to-face, at job fairs, during on-campus screenings, while you network, and in response to the request, "Tell me about yourself." On one hand, you might think you don't have enough material to fill ninety seconds. On the other hand, you'll soon realize that "time flies" was likely coined by someone interviewing for a much-coveted job.

First of all, read ahead to understand the KISS document before you go any further. Distilling your attributes along the lines of a KISS will establish the basis for your GEAKE pitch.

Second, understand that most interviewers don't know much about you and don't have the time to get up close and personal. Rather, they want to know what you can do for them. Keep this in mind as you develop your GEAKE approach. You can wistfully, but confidently, leave out "Penny the cat" stories from your youth.

Third, develop and deliver your GEAKE pitch like a pro. Shape and reshape it, ultimately learning it cold. Basically, lack of preparation shows and is a huge strike against you. Since you often lead with this song and dance, you're scrambling from the get-go if you're off-key or forget your choreography. Many recruiters advise that the first minutes of an interview are among the most critical.

And even though you might know the pitch in your sleep, you have another hurdle: it's hard to not sound contrived. Everyone bears this burden; just try to break the mold and present more naturally. Review the rehearsal insights shared in chapter 3, and concentrate on those that help you master a captivating style.

Additionally, be aware that you may have to slightly edit your perfectly memorized pitch on the spur of the moment. As an example, if you've just talked about your graduation from Arizona State, or if you're sitting in the actual campus career office with a recruiter, you shouldn't start your GEAKE pitch with redundant information simply because you've rehearsed it a certain way for the past six weeks: "I just graduated from Arizona State …"

Knowing your pitch backward and forward will only be helpful in these instances; you should be able to pick up the beat midsentence without too much difficulty: "*As we just talked about,* I graduated from Arizona State in May." "I'll graduate *from here* in May." And while this might sound like superfluous advice, the need for such on-the-fly adjustments confounds many new-grad interviewees, who stumble needlessly at the onset and then have a hard time recovering their all-important rhythm.

Fourth, use a fail-safe formula. Since you can only focus on limited data, concentrate on key factual information and defining your interests and accomplishments. Build your GEAKE infomercial step-by-step, weave in your theme, and underscore a fit with the organization, along the following lines:

1. Specify your graduation date, college, major, and whether you helped pay your way. Use a one-liner to plug your school if you suspect the interviewer might not know enough about the institution's prestige.
2. Describe campus involvements, noting outstanding accomplishments, rigorous course loads taken, and so on.
3. Focus on job experiences, highlighting significant training or circumstances.
4. Personalize your GEAKE pitch for each interview by using buzzwords from the organization's Web site.
5. Close with a feel-good sense about who you are, remembering that employers are seeking able, willing, and team-oriented, problem-solving professionals.

Below are a few examples of GEAKE pitches that receive high marks from seasoned recruiters. Remember that any stiltedness inherent in a written passage is diminished by the confidence and energy you display in a face-to-face meeting.

Kristina's GEAKE Pitch

"I graduated from Davidson College in June with a major in economics. Davidson has long been ranked in the top ten by *U.S. News & World Report's* 'America's Best Colleges.' Early in high school, I worked to help finance my education, and I've successfully balanced a number of responsibilities for the past eight years.

"Davidson is one of a few schools that provides economics majors the chance to participate in a program called Comparative Advantage. This program was both enlightening and rewarding. Those of us selected to participate by the Economics Honor Society interfaced with local business professionals. While I gained many insights through this experience, I was pleased to learn that my team-building and technology skills were meaningful beyond a school setting. I witnessed firsthand what a positive impact I could make in a corporate setting.

My mentor also singled me out for these exact attributes.

"I was also involved in the Community Action Initiative on campus. I tutored local elementary-school children in math. I know this experience was worthwhile for the students I taught, and it was something I personally looked forward to every week. I would like to find a similar opportunity once I start to work full-time.

"I can be counted upon for my interpersonal skills, professionalism, and responsive attitude. I believe these traits mesh with your emphasis on employees being 'customer custodians.' I would like a chance to demonstrate my fit with this mandate."

Jack's GEAKE Pitch

"I'll graduate from the University of Dayton in May as a sports-management major. Dayton is well-known for its business programs and is among a select number of schools that offer this degree.

"I've worked on campus in the fitness center since I was a freshman, and for the last few years I've held the same lifeguard job during the summers with our local park district. Last year, the head of the park district hand-picked me to participate in a supervisory training program. I completed this seminar, with special recognition from the instructor, while fulfilling my day-to-day responsibilities at work. These two jobs contributed toward financing a majority of my expenses at college.

"I enthusiastically participated on three intramural teams at Dayton, and I helped organize our annual Christmas on Campus event each December. This program brought our student body together with the local community, and I was proud to be involved with something that made a positive impact and created so much goodwill.

"Sports have always been a part of my life. I'm a passionate participant and spectator. I knew quite a while ago that I wanted to pursue a career along these lines. In addition, I'm comfortable around all kinds of people and have a knack for putting others at ease. When I combine these interests and skills with my solid background in business courses and my strength in math, I'm confident that I have a lot to offer—and am eager to do so. I embody your 'we want to win' approach.

"I am energetic and accomplish more than I'm asked to do. You can count on me to go the extra mile no matter what."

Seal It with a KISS

Your KISS—key information sell sheet—is a one-page leave-behind with four to six points that emphasize your viability and energy. The KISS is a spec sheet, of sorts—all about you. The purpose of yet another piece of paper in addition to your résumé and cover letter is primarily to remind the employer about you and your fit with the organization.

You should use the KISS only if you are comfortable doing so and sense that the document will enhance your candidacy. This is one of many instances where you will trust your instincts.

While you lead with your résumé and GEAKE, you most often use your KISS on the tail end of your interviews—or even after you've said good-bye. Still, it is helpful to construct your KISS before you tackle much else. This exercise allows you to distill your experiences, passions, and key attributes; the earlier you accomplish this, the better. Even if you never hand your KISS to an employer, you will use this information repeatedly throughout your interview process.

Anything you give to a prospective employer must be of the highest quality. The paper should be the same you use for your résumé, and the detail and overall appearance must be of the same quality. Many candidates include a picture when it's a professional looking, high-quality JPEG inserted into the electronic document itself (as in: do not rubber cement a passport photo to this sheet of paper).

Your KISS should be brief and newsworthy—but also compelling. Ask yourself, "If this were left at a recruiter's doorway, what pieces of information would prompt that person to seek me out?" Your sell statement is a crisp, bulleted list that uses active verbs (see chapter 10, "Talk Turkey") and strong adjectives easily reminiscent of you, your conversations, and your résumé. In other words, nothing on that page should be surprising or new; you are simply condensing, repackaging, and hitting hard with bold underlining.

While the temptation is great to be unusually clever or brilliant, stick to straightforward and succinct. If you're having a hard time eking out one more way to say how fabulous you are, go back to the list in this chapter that details common perceptions about Generation Y in the workplace. Extract what makes sense, using what employers largely love about you already. Or borrow words and phrases from your reference letters or from the recruiting organization's Web site. If Hillcrest Bank advertises that it comprises a team of "innovative thinkers," tell them you are an "innovative thinker."

Include as many of the following as possible in your KISS, remembering that being concise is important:

- Your theme and branding advantage
- Generalized reference to accomplishments
- Professional values
- Passion triggers (these include feel-good involvements such as volunteer work, charitable endeavors, and community participation)
- Key words and phrases pulled from the organization's Web site

Organize your KISS on one page along these lines:

1. Begin with a title such as "Key Information," "Key Qualifications," or "Key Information and Qualifications."
2. Below the title, add your name and contact information, similar to your résumé.
3. If you like, include a small but discernible picture of yourself that smacks of professionalism and energy (printed onto the page).
4. List what you bring to the table by using bullet points.

Here are two examples of hard-hitting KISS strategies (note that both Clive and Kasey pulled terms from the interviewing organization's Web site, "passionate innovation" and "customer custodian," to use in their summaries):

Clive's KISS

KEY INFORMATION
Clive Forbes
249 S. Indiana Avenue
Bloomington, Indiana 47405
cforbes@indiana.edu   812-555-9911

- Possesses outstanding interpersonal, leadership, and organizational skills.
- Resourceful self-starter as evidenced by two jobs held

throughout high school and college to finance education, including junior year internship at Goldwater Inc.

- Goal-oriented and conscientious, as shown by a rigorous course load, including a study-abroad program in Florence, Italy, and stellar academic performance throughout college.
- Interested in creating a long-term impact and contributing to a team through hard work, exemplary customer service, and passionate innovation.

Kasey's KISS

KEY INFORMATION AND QUALIFICATIONS
Kasey Obermeier
Clemson University
Mell Hall #1612013 Clemson, South Carolina 29634
kdobermeier@clemson.edu   864-555-6566

- Earned reputation among professors and employers for outstanding communication and critical thinking skills.
- Able to successfully balance priorities, as evidenced by academic load, participation in extracurricular activities, and employment throughout college.
- Possesses strong technology background and acumen consistently tapped at various jobs, most recently at Norridge Partners.
- Committed to community-related causes, such as Thresholds, that positively impact disadvantaged populations.
- An enthusiastic customer custodian through and through.

Friends with Benefits

You will need a network of individuals to establish your legitimacy and to offer you advice throughout the interview process. If you don't use others to your advantage, someone else will. It's wise to lose this mantra of the unemployed: "If I can't do it on my own, I'm not interested." Instead, concentrate on enlisting the support of two distinct sets of people. Included are rock-solid references and someone who will assume the role of your confidant.

Secure Rock-Solid References

Once you publish and disseminate a résumé, it's implied that you have reputable people waiting in the wings to bestow halo after halo onto your mortarboard. Since requests for your references are likely to start pouring in at interview time, it's important to organize this roster, if you haven't done so already. Actually, it's important to use recommendation letters as a part of your sell package—your offensive arsenal—when you need to keep yourself in the running or close the sale.

When choosing individuals to approach for references, concentrate on four people who know you well and think very highly of you. You should be confident that their portrayal will put you in a favorable light. Try to fill in weaknesses or areas of concern through your letters of recommendation. For example, if your grades are not stellar, try to find a professor who will write about your active class participation.

Look outside the family to the following individuals, and strive for variety, when it comes to your references:

- An inside-track person who knows you (this is an individual connected to the organization you are targeting as your potential employer)
- Professors
- Advisers
- Coaches
- Previous employers

Once you've identified four appropriate people who will likely go to bat for you, coordinate your reference materials along these lines:

1. **Ask each of the four people if they are willing to be a reference for you.**
2. **Once you have agreement, request a letter of recommendation from each of the four individuals.** This correspondence should be on their letterhead and must include information about how long they have known you, what capacity they've known you in, what your strengths are, and why they are recommending you. Kindly request they provide this letter within a few weeks. It's best to get this correspondence in hard copy (it's appropriate to provide a

stamped, addressed envelope if you are asking for the letter to be mailed to you) and also as a Word document. If you notice typos on any recommendation letter, politely request a redo.

3. **Choose the three best reference letters from among the four.** As you make your selections, be mindful that as much is revealed by what isn't said as by what someone chooses to say about you.

4. **Consider enlisting a very mature friend to pose as a potential employer.** A number of recently employed college grads, and even some HR pros, suggest using this ruse as a way to validate each one of your recommenders. The idea is to engage your benefactors in conversation about your candidacy and any underlying concerns they may have about you. Are there any deal-breaking insights mentioned in one-on-one "confidence"?

   Please keep in mind that this is a risky gambit. It's difficult to proceed without any hint of a connection to your backstage machinations. For example, consider that telephone tag is often the name of this game. Your impostor's contact information might seem odd; it would be unusual to offer only a cell number, without any office contact information.

5. **Hightail it back to the drawing board to come up with three good-as-gold references, if you must.** It isn't worth your time or energy to confront a recommender who portrays you in a lukewarm fashion in the hopes that he or she will change. You're far better off moving on, even if the matter feels like unfinished business. While your imagination may run rampant on how to get back at a professor who details your tendency toward tardiness more than your sterling class participation, you're smart to adhere to the adage: "success is the best revenge."

6. **Collect detailed, specific contact information for each recommender.** Any employer who wishes to call or e-mail should be able to easily get in touch with your references.

7. **Create both a hard-copy and Word cover page listing your references.** Use similar paper as your résumé and pay attention to overall appearance and detail. Organize the information onto one page as follows:

- Title as: "References for [Your Name]."
- List your personal contact information, similar to your résumé, immediately below the title.
- Organize and list references by number: 1, 2, 3.
- Include the same information, in the same order, for each reference:
  Recommender's name
  Recommender's title
  Organization affiliation
  Address
  Phone number(s)
  E-mail address(es)
  Brief note regarding the connection

8. **Hand over your reference packet at the right time.** Since you are in the position of providing yet more paperwork to an overworked recruiter, you should be sensitive about when to hand over these documents. You want your pearls of praise to create advantage with employers, rather than overwhelming or annoying them. If given a choice (some recruiters will ask you for your references, but many will not), consider that complimentary insights often tip the scale in your favor. If you sense that you need a boost to make it to the next round in the interview process, hand over your reference packet sooner rather than later. You'll either go down swinging or you'll keep the dream alive. On the other hand, your desire for a boost might be the very reason to be patient. If you make it to the homestretch when fewer candidates are in the running, you could create a strategic edge, as you close in on your goal. Clearly, you will need to rely on your instincts to guide you regarding timing.

9. **Write a personal note of thanks to each person.** Do this at the time they agree to write a letter of recommendation for you, and again after you clinch your job.

Enlist a Confidant

As you hop on the roller-coaster ride of interviewing, you'll need a confidant to hold your hand throughout the ups and downs. It's important to use this person to charge up, regroup, and celebrate.

Your confidant will scaffold you when you require it most and open your eyes wide just when you thought you knew it all. Therefore, it's beneficial to recruit someone who brings experience and level-headed professionalism to your efforts.

Consider what you need and who might best fit the bill. Then, decide how to coordinate this alliance so it is meaningful and manageable for both of you.

Create an Agenda

Aside from wondering who this confidant is going to be, you're probably wondering what the two of you will do—beyond downing a few when the going gets tough. Count on this crony to:

- Drill you on facts and figures about the company, market, and interviewers
- Expand your network
- Assist with your overall appearance (clothes, hair, makeup, and so on)
- Brainstorm alternatives related to your preparation efforts
- Rehearse with you for the interview
- Rehearse with you for the interview again
- Send you off with a pat on the back and a thumbs-up
- Congratulate you when the interview is over
- Proofread your communications
- Pick you up and dust you off just when you need it
- Do everything all over again until the day arrives when you accept a job offer
- Share in the celebration

Decide Who Fits the Bill

Given the diverse job description, the position of confidant is not an easy one to fill. But understanding what comprises a good fit helps you narrow the search and hone in on the perfect match. In addition to seeking out someone who has had experience with the interview process, look for a person who is:

- Interested in helping
- Reliable, experienced, available and trustworthy

- Supportive, yet unafraid to be tough as nails to make you better
- Even-keeled and focused
- Upbeat

While mothers and fathers are an outstanding resource throughout the interview process and should be tapped with tremendous frequency, it's typically not wise to use a parent in the confidant role. In many instances, the dynamics of the close, nurturing relationship you share supplant honesty and hinder productive prioritization. But you might view this strong connection as an upside in your particular situation, and you should certainly enlist a parent if this feels right.

Otherwise, there are many other people to consider, including:

- Relatives, such as an aunt or uncle
- Friends of the family, who may be your parents' close friends and people you've known your whole life
- Former bosses
- Former coaches
- Neighbors or more distant family friends whom you may not know well, but whom you admire and respect
- Former teachers
- Former co-workers

Ask

Just because you pick the right person doesn't mean you're done. You have to approach this certain someone and lay out your request and your hopes. Share this section of the book if it paints the best picture.

You don't want an individual who claims to be "kind of" on board or a person who "sort of" gets what you're talking about. The last thing you need is a work in progress—someone you will have to prod along and coddle. That said, this friend also has a life and most likely a full-time job of his or her own. The two of you should have a heart-to-heart spelling out expectations and ground rules that work to everyone's satisfaction. And then you need to honor your side of the bargain.

Be Real

This person is meant to provide support and guidance on a regular, but occasional basis; she's not here for you at three in the morning when you realize your honey-toned shoes don't match the wheat-colored belt that suddenly screams pink. Nor is this individual supposed to be your work minion who marches to a "Must Have By" list at the beginning of each week.

This confidant is a generous soul who has agreed to be a resource as you interview for jobs. Respect the relationship and the benefits you're getting from this alliance and give back frequently all along the way (send a note of thanks, pick up the tab for lunch, and so on). And down the road, this is someone you should always remember with tremendous fondness.

By adhering to the advice in chapter 1, you've built a critical foundation for your interview process right from your own backyard. All of these pieces instill the beginnings of purpose and effectiveness into your job search. As someone who took the time to do more than switch on autopilot after graduation, you'll undoubtedly proceed in a more compelling fashion now.

There's no better way to bolster your interview process than to have managed this first step so thoroughly and thoughtfully. Yes, challenge lies ahead ... but now, so does opportunity you can touch.

Chapter 2

Get the 411

"In my interview yesterday, I was asked what I know about the
company. All I came up with was that commercial about talking
to the hand. Half way into an explanation I pulled
from my after-school days in front of the TV,
I realized I was referring to a competitor."
—*Senior, Architecture Major, University of Illinois*

Her goal: "To build literal and figurative bridges."

IF YOU'VE EVER WITNESSED Donald Trump dress down an unsuspecting
minion inch by cowering inch, you know that corporate America
values information. Operating by the seat of your pants makes interviews
uncomfortable for everyone and places you at a conversational
disadvantage you can't afford in your meetings. With reliable facts
about the employer, the market, the interview, and the specific job on
the tip of your tongue, you can field questions and return answers in
a "feel good" volley style.

As you concentrate on learning the subject matter of the hour,
it's strategic to focus on the most pertinent details from all that are
available to you. An encyclopedic digestion of everything on Google
potentially overwhelms you and bogs down the interview process.
Once the list is narrowed, it's essential to understand which of the
particulars to emphasize and which to keep under wraps. Impressions
are formed according to the information you use or leave out, building
a case for your candidacy.

Keeping this impact in mind, thorough guidelines are summarized
in the "Information to Know" and "Touchy Subjects" sections of this
chapter. The "Where to Look" sections point you toward the best data

sources. These insights allow you to astutely further your chances with a recruiter. At the same time, you gain understanding that is meaningful to your personal agenda—now and down the road.

While the guidelines below can help you build the most useful outline of key facts, it's realistic to consider that you might be pressed for time on occasion. If this is the case, study the organization's Web site. Visit the "Home" page and the "About" and "Careers" sections. Pinpoint the company's mission and note buzzwords and emphasized phrases. Try to ascertain the entity's culture, its key players, and any breaking headlines. You're better off digging in to get a more thorough overview, but in a pinch, you can make a dent even if you spend just fifteen minutes in cyberspace.

The Employer

No, all consumer-products companies aren't the same. Nor are all high schools, banks, hospitals or architectural firms. In addition to having distinct personalities and cultures, like employers differ on variables that impact day-to-day operations and broader viability.

Information to Know
- Organization's mission
- General start-up details
- Growth story
- Ownership/legal structure (public, private, corporation, partnership, not-for-profit, and so on)
- Names of the top executives
- Type of organization (manufacturer, marketer, retailer, wholesaler, service provider, and so on)
- Business focus (key services, products, markets, and so on)
- Geographic scope of operations and markets
- Key factors affecting the growth or slowdown of the organization (demographics, fiscal policy, supply considerations, Mother Nature, and so on)
- Current growth trend of the organization
- Revenues
- Profit/loss
- Internal structure (divisions, subsidiaries, and so on)
- Number of employees

- Recent news/press
- Pattern of hiring new college graduates, especially from your school
- Notable affiliations with your college or university

Where to Look

Not so long ago, job applicants collected information by hoofing it around town to nab hard copies of annual reports and archived library documents on microfiche. This took time and occasionally served as a quasi-legitimate excuse for not being as conscientious as possible. Now, the Internet's availability as our window to the world makes it criminal to skip vigorous due diligence.

But before you smugly confine yourself to a keyboard, recognize that old-school research still has merit and produces more than a few "Bingo!" nuggets. Use a combination of the following avenues to explore your potential employers:

1. **The Internet**
   Search engines. There are a few ways to enter search criteria, all of which give you front- and back-door access to the information you need.
   - Company name (yes, you'll probably find an online version of that tried-and-true, information-laden annual report)
   - Subsidiary/division names
   - Names of the company's top executives
   - Product names (as specific as possible)
   - Specific markets (as pinpointed as possible)

   Specific sites.
   - hoovers.com
   - vault.com
   - metamoney.com/w100
   - irin.com
   - wetfeet.com
   - zapdata.com
   - mycareer.com.au
   - Google's news search (use a company name for the subject)
   - Your alma mater's Web site (search for the interviewing organization's name to see whether a campus affiliation

pops up)

2. **Campus career center**

On-campus professionals. The professionals in your campus career center are always on your side; they make it a point to know details that further your job chances. If you're no longer on campus, pick up the phone or e-mail a quick query about the company, asking whether the center has any information that might be pertinent or helpful to your upcoming interview.

Alumni resources. Most career offices have alumni directories with very explicit contact information included. Use these to get in touch with people working in your field. The directories may be separated into two groups: former students who have volunteered to help graduates as they look for a job, and alums who have not specifically noted a desire to mentor (although this does not mean you shouldn't contact these individuals, unless otherwise noted).

Any and all. In essence, use any of the resources this office routinely supplies to candidates in regard to employer education and information.

3. **Professors/college personnel**

Finance professors will likely be able to shed some light on your upcoming meeting with a recruiter from New York's number-two bank. Procter and Gamble has probably tickled the fancy of more than one of your marketing professors. Your teaching assistant in educational theory once taught at the junior high school where you have a meeting next week. Individuals on campus can be counted upon to share useful in-the-trenches tips and insights.

4. **Library**

Some potential employers (such as schools and privately held corporations) may not lend themselves to a full-blown Internet search. The reference section in your local library may be the answer in these cases. When an ace of a librarian pulls up hard-to-find information like a rabbit out of a hat, you know you've died and gone to interview-prep heaven.

5. **Friends and relatives**
    The more you ask, the more you find out—often in
    the strangest places. You may discover that a friend of a
    friend actually knows a meaningful tidbit or two about the
    organization you're scheduled to meet with next week.
6. **Human Resources** (at the organization where you are
    scheduled for an interview)
    This department may have an up-to-date organizational
    profile it shares with prospective and new employees. It's
    not out of line to ask for available background information
    in preparation for your interview. If possible, offer to swing
    by to pick up any materials, as opposed to requesting mail
    delivery.
7. **Local chamber of commerce office**
    This is admittedly a stretch, but may be your only hope
    in researching certain employers. You can approach the
    chamber in the town where the organization's local office,
    main branch, or headquarters is located. If nothing else,
    you'll learn about the surrounding area and where you
    might be spending many of your waking hours.

Touchy Subjects

You shouldn't bring up certain employer information in an
interview, simply because it isn't your place to do so. Despite your
best efforts at being a supersleuth, you don't have all the facts; in these
instances, conversation quickly careens toward a head-on collision with
the exit. And you quickly step out of your league when you assume a
self-appointed CEO position overnight.

It's true that some subjects may become less taboo as your interview
progresses and you're clearly in the running for a job. But this point
is miles down the road for most candidates and usually comes after
an offer is extended. Rather, keep in mind the old adage about a little
bit of knowledge and how it can make you dangerous. The following
are employer subjects to completely sidestep or tread around lightly
in most interviews:

- **Profit/loss.** While a summary of this financial information can be useful in a general way, specific numbers are not casually discussed in interviews with new college grads. The bottom line is a complex matter—one rarely without a few asterisks behind it.

- **Negative or suspect news/headlines.** Remember that the media is in business to sell glitz and glam ... and misery and strife. If, after several meetings, a particularly ugly headline continues to gnaw away at you, broach the specific news item by carefully asking about its impact on the employees and the company's business. Never accuse.

- **Surmised information about employment practices.** You may have gotten a scoop from someone, somewhere, about women being passed over for promotions left and right at this organization. Or perhaps race innuendo has floated around and surfaced one too many times for your comfort. Rather than playing the blame game and pointing fingers, you're better off to do more research on the matter. Reach your own conclusions behind closed doors. If you're compelled to bring up the issue in a meeting with a prospective employer, do so once you're clearly a thumbs-up candidate from their standpoint. Then, speak in general terms, without any indictment, inquiring about the organization's practices and goals regarding hiring and advancement. This is very tricky territory. The tables can be turned on you if the situation is not handled astutely. Proceed cautiously, and use your instincts.

- **Inferred preferential status by right of college/university affiliation.** It may be that the organization you're lunching with today has a campus building or two bearing its name. Nevertheless, this is not an automatic go-ahead to engage in "chip off the old block" banter. Nor are you a shoo-in simply because you graduated from the CEO's alma mater. Referencing the connection is strategic. Getting too cocky or cozy is interview suicide.

The Market

The market (also referred to as "the industry") is the arena within which your prospective employer operates. For example, a hospital operates within the healthcare industry. A school delivers services within the educational industry. Market information gives you broader insights about viability and enhances your overall understanding of why and how an organization functions.

Information to Know
- Key factors affecting the growth or slowdown of this industry (demographics, politics, fiscal policy, supply considerations, weather, foreign relations, and so on)
- General health of the industry and why (robust, flat, and so on)
- Major competitors and how they compare with the prospective employer

Where to Look
To understand the industry and the overall climate—economic and otherwise—consider these resources:

1. **The Internet**
   Search engines. As you've undoubtedly learned to do in your online exploration, let your search expand based on what you find as you go along; use those specific links and keywords as you navigate various Web sites. Search criteria with revealing possibilities include:
   - Industry name (e.g. healthcare, transportation, mail order, and so on)
   - Specific markets (e.g. home healthcare, domestically produced automobiles, mail-order, women's apparel, and so on)
   - Competitors' names

   Specific sites.
   - hoovers.com
   - vault.com
   - metamoney.com/w100
   - wetfeet.com

2. **Our government**

   Various governmental agencies collect a lot of data on
   the economy, demographics, trends, and other significant
   factors that come in handy as you try to paint a larger
   picture based on market dynamics. Fedstats.gov is an
   excellent Web site to start with, and it doesn't require a
   subscription. Or enter "government statistics about [industry
   or market name]" as your search criteria, and you'll be
   directed to a number of sites with data galore. These official
   agencies, and others, regularly provide summary reports you
   can access online:
   - U.S. Census Bureau
   - Bureau of Economic Analysis
   - Bureau of Justice Statistics
   - Bureau of Labor Statistics
   - Economic Research Service, U.S. Department of
     Agriculture
   - Energy Information Administration
   - Environmental Protection Agency
   - National Agricultural Statistics Service
   - National Center for Education Statistics
   - National Center for Health Statistics
   - National Center for Transportation Statistics

3. **Daily newspapers and periodicals**

   Beyond magazines such as *Newsweek* and *Fortune,* you may
   find industry-specific periodicals worth thumbing through
   for market knowledge. To find these, go online and enter
   the following for your search: "periodicals about [industry or
   market name]."

4. **Library**

   Libraries often subscribe to a number of sites and services
   that might otherwise require your paid membership. It's
   generally unnecessary to plunk down your own cash for any
   of this research.

5. **Campus career center, professors/college personnel, and friends and relatives**

   For all the same reasons noted above as you gathered information about a prospective employer, use these resources to their fullest when researching the market and its dynamics.

Touchy Subjects

Avoid trying too hard to be an expert after dedicating only cursory time and research to the study of the market. You may be miles ahead from where you were yesterday, but you're still light-years behind your interviewers. Once you understand this distinction, you'll be able to converse with confidence—in a respectful manner.

Addressing market specifics involves tiptoeing through a few minefields, with discretion. First of all, discuss trends carefully. Research data can be interpreted in a variety of ways. It's hard, as a quick study, to ascertain the reliability and validity of the facts you've gathered. You might come across as offensive or illogical if you espouse a hasty conclusion about overall strategy based on information that isn't deemed meaningful by the organization.

One way to demonstrate your base of knowledge is to ask the interviewer a question that uses the available facts, but assumes nothing about the organization or the impact of the statistic. For example, you might offer, "I know the population is shifting toward an older demographic on the whole. Is this a variable you believe is important to factor into customer-service capabilities beyond what you're doing now?" This is a far better approach than, "With an aging U.S. population, it's really necessary to revamp the way your customer-service operations function."

Second, avoid bad-mouthing the competition. This is the first of many instances during the interview process where you'll be reminded to keep a lid on trash-talking. Being politically correct is important, even though you're referring to the bad guys. Demonstrate your "go team" leaning in a more diplomatic way. Use words that suggest you know what you're talking about, but temper your discussion with terms such as, "appears," "seems," "probably," "I believe," "I feel," and so on.

"It seems that your major competitor, Holden Enterprises, isn't as streamlined in getting products to the end user, since they rely so heavily on their middlemen."

"I feel St. Regis does a better job of marketing to the community than many of the other area hospitals, because your print campaigns offer testimonials from actual patients who are local residents."

"Charlotte Country Day School appears to offer a few advantages—one being that students have a chance to develop close connections to faculty. These beneficial relationships are probably much harder to accomplish at the two area high schools, where populations are ten times the size of CCDS."

The Interviewers

A heads-up regarding your interviewers enhances your preparation. You might tweak your approach if you're lunching with advertising types as opposed to bean counters. Similarly, you'd want to bone up on the dynamics of group interviewing if this is the stated plan.

Additionally, if your research yields a warning from the campus career counselor about Ms. Garcia being a no-nonsense, by-the-book interviewer who sizes up candidates in fifteen minutes flat, you've got a clear marching order to perfect your GEAKE pitch.

And familiarity—a better insight into the man or woman behind the title—simply provides a level of comfort as you present yourself on interview day. If you learned through the local press that your prospective boss is a marathoner, you know a little more about this person's drive and commitment than you did a day or two ago. This tidbit should serve to tune you in and sharpen your conversational tactics.

Chances are excellent you'll be provided with the name of the person conducting your interview in advance. For campus screenings, you often access this information online through your campus careers network, or you will be informed when the interview is scheduled. When you are called in for an on-premise interview at the organization's offices, the person organizing the meeting typically indicates a brief agenda, with names included.

If this information isn't readily provided to you, it's all right to ask, "Do you mind telling me who I'll be meeting?" (If you don't have a specific contact who is coordinating the meeting, head to HR.) It's also acceptable to ask which position the named individual holds within the organization and whether you'll be meeting the person who would be your boss.

If you end up with a listing of names, you might pose another question, asking whether you will be engaged in individual or group interviews. But this is about it; probing further starts to exude a stalker's persona. Essentially, you're not granted much leeway for ramrod interrogation about your interviewers. And in the interest of professionalism, it's wise to consolidate any inquiry here with questions you may have regarding the other interviewees and the specific job on the table (both are reviewed further on in this chapter). In this way, you are involved in one point of contact, not several.

Information to Know
- Names and titles of your interviewers
- Format for the interview (one-to-one, large group, lunch, and so on)
- General information and insights about each interviewer

Where to Look
1. **The Internet**
   Enter the names of your interviewers into search engines and on the organization's Web site. Additionally, hoovers.com offers limited free content that might be useful.
2. **Campus contacts**
   Run names by the career-counseling office, your professors, and other campus personnel to see whether there is an association or knowledge base. "I'm interviewing with Noemi Garcia, Midwest region sales manager at Kimberly Brothers. I'm wondering if you have any insights about her, or perhaps another person who was in this position previously at the company." Someone may actually know Ms. Garcia rather well and give you a valuable tip to use.

Touchy Subjects
When it comes to your interviewers, anything is off-limits if it

isn't well-known information of a positive nature or a fact from the organization's Web site. And while it's wise to focus your conversation on business, there is a window of opportunity regarding particulars of a mildly personal nature.

Just be careful that you don't collide with trouble by trying too hard. As an example, attempts to identify yourself as a kindred spirit can backfire. You will look painfully obvious if you tout your newfound love for ballroom dancing after learning that your prospective boss recently scored big in the regional tango competition. However, if you've got a flair for skillful conversation that will showcase your enthusiasm and diligence, you should definitely waltz your way into a recruiter's good graces.

Other Interviewees

The enemy toils away laboriously to understand as much about the opponent as possible before game day. This is because the best defense is usually a good offense—the very reason you'll be better prepared for your interview if you know who you're up against. Armed with this knowledge, you can highlight your distinct advantage and position yourself ahead of the competition. "While I understand the rationale behind an insider stepping up into the job, I'd like to emphasize how I bring unique value worth considering."

Information to Know
- Type of competition (other recent college grads, individuals from within the organization, anybody and everybody, and so on)
- Approximate number in the running

Where to Look
Get your answers directly from the source. The same individual you questioned about the interviewers (the one inviting you in for the meeting) is the contact person for these specifics. "Do you mind my asking who else is interviewing for the position and how many candidates there are?"

If you get a retort questioning your specific interest in this information, you can honestly say, "I want to better understand my competition as I prepare to meet with you." Most savvy businesspeople will appreciate your response and interest in maximizing your position.

Touchy Subjects

If you stick to the politically correct script, you'll be fine. If you delve into any of the following while trying to learn who the other contenders are, however, you'll sink fast in Personnel's deepest waters:

- Gender
- Race/ethnicity
- Age
- Religious affiliation
- Sexual preference

The Job

Learning more about the job is a detail often forgotten in the excitement of landing a meeting, signing up for a campus slot, or attending a job fair. True, you won't always be in the running for a specific position in the early stages of some interviews. Recruiters may be looking for candidates to fill a variety of spots, all of which hold appeal. In these instances, you get channeled in one direction or another as you make each cut along the way.

But whenever possible, learn about the particulars of a specific position so you can focus on details that put you in a favorable light. "I know the Phoenix area well and really like it; I have close relatives living there whom I've visited for years." Information about the job also gives you insight into which interviewers likely hold the hiring trump cards.

Information to Know
- Job title/description/basic responsibilities
- Chain of command, reporting relationships
- Location of the job

Where to Look
1. **Campus career center or online campus career network**
   Through your career center, you can usually gather complete specifics about jobs being recruited on campus.
2. **Interview coordinator or the company's HR department**

It's perfectly all right to ask, "Do you have any information about the job I'm interviewing for? I'm specifically interested in a brief description about responsibilities, reporting relationships, and where the job is located."

3. **Organization's Web site**
   Job descriptions are routinely posted online.

Touchy Subjects

Candidates most often blow it here when they get obsessed about the details too early in the game. Title mania ("Is this equivalent to a vice president, or a second-tier manager, or what?"); chain-of-command hang-ups ("Wait, are you saying that I'd report to another product manager instead of having the opportunity to report to the department manager?"); vacation dismay ("Since I'm not used to ten days of vacation time each year, is there any way to increase this or get additional days off?"); and location panic ("Oh boy, I really can't see myself living in Little Rock, but hey, stranger things have happened.") make you look overly confident on one hand, and insecure on the other.

This isn't the time to get picky about the particulars. You'll travel miles on the interview highway within one organization. Titles, locations, and bosses often change overnight. Your goal is to concentrate on selling yourself; you can ask for clarification after you've been invited to join an organization. Chapter 11 reviews how to get the lowdown on anything and everything after you have an offer to your name.

Chapter 3

Draw Some Blood

"Whoa. They asked me what kind of a tree I want to be. Then they asked me to describe my greatest failure. As I tried to keep my left knee from twitching uncontrollably, I explained that my biggest defeat was not being able to figure out what kind of a tree I want to be. No one laughed. Again with the knee."
—*Senior, Biology Major, Beloit College*

His goal: "Plastics."

IT MIGHT SEEM ODD to compare the next phase of the interview prep process to flossing your teeth, but it's actually a very appropriate metaphor. Both are vitally important for a variety of reasons and deserve your fastidious attention. At the same time, each is tedious and occasionally draws blood. As you approach the sometimes uncomfortable tasks ahead, keep repeating to yourself, "No pain, no gain."

After all, hard-core fine-tuning is never easy. But this is a time for aggressive tweaking. You steadily inch ahead of your competition when you smooth out rough edges and add overall spit and polish. You won't be sorry if you go the extra (and slightly agonizing) mile here.

Clean Out Your Closets

No, this section isn't about your clothing. Rather, it deals with eliminating or massaging personal information that is either incriminating or might be construed as such. You should spruce up your Facebook and MySpace profiles, for example. (Chapter 9 reviews redoing your voicemail message if it is anything but professional and straightforward.)

It isn't uncommon for a potential employer to take note of online photos in which revelers, identified by name, are in compromising positions. If you believe that passwords will protect this information, you should know that organizations are actively seeking to uncover trash—and are finding ways to gain access.

What qualifies as a skeleton? Suffice it to say that references to lewd and unlawful behavior, along with sexual or drunken innuendo, should be removed. Other circumstances are not so clear-cut. Unfortunately, individuals involved in same-sex or interracial relationships are often viewed with prejudice. Additionally, students passionately committed to organizations that purport extreme positions or lifestyles are similarly treading in questionable waters.

It's true that contemplating the notion of rejection based on your personal choices and loyalties likely creates discomfort of the first order (and such rejection may even be unlawful), but it is a reality you should consider very carefully. You might decide it's prudent to keep certain information under wraps throughout the interview process and even beyond. If the particulars are available to the world at large through a Web site, figure out whether you will get rid of these online references.

Your day-to-day existence is slowly but surely transforming. Your opportunities will now be furthered by decorum and a pristine reputation (as defined by professional—and sometimes outdated— standards). Play it safe: project outstanding character in every aspect of your life. And if you deem appropriate, also subdue other facts that might be used against you by more conservative (and, yes, even ignorant) individuals still running a great number of our businesses.

Bring It Down a Notch

Despite the fact that you're young, bright, and heading toward a better version of MTV's *Real World,* you can't sashay into your interviews with a hot, you-know-what swagger. An overinflated ego or an insinuation of entitlement turns off recruiters like nothing else.

While you're clearly qualified for a professional opportunity that is challenging and pays commensurately, you have to face up to the less provocative side of your candidacy. Prospective employers fully understand that you don't yet bring experience to the mix. As chapter

1 pointed out, this is actually part of your appeal in the hiring process. Consequently, your demeanor can reflect confidence in all that you genuinely bring to the table. At the same time, however, temper your self-assurance with an understanding of your ground-floor place in the hierarchy. It's wise to show respect for the rules as well as the veterans who are the bread and butter of the organization.

Also be aware that pompous bravado often slips into the equation when you are in the thick of interviews and have a particularly feel-good moment with a recruiter. It's easy to get cocky when someone recognizes just how smashing you are as a candidate. While you should accept this feather in your cap without hesitation, don't let it define your interview process from that point on. You may end up feeling double-crossed if you aren't extended an offer. Nothing is in the bag until it's in the bag. Don't let down your sense of urgency until a paycheck is guaranteed.

More than one HR manager suggests that it's worth taking a hard look at professional athletes who speak to the media after they come off the field. Many of these jocks have gotten good advice because they consistently convey a winning blend of confidence and humbleness. Try to emulate this same respectful, optimistic approach in your interviews.

Do Extra Credit

Additional interviewing resources offer two advantages as you prepare to meet with recruiters. For starters, broader insights enhance your approach and fortify your self-assurance. While this book provides a very comprehensive overview, using it in tandem with a number of other carefully selected resources elevates you to another level of preparedness. You will understand more about what lies ahead and, as a result, better manage a variety of situations, including interviewing's quirkiest moments.

Second, interviews within certain industries may entail off-the-beaten-path specifics that should be considered and understood ahead of time. For example, entire books are dedicated to mapping out the interview process within the technology arena because of very unique recruitment tactics (including the line of questioning taken). Sales, consulting, engineering, teaching, journalism, and the service industry are additional fields where expanded resources regarding interview particulars are available and helpful.

The key is to avoid getting sidetracked or overwhelmed in your endeavor toward further enlightenment. The volume of available job-hunt information is best described as daunting. As a shortcut to wading through thousands of options just to find a useful tidbit here or there, try the pinpointed suggestions below to gain meaningful insights into your interview process:

1. **Web sites**
   Surfing the Web, when you know where to navigate in the vast cyberspace, yields very positive results when it comes to interviewing advice.
   - monster.com
   - hotjobs.com
   - quintcareers.com
   - careerjournal.com
   - mycareer.com.au
   - collegegrad.com
   - job-interview.net
   - parachute.com

2. **Books**
   Most current publications about interviewing are not specific to the new college graduate. Therefore, you should carefully pick and choose your reading material, then understand that you may have to massage the data to fit your circumstances. Each of the following books has been thoughtfully reviewed. The notation by each title suggests which sections or chapters will be most helpful to recent degree holders.
   - *Boost Your Interview IQ,* by Carole Martin
     (Part 1) This IQ test helps you isolate areas of weakness as you prepare for your job interviews.
   - *Winning Job Interviews,* by Dr. Paul Powers
     (Chapter 9) Based on broad industry experience, this text offers guidelines for creating a winning interview toolkit.
   - *Fearless Interviewing: How to Win the Job by Communicating with Confidence,* by Marky Stein
     (Chapter One) Useful insights on managing interview anxiety are thoughtfully provided in this chapter and

throughout the book.

- *Monster Careers: Interviewing,* by Jeffrey Taylor and Doug Hardy
  (Chapter 3) A comprehensive checklist for a traditional interview is provided in this chapter. Because this information is new territory for most recent college grads, it's worth reviewing the particulars yet one more time and from a different perspective.

- *The Unofficial Guide to Acing the Interview,* by Michelle Tullier
  (Chapter 2) The five biggest mistakes interviewees make are dissected in this chapter, and realistic recommendations for improvement are included.

- *Power Interviews: Job-Winning Tactics from Fortune 500 Recruiters,* by Neil Yeager and Lee Hough
  (Chapter 4) This chapter details the key business trends for the twenty-first century. This information should be helpful to your overall job search as well as to your individual interviews.

- *Knock 'em Dead: The Ultimate Job Seekers Guide,* by Martin Yate
  (Chapter 3) The "secrets of the hire" are disclosed by an industry guru who has the attention and respect of recruiters from a variety of industries.

- *Have No Career Fear: A College Grad's Guide to Snagging Work, Blazing a Career Path, and Reaching Job Nirvana,* by Students Helping Students
  (Chapter 4) Accepting or declining an offer is often among the most confounding details of the interview process. This chapter provides additional insight into the predicament.

- *From College to the Real World: Street-Smart Strategies for Landing Your Dream Job and Creating a Successful Future!,* by James Malinchak
  (Chapter 10) Employers weigh in on standout tactics to use in your interview follow-up.

The following volumes all provide hard-hitting Q&A
rehearsal details and are highly recommended:

- *101 Great Answers to the Toughest Interview Questions,*
  by Ron Fry
- *201 Best Questions to Ask on Your Interview,*
  by John Kador
- *Best Answers to the 201 Most Frequently Asked
  Interview Questions,* by Matthew DeLuca
- *Great Answers! Great Questions! For Your Job
  Interview,* by Jay A. Block

For specific industry guides, visit Amazon.com and enter
your search criteria (in the "Books" section of the site) by
playing around with various key words, such as "interviewing
for teaching jobs," "IT interviews," "retail jobs interviewing,"
"applying for accounting jobs," and so on.

3. **Familiar faces and places**

   As you've learned by now, many important interviewing needs
   are best fulfilled by resources found in your own backyard.
   A number of campus contacts, as an example, are all about
   helping you get a job; graduate in a blaze of glory by utilizing
   these "freebies" to the max before you finish that last final.
   And remember what they say about six degrees of separation.
   Everywhere around you are people who have been both
   interviewer and interviewee. Their experiences are worth
   your rapt attention; they can offer insights that will open
   doors, shed light on specifics, and point you in new, better
   directions. Yes, your own neck of the woods is definitely a fine
   place to be with these resources at your fingertips:

   - Campus career-counseling office
   - Professors/advisers/coaches
   - Local library
   - Family
   - Friends

4. **The horse's mouth**

   If you can get your hands on the DVDs chronicling Donald
   Trump's famous televised four-month-long job interviews,
   it's well worth your time. *The Apprentice,* despite focusing
   on ratings and allowing Mr. Trump's extreme wealth to
   occasionally steal the show, addresses how to sell yourself

while in the sizzler of all hot seats. The series also provides decent advice on how to perform most effectively once on the payroll.

Answer the Tough Questions Now

As is apparent by the number of top-selling books dedicated to the subject, the Q&A behemoth is at the crux of interview prep. And even though lists like the one immediately below summarize the most frequently asked questions of new college grads, there are no guarantees. The possibilities are diverse and seemingly endless.

Still, because you will be bombarded with a great number of questions as you sit across from a prospective employer, you're wise to familiarize yourself with recruiters' favorites. Interview inquisition is often reminiscent of a starved dog attacking a bone. Remember that you're not the Great Dane.

Frequently Asked Questions of New College Grads

- Tell me about yourself.
- What are your career goals?
- What is your most memorable accomplishment?
- Why do you want this job?
- What strengths do you bring to this job?
- What is your major weakness?"
- Why did you choose your specific college and major?
- Describe a situation in which you successfully persuaded someone to see things your way.
- Tell me about a time when you triumphed at a particular task in school or in a work situation. Explain how you got to the finish line and how this changed your life.
- Apply the same analysis to a time when you failed at something in your life.
- Explain how you have operated in group projects.
- Explain how you typically resolve conflicts.
- What do you see yourself doing in five years?
- Give me a specific example of a time when you used good judgment and logic in solving a problem.
- How long do you plan to stay at this job?
- What makes you better than the other candidates?

- What do you know about this organization and our place in the market?
- What do you do when you're not working?
- Give me an example of when you showed initiative and took the lead.
- Tell me about a time when you were forced to make an unpopular decision.
- What other opportunities are you looking at right now?
- Describe your ideal job.
- What would you like to change about yourself?
- What is your definition of success?
- Give me a specific example of a time when you had to conform to a policy with which you did not agree.
- How do you handle stress?
- Go through your decision-making process.
- Tell me about a time when you had too many things to do, and you were required to prioritize your tasks.
- How would your favorite professor describe you?
- What was your favorite (or least favorite) class and why?
- Do you have any questions?

The following shockeroos are not asked as frequently, but are worth mentioning so you won't be blindsided:

- If you could be a tree (or car, or flower) what kind would you be and why?
- If you were required to take a trip to the moon, what three things would you insist on taking along?

Strategic Management of the Q&A Onslaught

After reading the long list above, you've likely surmised that it's virtually impossible to prepare comprehensive answers to hundreds of interview questions ahead of time. As a result, it's wise to consider a more manageable framework for Q&A prep. Concentrate on a strategy that ensures your success, no matter what you're hit with from a recruiter. Which of these approaches you take depends on your personal capabilities and goals:

1. Familiarize yourself with the general Q&A process and learn what comprises a winning answer in most situations.
2. Get comfortable with a sampling of common questions and astute answers.
3. Briefly review as many potential questions and answers as possible.
4. Thoroughly review as many potential questions and answers as possible.

This book concentrates on a combination of numbers 1 and 2, strongly encouraging the use of additional resources (noted further above) for expanded reviews. This plan of attack generally affords very sufficient preparation and avoids burnout.

To accomplish these goals, it's important to learn more about the four types of questions asked in job interviews: screening, general, behavioral, and stress. You will be light-years ahead of your competition if you understand the basic differences and what is expected of you in each instance. The four question types are evaluated below according to their purpose ("About"); input provided by HR professionals ("Insights"); and actual samples ("Examples of …").

Screening Questions
About

From campus to corporate office, HR assistant to head honcho, and everything in between, you'll likely engage in one or more screening sessions. Screenings, conducted over the phone, in person, and even online, are meant to quickly identify the best and the brightest candidates. Your interview journey can be cut short rather quickly if you are tossed into the no pile.

Screening questions focus on collecting and validating a great deal of factual information while also gathering insights about professional basics, including reliability, honesty, group skills, leadership indicators, and so on. These interviews also focus on your overall presentation, conversational skills, and acceptable appearance.

Insights

- Be honest. The information you share must be legitimate, because the details *will* be scrutinized and validated. You can quickly end up digging yourself into a deep hole with no way out if you lie.
- Provide concise, thoughtful answers that address professional circumstances. Advice from the pros typically emphasizes short, zippy responses. While it is important to be focused, it is also critical to be thorough. If you have compelling information to share, your response will rarely be perceived as too lengthy.
- Respond in a straightforward, positive manner. Apologetic, flip, or flirtatious comments, or an attempt at sophomoric humor, detract from your professionalism. Similarly, avoid complaining or bringing up controversial topics (politics, religion, sports rivalries) or emotional subjects (recent relationship breakups, money woes, family issues).
- Highlight skills and attributes that make you stand out.
- Quantify your experiences, if the facts are meaningful and impressive.
- Use a considered, moderate tempo to establish the pace of your conversational style.
- Understand that the way in which you handle yourself is just as important as the specific answers you supply.

Examples of Screening Questions

1. **Question:** "What supervisory responsibilities did you have while working at the campus information center?"
   Answer: "I was responsible for scheduling and supervising two shifts of workers. I especially enjoyed the training aspect, and I was the first person to standardize training by creating a manual and implementing a qualifying test. Because I am very goal-directed and creative, this project came together quickly, at a quality level that encouraged employees to learn more."
   Analysis: This concise answer immediately provides the factual information requested, but also adds a brief plug (her branding advantage or theme) that causes the candidate to stand out.

2. **Question:** "You worked in the tutoring center during your freshman, sophomore, and senior years. Why weren't you tutoring during your junior year?"

    Answer: "After my sophomore year, I decided to take some time off from the tutoring center to focus on my major. I specifically wanted to finish as many course requirements as possible, so I'd be free for one of the few internships available to seniors during the January term. My plan worked, because I ended up with a great internship. I was able to get back to the tutoring center this year."

    Analysis: The answer is to the point and focuses the interviewer on the benefits of the decision. Rather than coming across as lazy, the interviewee positions herself as someone who made a clearheaded choice and realized a worthwhile outcome.

3. **Question:** "On your résumé, you list two years working at the library. How many months was this actually?"

    Answer: "Six months during the 2007-08 academic year. Since I'm a very organized and focused worker, the library increased my hours from five to sixteen hours a week after the first month."

    Analysis: The interviewer is trying to weed out some of the fluff produced by skillful résumé writing. When asking questions such as this, the recruiter may be interested in gauging how a candidate handles the question, as opposed to being vitally curious about the specifics. The candidate's direct, honest answer is not apologetic; it indicates that he has nothing to hide. The detail about increased hours recasts the subject into a very favorable light.

4. **Question:** "What is your cumulative GPA?"

    Answer: "Since my freshman year, I've always taken a challenging course load. My professors would attest to my investment in the coursework, specifically pointing to my outstanding classroom attendance and participation. Middlebury is well-known for its overall rigor and does not subscribe to grade inflation. My overall GPA is a B-, or a 2.8."

Analysis: While it might seem as if this interviewee is pouring it on thick and taking a bit of a defensive posture here, his response is necessary, because he lacks the magic GPA of 3.0 and above. It's a shame that many interviewers classify GPAs similarly, regardless of the respective school's rigor, but the sheer number of qualified applicants these days makes this a reality. GPA is often used to make the first cut—often by a computer scanning your online application. Still, when you have a chance to talk your way through it, by all means, lay it on as thick as this earnest candidate did.

General Questions
About

General questions are the probes most frequently employed in face-to-face interviews, no matter where your meeting takes place. This Q&A format most clearly resembles everyday conversation. However, unlike a heart-to-heart with a good buddy, this conversation has an agenda to get through in thirty to sixty minutes.

You will be asked to relate your experiences, share personal information, and respond to seemingly idle questions; then you will be given leeway to make inquiries of your own. For example, the line of questioning could proceed as follows:

1. What is your major strength?
2. Tell me about yourself.
3. How about those Red Sox?
4. What is your family like?
5. Do you have any questions for me?

Yes, interviewers cover a lot of ground in a short period of time. This is a key reason preparing and rehearsing are so critical for the general question-and-answer interview. Just as ACT and SAT preparations proved helpful the day of the test, your familiarity with this interview format will enable you to offer cogent information on a variety of topics.

Insights
- Review the insights suggested above for screening questions, which are similarly helpful in general interviewing sessions.

- Focus your answers on recent events, rather than experiences from your childhood.
- Always consider the job you're interviewing for, relating your skills and education to this opportunity and to the company. Use the organization's buzzwords without overdoing it.
- Weave in your theme to create branding advantage and choose a story that breathes life into your résumé and candidacy.
- Skillfully rewrite your experiences as you learned to do in chapter 1. Using adjectives and substituting certain phrases for others make all the difference when responding to general questions. "Yes, I worked at a day camp for a couple of weeks last summer" sounds far less impressive than "Yes, this past summer I was a senior counselor at an elite day camp, where I led a record number of campers on a wide variety of activities, utilizing my creativity and leadership skills."
- Don't worry too much about sounding suspiciously perfect. It's far better to lean toward canned and polished than "uh" and "um" any day.
- Show your human side and exude passion.

Examples of General Questions

1. **Question:** "Tell me about yourself."
    If you remember that this question is asking you to provide verification that you are worth a job offer, it's manageable. Choose a context within which to portray yourself and build within this structure to achieve the focus you need. Your GEAKE pitch (chapter 1) might also satisfy this oft-used request. Below are examples that take a slightly different approach than a more formulaic GEAKE response.
    Answer: "When I chose to major in information technology and operations management, I didn't struggle with the decision for very long. From the time I applied to Cox as a freshman and got into a business program that only admits ten percent of its applicants, I knew I wanted to target a career that allows me to do what I've enjoyed doing for years.
    "Technology and problem solving are two areas that

have captured my interest for as long as I can remember. These are the focus behind a business I established in our community when I was in high school. Word-of-mouth and repeat business fuel this venture, which provides a variety of software and hardware architecture support to individuals and small businesses.

"I'm involved with installation, troubleshooting, conceptual design, training and maintenance. I've trained up to forty users at a time in a single location, and I've been held accountable to a budget as large as one hundred thousand dollars. I'm happy to say that I fulfilled my responsibilities to the letter, establishing a very satisfied customer clientele that continues to hire me.

"I've worked at this entrepreneurial venture for the past six years, during the school year and throughout the summers. I even managed to maintain ongoing business with a few of my larger customers during my two summer internships at Rodie and Metropolitan. All of this effort contributed to paying for my college education.

"It might seem as if I'm all work and no play, but this isn't the case. I've always found time for my friends, and also for hockey. I was actually on the club team throughout all four years of college, and we didn't do so badly, placing second in our league this past season. I'd actually like to get involved with coaching a mite or squirt hockey team in the future.

"I believe that my IT skills, along with my ability to solve problems and implement solutions, are especially important to a consultant-trainee position. I've had the chance to demonstrate that I am a 'passionate innovator' and I'm excited about discussing career possibilities with you."

Analysis: This interviewee has clearly been around the block a few times; he does a great job of highlighting the sexiest parts of his life—from an employer's vantage point, anyway. By framing his response around "for as long as I can remember," he removes the enormity of the "tell me about yourself" question and effectively brings it down to a two-minute summary that manages to paint an in-depth picture of his life using recent experiences. The anecdotes about the friends and the hockey team help to soften this candidate's overall image. Otherwise, he might come across as being twenty-two going on fifty-three.

2. **Question:** "Tell me about yourself."
Answer: "On the last paper of the term, my junior-year American lit professor wrote, 'I expect to be reading your material following graduation, and I look forward to it.' For as long as I can remember, I've always been a storyteller, organizing facts and adding creative turns and twists to grab an audience.

"Not only do I enjoy communicating through my writing, but I've concentrated on developing it for years, as my education and work experience show. Most recently, I worked as circulation manager and lead feature writer for our college newspaper, which was published daily and read by 80 percent of our student body. Readership increased 12 percent during my three-year tenure.

"This arena appealed to me because it was fast paced, but still required thoughtful, top-notch journalism. As you might suspect, a college audience has no problem levying criticism at the drop of a hat. More than anything, I found this challenge exciting.

"In addition, I'm an astute worker who understands the importance of details and getting along with people from all walks of life. Each year, I was selected by my sorority to negotiate our food-service contract with Flo. Flo had worked on campus for the past forty years and knew just what she wanted and how to get it. At the same time, I had a budget and a lot of menu requests from my sorority sisters. I'm pleased to say that Flo was content, and we had decent meals at a reasonable price while I was signing on the dotted line.

"Now that I've graduated with honors, and a demanding course of study with a double major is behind me, I'd very much like to launch my full-time career in journalism. Not only do I bring meaningful experience and desire, but I'm organized, creative, and very willing to take the risks with my writing that your cutting-edge mandate calls for."
Analysis: This candidate, like any good journalist, grabs her audience from word one. She then builds a credible case,

supplying facts, human interest, and a summary (using the
organization's buzzwords) that screams, "Look no further."
She also effectively uses "for as long as I can remember" to
her advantage; the interviewer gets the idea that journalism
has simply coursed through her veins since she was able
to hold a pen. Similar to the hockey reference used by the
interviewee above, the anecdote about the sorority lightens
the mood and underscores a bankable attribute.

3. **Question:** "What is your most memorable accomplishment?"
    Answer: "My most memorable accomplishment is delivering
    a fitting eulogy for my grandmother. My grandmother was
    a remarkable woman for all she achieved in her ninety-two
    years of life. I was honored to impart her story to over 250
    people attending the funeral.

    "Since I was the author of the eulogy and felt deeply about
    what I chose to share, I was especially moved when a number
    of the attendees asked for a copy of what I had spoken
    about and indicated they were very touched and inspired. I
    continued to receive many requests for weeks after the service.

    "Quite a few of these individuals expressed keen interest
    in my grandmother's journey to America from Russia as
    a teenage girl without family by her side. She went on to
    become Cornell's first female engineering graduate. I
    wanted people to understand so much more about this
    woman than what had been seen on a daily basis in her
    final years; I'm satisfied that I succeeded, and I know my
    grandmother would be pleased and proud.

    "Along with other experiences relating to my degree
    in communications, this personal accomplishment
    demonstrates my ability to take in a great deal of
    information, consolidate it to fit the circumstances, and
    ultimately reach an audience in a compelling way—no
    matter what."
    Analysis: While college-admissions staff bemoan one more
    story about grandparents, this candidate is obviously
    speaking from her heart. Besides, the admissions
    department is not sharing college-application essays from
    eighteen-year-olds with your job recruiters. This interviewee

commands attention for the respect she pays her elder grandmother and for stepping up to the plate to deliver this eulogy to a packed house. In essence, she managed this interview question nicely because she specifically:

- Told a story
- Explained why the accomplishment was important to her
- Related it back to the business at hand

4. **Question:** "What is your major weakness?"
   Answer: "I've been accused of being a workaholic, and I admit to burning the midnight oil. It's not that I can't get work done within a reasonable time frame, it's that I have a hard time stepping away, because I'm motivated to excel. While I know this has an upside, I'm also aware that all work and no play potentially skews my perspective and may lead to burnout.

   "Understanding this, I've made a conscious effort to stay involved with sports. I just finished up with intramural softball and am now heading into what I hear is an enthusiastic bunch of alums in a local baseball league. These casual connections and commitments are important to me as a way to stay balanced, with priorities in check."
   Analysis: If there is ever a moment where the canned answer rears its ugly head, it's usually with this question. The key is to choose a weakness that doesn't knock you out of the running for the job. It should also be one that you genuinely recognize as problematic—one you have chosen to remedy for that reason. This interviewee is on target on both accounts. Simply stating a weakness isn't enough. You must relate it to the work situation, head off concerns (this candidate's identification of himself as motivated, rather than inefficient, is a skillful defensive move), and then explain how you make lemonade out of lemons.

5. **Question:** "What is your major weakness?"
   Answer: "I've had a tendency to overly focus on details. I now take time each day to factor in the bigger picture, and I set priorities based on this general overview. The simple switch in focus has really made a difference to my overall effectiveness and ability to get things done—often ahead of

time now."

Analysis: This interviewee doesn't mince words, and she offers a solid, concise answer that has all the right bells and whistles:

1. Identify a weakness that isn't overly concerning.
2. Define how you fixed the problem.
3. Relate it back to the job and work.

6. **Question:** "Explain how you operate in group projects."

    Answer: "I enjoyed group projects all through college and had an opportunity to participate a number of times. I was always a solid, steady contributor, and I stepped up to lead when I was in a position to do so effectively. I was also willing to let someone else take charge when it made sense. Perhaps it's easier for me to be productive in group settings, because I am naturally very goal-directed and astute when it comes to dealing with other people.

    "I remember working as project leader for an assignment in film class during freshman year. I quickly realized that the most important components of working with a group were creating an overall positive attitude, fulfilling responsibilities on schedule, allowing for different opinions, and staying focused on the goal. A sense of humor, and the ultimate camaraderie we developed, certainly helped as we watched one Alfred Hitchcock thriller after another until three in the morning.

    "We delivered on all counts, to the tune of an A, and I used this experience as a framework for group projects I've been involved with since. It's a model that works time and time again, and I'm personally committed to it as my way to get the best job done when working with others. I sense that a similar approach would be important as an account-management trainee here."

    Analysis: Keeping in mind that employers consistently stress that they are looking for team players, this is an answer to hone and polish until it shimmers. Right away, this interviewee states that he knows what he's talking about since he's been involved with group projects all through college. The candidate presses on and quickly positions himself as a ready, willing, and able participant who will do whatever is necessary. He also sneaks in his branding advantage—which he will undoubtedly use as a theme throughout his entire interview, across as many questions as possible. And this interviewee ends with a bang by appropriately bringing his response right back to the opportunity on the table.

7. **Question:** "What do you see yourself doing in five years?"
   Answer: "I'd like to be here, with five years of tenure under my belt. Since I've always been one to think on my feet, and I enjoy solving problems through collaboration, I suspect I'll remain challenged by a position within the sales department.
   "But within sales I'd like to step up into a managerial position with greater accountability for the bottom line, possibly through new product introductions or in another regional market of the company."
   Analysis: This candidate would really like to say that she hopes to win the lottery and then kiss this sucker good-bye. But she takes the high road, and appropriately so. Employers want willingness and professionalism. This interviewee delivers, while also sticking to her theme and letting the interviewer know she's focused on business variables that make a difference to success (stepping up, bottom-line accountability, new products, and possible relocation).

8. **Question:** "What do you do when you're not working?"
   Answer: "I'm a pretty hard partyer."
   Analysis: It might seem as if the interviewer is a regular Joe—one who likes the Bud commercials during Super Bowl and beyond—but this college grad's response doesn't cut it. The insight isn't professional, and it's a deal breaker. Even if you are a hard partyer, this is information to keep to yourself.

9. **Question:** "What do you do when you're not working?"
   Answer: "I've always been a runner, and I recently decided to train for the Humphrey Triathlon coming up in the fall. I still play some tennis on the weekends, but for the next several months, I'm concentrating on my swimming. Since

I'm someone who likes to cross a finish line, I'm counting on having a decent showing in October."

Analysis: Bingo. The interviewee hits the nail on the head this time around and even strikes a chord with the interviewer with, "Since I'm someone who likes to cross a finish line ..." Pursuits that require dedication, training, long-standing interest, and so on are all on the A-list. Talking too much about relationships (parents, siblings, significant others) can feel maudlin or needy if you're not careful. You also want to be sure that you don't boast, portray yourself as someone you're not, come across as privileged ("I have a personal trainer who comes in three times a week"), or act disinterested ("Not much, to tell you the truth"). It's best to concentrate on leisure that hints at energy and an involved, active lifestyle, such as sports, the arts, travel, alumni relationships, and volunteering.

10. **Question:** "How do you handle stress?"

Answer: "Usually by taking a deep breath and diving in quickly and calmly. While I was manager of our lacrosse team, our equipment wasn't delivered to the locker room on time on two separate occasions. It was my job to defuse the situation and make it right while the clock ticked toward game time.

"There's no question that I felt the stress of the moment, but I hammered away at the problem in a way I've learned is most effective. I stayed calm, asked who was available to help, and quickly reached out for assistance. And then I hustled. Both times, we made it under the wire. In the second instance, no one else even knew we had a problem; I'd fixed it before the mishap was noticed.

"I now use this approach without hesitation when I'm in any stressful situation, including professional ones. I'm confident that a combination of positive action and calm get the job done, making stress less likely to cannibalize the moment."

Analysis: This college senior nicely relates a personal story that gives his explanation merit. Additionally, he does a commendable job identifying a very realistic action plan

that makes sense. And always wonderful is the fact that
this interviewee emphasizes the professional merits of his
strategy.

11. **Question:** "Why did you choose your college?"
    Answer: "For the same reasons that I would do it all over again,
    knowing what I know now. The admissions literature painted a
    picture that was very seductive. I wasn't sure it would all unfold
    in such bold, four-color style, but I hoped to pursue a financial
    career at a top-notch institution. I wasn't disappointed. The
    business program is dynamic and hands-on.

    "The professors were engaging, the internships were
    available for the taking, and our classroom experiences
    related to the real world. I can't say enough about what I
    learned and how it was taught.

    "Aside from the academics, I sensed that college life there
    would be filled with some of the most interesting, nicest
    people I'd ever meet. Again, I turned out to be right and my
    choice resulted in lifelong friends."
    Analysis: This is a tough question, because it asks you to
    think back several years to the time you enrolled, before you
    knew everything you now understand so well. Granted, the
    question is slightly awkward, but you should answer what was
    asked. By mentioning the people on campus, the interviewee
    accomplishes a winning strategy; there's something very
    appealing about a person who has lifelong friends.

12. **Question:** "If you could be a tree, what kind would you
    choose and why?"
    Answer: "I'd like to be a redwood because I think this
    matches who I am the best: sturdy and constantly growing,
    ultimately reaching great heights."
    Analysis: This college senior gives it his best shot. While he
    wanted to start off by intoning, "You've got to be kidding
    me," he headed in a loftier direction and is better off for
    doing so. If you're asked this type of a question, concentrate
    on attributes that position you as a strong employee. This is
    an answer to keep very short and to the point.

Behavioral Questions
About

Structuring an interview around behavioral questions is known in the business as a highly reliable interview probe. Human Resources often delves with a behavioral assessment, and other individuals within the organization may also take this tack in a one-to-one exchange. These questions may be asked as easily as inquiries about your spring break, but they're formulated and analyzed quite a bit more assiduously.

Behavioral assessments are an attempt to understand more by asking you to recount how you previously acted in certain situations. The employer designs questions to determine whether a candidate possesses desired characteristics vital to the organization's success. Your answer helps determine your potential. Do you or don't you have the necessary traits for this position or company? The assumption is that your past behavior is a good predictor of how you will act in the future. It is commonly reported that behavioral assessments have a better-than-average chance of making the right call.

You might be asked why you did something, to give specific examples, and to explain reasons for an outcome. The questions are likely to begin with phrasings such as, "Tell me about a time ..." or "Describe a situation ..." The research you've done in preparation for your meeting (chapter 2) should be helpful in framing your responses. Employer and market knowledge provides insight into the important characteristics it takes to be a contributor within a specific organization. Any experiences emphasizing these exact same qualities are excellent material.

Beyond specific employer-required traits, there are attributes that a majority of organizations hope to uncover during a behavioral assessment. Instances from your colorful past that drive home at least one or two of the key qualities noted below will underscore your paycheck worthiness in today's market. Consider this list carefully as you create your branding advantage (chapter 1) so you weave stories that are consistent, hard-hitting, and believable:

- Energy
- Leadership
- Flexibility
- Decisiveness

- Adaptability
- Motivation
- Initiative
- Organizational skills
- Communication skills
- Risk-taking
- Teamwork
- Integrity

Insights

- Adhere to the insights detailed above for screening questions and general questions, being sure to offer *exceedingly* thoughtful and thorough answers.
- Decide, ahead of time, which personal experiences you will recount.
- Review your employer and market research to ascertain which characteristics are most valuable to this type of organization, culture, industry, and so on.
- Include information from your past demonstrating that you possess these specific qualities.
- Share experiences that involve both positive and negative circumstances. However, be sure that the negative instances demonstrate satisfactory resolution or proactive lessons learned.
- Formulate your answers as follows:
  1. Briefly describe a specific situation or event.
  2. Explain the action you took.
  3. Define the results in terms of outcomes and what you learned.

Examples of Behavioral Questions

1. **Question:** "Describe a time when you were put into an uncomfortable position and explain how you dealt with it."
   Answer: "I was faced with a challenge the past two summers, when I was the lead lifeguard with a lot of my friends reporting to me. There were expectations placed on me by these friends, who sometimes wanted to be treated preferentially. I was able to actually turn the tables and make the situation a positive one for our boss, the New Holland Park District.

"By being fair in my scheduling, rotating the early-morning slots, and routinely scheduling myself for a variety of shifts throughout the summer, I showed my friends that I worked hard and was committed to my responsibilities. I also made sure to tell them this in a casual, but serious way when our professional relationship got a little too easygoing. My buddies actually ended up helping out and pitching in more, rather than taking advantage of me or the situation."
Analysis: This candidate follows the model perfectly, stating the situation, explaining his actions and then defining the outcome. His example is pertinent, because it is work related and highlights responsibility—not to mention his ability to manage a difficult situation with an honest, up-front approach.

2. **Question:** "Tell me about a time when you were put into a situation and had to get up to speed quickly."
Answer: "During my six-week internship at Chronicle last summer, I felt that it was important to add value. I knew this was the only way the experience would be meaningful, and I felt an obligation to become a contributor, even if it was only for a month and a half. As a result, I made a point to transform this opportunity into more than a tour of the office.

"I contacted the person who was to be my boss during the internship and asked if we could have a brief meeting before I started. She listened as I described my desire to contribute during the summer. I told her I thought this would be the most worthwhile situation for both of us, and she agreed, pleased that I had taken the initiative.

"Together, we came up with the idea that I would work on generating a follow-up campaign to thank businesses for contributions made toward a specific cause backed by Chronicle. I was able to do some research that allowed me to be productive from the first day on the job.

"Not only was I able to learn a great deal from many different people, but I also created a database and an attractive mailing that Chronicle will continue to use. I attribute the positive outcome to my willingness to go the extra mile ... and to planning, which is a particular strength of mine."

Analysis: This candidate followed the model by defining the situation, then explaining her actions and the outcome that resulted. She did a noteworthy job of underlining her strengths—ones that are particularly attractive to recruiters.

3. **Question:** "Describe a time when you were confronted by a challenge and the outcome wasn't what you expected or planned."

   Answer: "When I joined the executive committee of our Environmental Club at school, we had to overcome a few obstacles to educate the college population and increase membership. Expanded membership was critical to funding and attracting sponsors.

   "We tried a few different approaches and eventually came up with a fun spin on a serious topic to encourage involvement. Our annual Pitch-In Fest got students in the door and kept them coming back each year for the food and entertainment we provided. The problem was that attendance didn't turn into increased membership. The event essentially operated in a vacuum.

   "Before we threw in the towel on Pitch-In, we noted that the Fest actually provided increased funding to our organization. So we shifted our focus away from the Fest as a means to increase membership and used it as a cash stream toward improving environmental programs on campus—and to mail a targeted solicitation to forestry and agriculture majors. As a result, our membership did increase.

   "Through this experience, I realized the value of looking at issues from different angles and the importance of using resources in a variety of ways to reach goals. I believe I'll apply these lessons repeatedly in my business career."

   Analysis: This interviewee is asked to address a negative outcome. He did this, then wisely pointed out how the situation had been saved from doom, which is always critical to do in a job interview. He astutely emphasized the lessons he learned and how these will be useful to him in his career. Even if Pitch-In hadn't ultimately saved the day, this candidate could have emphasized one or two positive lessons learned from the experience and still ended up with a very decent response to the question.

Stress Questions
About

Stress interviews are purposefully orchestrated to intentionally introduce taxing elements into your meeting (not to be confused with the stress naturally resulting from this entire process). Tactics include blatantly disagreeing with your opinions; challenging your credentials; inserting long, uncomfortable silences; making you wait for extended periods of time; and so on. Imagine an Interpol interrogation, and you've got the prematurely graying picture. The misguided goal seems to revolve around understanding just what you're made of and how easily you crack under pressure.

Insights

There isn't much to say about this format other than to suggest you stick to your game plan and all you've learned about professionalism, staying positive, and highlighting your skills. You can take heart in the fact that a full-blown stress session is fortunately not all that common. If you are ever caught in the predicament, try to recognize the exercise for what it is, as opposed to taking it personally.

Still, be aware that barbed, stress-laden zingers may come your way in the midst of a general Q&A interview. These inquiries are uncomfortable, because you likely have to address a glaring weakness in your candidacy.

Examples of Stress Questions

In response to the occasional high-stress question that pops up in new-grad interviews, such as, "Why isn't your GPA any higher?" or "Why didn't you get involved while on campus?" you can't be humorous or avoid answering. Be straightforward without being defensive or maudlin. Definitely reorient the session back toward the positive. You can't be too farfetched, but you can push and slightly massage an adjective or two to your advantage.

"I understand that my GPA is perhaps lower than what you would like to see. As my references show, I was invested in my courses, and I was an eager, contributing class participant across the board. I did stretch myself at college, taking courses that were challenging and interesting, rather than enrolling in those that were known to be an easy grade. I also spread myself in many different directions through extracurriculars and work, so I bring a broad skill set and valuable experience to the job."

If you just can't dust the cobwebs off anything remotely positive about your experiences—as in, you really were checked out during college—share what you've learned, how you've changed, and how this job fits in with your epiphany.

No one ever got a meaningful job offer by saying, "Hey, I messed up bad, man. Think *Pimp My Ride* with me here. I'm ready for a makeover, and this is the place."

You have to package the same sentiment in a more professional manner, understanding that some recruiters will bite and some will not (pulling out a reference from someone vouching for the new, improved you would be a nice touch right about now).

"I missed some opportunities in college, and this was a mistake. Fortunately, I understand what I should have done and I'm committed to being a person who is focused and goal-oriented. I don't want to let opportunities pass me by, and I know I'm in charge of making sure this doesn't happen. I've learned a lot and actually believe this will make me a much better, harder-working employee."

Rehearse, and Rehearse Again

It might help to remember that the best candidate doesn't always win the job; that particular prize often goes to the one who interviews best. After all, employers unanimously claim that lack of preparation is the number-one problem confounding recent grads in their job interviews. You can imagine how dramatically a young candidate who owns the moment stands out.

Consequently, rehearsing for your interviews is never a waste of time. Pull up some sample questions and answers and stand in front of the mirror to give it a run-through. Or enlist your confidant to help you practice—as well as the campus career office, which is often ideally equipped for mock interviews. Videotaping and voice recording are similarly enlightening techniques. All of these exercises take the "um" out of your presentation.

It's true that rehearsing, no matter how you do it, is contrived and awkward. You're operating in a vacuum without the real leading characters and minus the script you will be asked to follow. But with trusty insights and a focus on the big three—content, body language, and overall flow—you have an opportunity to turn practice into profit. These variables can be effectively managed using the advice on the following pages; the effort generally separates sink from swim.

Therefore, it's best to tackle rehearsal by focusing on this core. Understand what content, body language, and overall flow are all about. Then take note of the stumbling blocks typically afflicting new grad candidates. With this knowledge in hand, you can fix your presentation accordingly, before you meet your prospective boss.

Content

Content is all about the words, phrases, and stories you use in your interviews. You can say the same thing in a variety of ways. The goal, of course, is to make sure you speak as clearly and vividly as possible. This doesn't necessarily mean using a lot of fifty-cent words, by the way. Forethought and conscientious effort are just fine—in fact, they're better than a thesaurus any day.

You come across very differently when you enter a room with, "Uh, hi there. Where do you want me?" as opposed to, "Hello, I'm Graham Newton, and I've got a ten o'clock meeting with Mr. Paulsen." It's a matter of "What do you guys plan on doing next?" versus "An article I just read in *CityWatch* indicates that you put the museum on the map this past year. How do you plan to keep this momentum going?"

Many young candidates express amazement at how their message "changes" when they bother to speak aloud as opposed to composing and rehearsing in their heads or on a piece of paper. If the meaning isn't clear, or your words are getting tangled up, you'll hear this as you share your story with others or the room at large. Over time, and as you persevere with rehearsal, you will get more comfortable with this new conversational style and the words you must use to sell yourself. All of this enhances your confidence in front of recruiters.

Rehearsing sample questions and answers is a given, but you need to expand your focus. Practice a wide range of topics, concentrating on how you will greet people, excuse yourself, express thanks, and bid a fond farewell. Since you're not used to being unusually gracious and disarming from dawn to dusk (very few of us are), this is new territory that can cause a stumble or two if you're not prepared. Then, if you can't warm up to one set of words as you rehearse, try on another for size to get your point across effectively, but in a way that suits your style. The following are examples of common statements made with professional finesse:

- "It's very nice to meet you. Thank you for having me in today; I'm excited to be here."
- "Hi, I'm Amanda Cleary. Thanks a lot for this opportunity."

- "Thanks for asking. The directions were great; I didn't have any problem finding the office."
- "Yes, thank you. Everything went very smoothly this morning."

- "Will you excuse me, please? I'd like to know where the nearest restroom is."
- "I'd like to take a quick break, if that's all right with you. Where are the washrooms?"

- "Yes, a glass of water would be great. Thank you. If you point me in the right direction, I'm happy to get it myself."
- "Yes, thank you very much. I'd like some coffee, please."

- "Lunch was great. Thanks a lot for inviting me."
- "It was nice to take the time to have lunch together. I'm glad we had this chance to talk. I hope you also had a better opportunity to learn more about me. Thank you very much."

- "Thank you very much for having me in to interview today. I appreciate your time and I've learned a lot. I'm very interested in the position and hope that we can proceed to the next step."
- "I'd like to leave by mentioning that I'm very interested in this position and hope that you will seriously consider me for the job."

Similarly, go through the paces of small talk, which are always an integral part of your meetings. This too is a whole new challenge in many ways. Chapter 10 has a specific section on establishing rapport, and casual chitchat is certainly part of this interview necessity.

Stumbling Blocks

Interviewing is awkward for young applicants, because the conversation style is so far removed from the day-to-day exchanges they've had for the past twenty-two or so years. Older candidates have been around the water cooler for a while and are naturally familiar with a more formal, professional manner. As you rehearse, listen to the content of your speech to make sure you sidestep these common stumbling blocks:

- Canned dialogue
- Repetitive use of words/phrases/ideas
- Incorrect word usage and phrases that don't fit your style or demeanor
- Illogical flow, making it difficult to follow the story or understand the point
- Too much of the wrong information and too little of the right information
- Lacking refinement
- Too many "um"s and "uh"s

The Fix

Concentrate on the following as you craft the content of your interviews:

- **Occasionally use contractions to eliminate some of the stiltedness.** Use "aren't" versus "are not," "couldn't" versus "could not," "I'm" versus "I am," and so on.
- **Choose words and phrases you are comfortable with and understand.**
- **Make sure there is a concise beginning, middle, and end when telling a story (and do tell!).**
- **Focus on professional, job-related topics, along with your theme and branding advantage.** (Hopefully, you've already

become aware of the importance of this.)

- **Since there is no substitute for politeness, inject manners into the content of your conversation as much as possible without being obnoxious.**
- **Present aloud to another person and ask them to critique the content.** Did it make sense? Sound professional? Convey the right information? Was the choice of words as natural sounding as possible?
- **Eliminate awkward pauses.** Continue rehearsing your interview until you reduce the "um"s and "uh"s by at least 75 percent.

Body Language

Suddenly, you're an adolescent again. You're all legs and arms, and nothing is quite right. Body language during an interview is definitely a head-to-toe factor, encompassing every movable part. And as any decent cop knows, the guilty ones squirm the most. Those who prepare the least for an interview are similarly charged. Poise and a confident stature result from knowledge and practice.

Stumbling Blocks

You're meeting with a recruiter, not a military general, so there isn't a need to go overboard on formality and precision. But you are in body-language boot camp, training for a life-changing maneuver. Based on the persistent number of problems confounding new college grads, there's good reason to rise at the crack of dawn:

- Limp handshake
- Hunched posture
- Poor eye contact
- Perpetually pushing hair off the face or rearranging stray locks
- Chewing gum or sucking on a mint
- Twiddling with paper or pens or items on the desk
- Squirming or fidgeting
- Folding arms
- Massaging facial hair (mustache, beard)
- Slumping in the chair
- Spreading legs too far apart

The Fix

Concentrate on body language that communicates self-assurance in the following ways:

- **Shake hands using a firm, but not a "let's arm wrestle" grip.** Unobtrusively dry your hands on your pant leg or skirt if you lean toward sweaty palms.
- **Hold your head up high and your body straight in a relaxed style, so you look eager, but not overly stiff.**
- **Look your interviewer in the eye without coming across as a crazed hypnotist.**
- **Deal with hair issues before you get into the interview.** If your locks have a tendency to fall in your face, come up with a way to control the bangs or unruly strands.
- **Don't use mints or gum during an interview.** Period.
- **Keep your hands occupied with a pad of paper and a pen for note taking.** This has a way of controlling extraneous fidgeting, leg movements, and toe tapping.
- **Sit up tall and lean slightly forward in your chair, so you look attentive and interested.**
- **Position your legs close together.** Males should keep both feet planted firmly on the floor, and females are wise to do the same, or cross their legs.

Overall Flow

The tin man in *The Wizard of Oz* was looking for a heart. You are as well. And while you journey on the yellow-brick road to clinching a job, bolster your arsenal with the scarecrow's brain and the lion's courage. Let your passion, knowledge, and forthright essence shine through by connecting the dots and presenting yourself as a captivating total package in the interview.

Stumbling Blocks

"Wait, is it all right if I start over?" You guessed right. This question was asked and answered in an actual interview as a candidate attempted to rattle off her very well-memorized response to the request, "Tell me about yourself."

Even though you've sharpened the content and toned the specifics behind your body language, you haven't tied it all together with showmanship and confidence. Here's what typically goes wrong, short-circuiting your overall presentation style:

- You still sound and look too exacting and unnatural—in other words, amateurish, insincere, and dull.
- Anything slightly askew throws you far afield.
- "Backpedaler" is used to describe you more often than "suave."

The Fix

Adhere to the following insights about creating an appealing package that is interesting, natural, and full of "hire-me" warmth:

- **Memorize your answers ... kind of.** Many candidates claim that the most effective presentations result when you allow yourself to practice the essence of what you want to say. This is as opposed to focusing on all of the exact words, as our friend above did to her disadvantage. A slightly relaxed standard has a way of relaxing you and your delivery.
- **Include a smattering of interesting intonations and pitch variations into your speech.** This transports black and white into 3D animation like nothing else. And even though it's better to sound like a baritone than a monotone any day, make sure you don't submit your interviewer to the full range of a church-choir tryout.
- **Practice inserting an interviewer's name into your responses.** Your exchanges suddenly seem less prefabricated if you say, "I'd like to tell you more about my experiences at Lewis & Clark, Mr. Townsend."
- **Rehearse pulling documents (résumé, KISS, references, and so on) out of your portfolio, binder, or briefcase to hand to the recruiter.** This juggling act can trip up the most sure-fingered candidate at the most inappropriate times; practice will make perfect.
- **Rehearse in the clothes you'll wear to your meetings.** Interview day carries enough shock value without the ill-fitting introduction of numbing dress shoes, strangulating neckties, and ... well, let's not talk about what pantyhose does to otherwise happy, focused women. The sooner you

embrace your new professional style and all its boundaries, the easier it is to be yourself in these new duds.

- **If a beverage is offered, take it if it's to your liking—or simply ask for water.** Sipping a mug of java lends a casual, coffee-klatch feel that dilutes the formality of the meeting. It also gives you something to do with your hands, and the liquid infusion will come to the rescue if your voice cracks under pressure.

- **Be as satisfied as possible with what you are saying and how you look.** We all manage to put our best foot forward when we have the confidence to back it up. If you aren't happy about something at the eleventh rehearsal hour, change it. Despite your fatigue, squeeze out another fifteen minutes to make it right.

- **Think about someone who has a compelling delivery.** Decipher what attracts you to this person as they speak. As much as possible, inject these characteristics into your presentation, so you are equally irresistible.

- **Smile and be enthusiastic to a fault.** It's amazing how strongly a positive disposition can attract people and pull them onto your side, no matter what. If you're slightly canned, or if you stumble, you'll be forgiven if you exude good, old-fashioned sunshine.

Chapter 4

Step Outside the Box

"When I was applying to colleges they frequently reminded us that
our class had the largest number of applicants in the history of admissions.
And the truth is, I did have to get creative just to get deferred.
If I do the math correctly, I've got a similar challenge now.
I'm looking for a job and competing with the
exact same group from four years ago."
—Rising Senior, English Major and
Art History Minor, Emory University

Her goal: "To teach overseas for at least three years
in an exotic locale."

YOU CAN START UNLEVELING the playing field in your favor even before
you walk into your scheduled interviews. Via a simple, astute
communication, you solidify the notion that you're a person worth
talking to. This is one more piece of the puzzle firmly planting you in
the "good vibe" pile.

If you think you lack the aplomb to pull off a plucky maneuver
like this, think again. Colleges and universities are stellar incubators
for hatching hustlers who understand how to break out of their
shells and chirp for attention. Most college students confirm that
"the squeaky wheel gets the grease." After all, you successfully gained
admission to classes closed for weeks, convinced roommates to do …
well … you know what, and persuaded your parents to chip in for that
"educational experience" in Cancun. And then, fancying Cabo's West
Coast landscape, you talked them into another south-of-the-border

foray the following year.

As you learned, the key is to ease into your benefactor's good graces, as opposed to leading the charge with a steamroller. And while bribery has appeal, it emotes desperation and shadiness here. Basically, shelve any notions of skywriting, Super Bowl tickets, or a pop-up box of tchotchkes.

Recruiters sit up and take notice early on when your approach employs strategies that make a subtle but memorable statement. If you offer an enticing preview with an appropriate script that is well choreographed, your fresh face will be a very welcome sight when the curtain goes up on interview day.

Pregame Buzz

Figure out the best message to convey about yourself. Pinpoint the seductive high notes of your candidacy, but remember that you're in the early wannabe stage. Whet a recruiter's appetite instead of totally satiating it. Build excitement and anticipation as opposed to filling in all the blanks. There are four possible areas—proven topics—to draw alluring, appropriate details from right now: heartfelt desire, college experiences, personal tidbits, and work-related particulars.

Heartfelt Desire

We all enjoy hearing that someone is pleased to be included as a guest at our upcoming party. Recruiters are similarly gratified when you invest the time to say, "I'm excited about our upcoming meeting. Thank you for this opportunity." This type of enthusiasm is always appropriate and usually warmly received.

You avoid sounding formulaic by throwing in a buzzword or two you picked up from the organization's Web site. "I'm excited about our upcoming meeting and want to thank you for the opportunity to learn more about your 'one company, one team' approach." You can convey heartfelt desire of this sort on its own, or you can include the sentiment along with one of the other strategies noted below.

College Experiences

Using college experiences as a part of your pregame message isn't only for Rhodes Scholars. Most students can pull up an appropriate attention grabber from the past several years on campus. Choose the focal point of your warm-up strategy from the following school-related instances:

- **A quotation from one of your reference letters.** "I'm looking forward to discussing employment opportunities and am anxious to share what I can bring to the organization and its 'one company, one team' approach. A former boss pointed out that I am a 'highly committed and industrious individual with a lot to offer on a daily basis.' I hope to convince you that my high standards and energy will be evident from day one on the job."

- **Information from a professor, peer, adviser, or coach.** "Thank you for the opportunity to talk further about career opportunities on February 19. As you mentioned when we met on campus, you are looking for individuals who are creative and hard charging. My former swim coach, Cal Meyer, often commented on my inordinate determination and drive. The portfolio that I will share at our meeting should highlight my fresh, innovative style. I very much look forward to seeing you in a few weeks."

- **Notable pursuits, leadership moments, accomplishments, or awards.** Included are exemplary grades and academic achievements; college- sponsored trips and their impact on you; campus involvements that have been particularly meaningful; distinctions relating to your major; internships; and sports triumphs. "I hope to connect with you at the Hallmark Job Fair at the end of the month. Last summer, I interned at Juno Enterprises and quickly realized that operations management both interests me and capitalizes on my strengths. I am particularly intrigued by the opportunities to improve overall systems through innovative inventory control. Since last summer, I've completed coursework to bolster my knowledge base even further. I'll make it a point to stop by early on April 11 in the hopes we can have a quick lunch together that day; I'd like to learn more about how you consistently end up 'a cut above' in the marketplace."

- **Information about the interviewing organization's affiliation with the college, either through philanthropy or**

an impressive roster of alums on the payroll. "I appreciate the opportunity to meet with you about the management-trainee position at Dymatech. I would bring the same traits and skills to Dymatech that you have come to associate with Emory grads. I look forward to sharing more information about my coursework and experiences on November 2, and I'm anxious to learn more about your 'cutting-edge' methodologies."

Personal Tidbits

There are insights about your daily life that paint a picture worth a thousand words—the two most important of those words being "hire me." As always, it's wise to remain politically correct and avoid overly intimate details. Focus on information that emphasizes your drive, motivation, skill set, and any meaningful personal connection.

- **Personal or family connections that are meaningful to the organization or interviewer.** "As I learned more about Pathways Inc. over the past few weeks, I realized that my next-door neighbor, Doug Chaston, has a longstanding association with your president. After an in-depth conversation with Mr. Chaston, I came away further convinced that Pathways, with its 'passionate-innovation' approach, is an organization where I could flourish and make a contribution. I appreciate the opportunity to talk with you and other members of the Pathways team about career opportunities, and I look forward to seeing you on June 16."

- **Interesting hobbies, sports, or avocations.** "I appreciate the opportunity to meet with you early next month to talk further about the Midwest sales position. As I continued training for the Chicago Marathon this past weekend, I realized that the very attributes fueling my athletic interests are ones that would allow me to make a substantial imprint as a sales associate for Clemson Freightways, with its 'one company, one team' approach. I would bring similar enthusiasm and determination to the position; I look forward to convincing you of this on March 2."

- **Notable involvements or accomplishments in the community**

through volunteer work and civic duties. "Thank you for setting up my interview on January 26. I appreciate the chance to meet individuals from Crossroads and hope that I'm able to impart my strong desire to be a part of your 'committed to excellence' organization. I'll bring along photos and media releases reviewing the recent dance-a-thon I chaired where we raised over $13,000 for Orchard Village, a premiere nonprofit supporting individuals with developmental disabilities. I am hopeful that this information, along with other insights, solidifies the viability of my candidacy."

Work-Related Particulars

Park-district employment and babysitting say a lot about you. Don't shy away from talking about the jobs you've held simply because you haven't yet been the CEO of a Fortune 500 monolith. You're in the same boat as everyone else—and it's a decent, seaworthy vessel. Consider sharing these details:

- **Responsibilities that caused you to stretch and grow, and those you personally embraced.** "Thank you for the chance to further discuss the kinetic wellness teaching position at Sunrise Elementary, where you subscribe to the philosophy of 'one school, one team.' I feel that I am an ideal candidate for a number of reasons, including the opportunity I had last summer to plan and lead the morning sessions for the most popular day camp in town. I look forward to sharing the details and more with you on February 8."
- **Explicit supervisory and training opportunities.** "I'm excited about our upcoming meeting to discuss a research-assistant position with Facts, Figures and Formulas. My interest in your business is longstanding, and I've made a point of gaining meaningful experience. In an unprecedented move, I was allowed to conduct the opening session of a focus group for the market-research organization I interned for last summer. I look forward to sharing more information about this when I see you on October 4; thank you for the opportunity."
- **Promotions based on performance.** "Thank you for meeting

with me on January 23 to discuss job opportunities with Vital
Med. I look forward to sharing more information about my
work experience at our community hospital. I have been
given greater responsibilities over the past few years and
have increased my pay through various promotions based
on merit. I appreciate the chance to interview, and I look
forward to seeing you and learning more about your 'focus
on the future' campaign."

- **Cache-laden experiences.** Included are lessons and
  circumstances revolving around age-old hot buttons, such
  as customer service, sales tactics, employee relations, time
  management, and so on. "I'm excited about meeting with
  you to talk further about the nutritionist position and to
  learn more about your 'spotlight on fitness' initiative. I
  look forward to filling you in regarding my background
  and am particularly excited to share more about my unique
  educational experience in New York this past summer. I
  attended a two-week seminar dedicated to lifestyle trends
  that was both inspirational and highly informative. The
  insights and updates seem pertinent to the population you
  serve. Thank you for the opportunity, and I'll see you on
  November 19."

Finesse-Filled Execution

Your execution strategy is as important as the content cornerstone
you just chose for your mini ad blitz. You shouldn't be intrusive, but
you can't be so understated that it isn't worth the effort. Actually, if
smooth-as-silk were ever required, this is the time.

Given the parameters, and keeping in mind that this is an enticing
teaser and no more, there are only a few staid ways to get your message
across in an acceptable fashion. Strategies that have proven to work
well involve carefully calculating the who, when, and how of the
moment. ("Carefully" is the operative word—examples further below
demonstrate how, if you're not careful, you can misplace the advantage
you're far better off carrying in your hip pocket.) By doing your
homework, you advance in the process and enhance your interview-
day confidence. Remember that by making a concerted effort here,
you steadily inch ahead of the less diligent crowd.

Calculate Who

The individuals conducting your interviews are your target audience and should receive the communication you just crafted. If you researched your recruiters as suggested in chapter 2, you understand this roster very well.

Now is the time to be absolutely certain about the spelling of names, and of which exact title applies to each person. A vice president of customer service is unhappy when you demote him to a manager or completely ignore his position in formal correspondence by omitting his title. Knowing the correct name of the organization is also key. There are nuances worth paying attention to, such as "The McAllister Corporation" versus "McAllister," and "Claremont High School" instead of "Claremont City High School." You potentially do more harm than good if you miss any of these important details.

Calculate When

Given that inboxes are jam-packed, travel itineraries are intense, and employees take vacations, the quicker you put your plan into action, the greater the likelihood you will get the attention you're aiming for. This may be easier said than done, given that interview schedules are often not finalized until the last minute. But don't let this deter you from carrying on with haste.

Calculate How

Ah, those creative juices are really working overtime. Even ignoring the Super Bowl ticket bribery angle, resourcefulness and a keen imagination are still taking you down other colorful, standing ovation roads. What's wrong with artfully presenting your pregame message on a mocked-up box of Frosted Flakes? After all, you're interviewing with the leading ready-to-eat cereal company in the country.

More often than not, "too much, too soon" is ... well, too much, too soon. A possible finale played out at the onset sets the stage all wrong. You might come across as desperate or brash, or you create a benchmark that you have to beat with each subsequent point of contact. As the interview process comes to a close, the ante might be up high enough where you need a Tony the Tiger getup and voice lessons to help you project out of twenty pounds of fur.

As with most relationships, it's wise to ease into the dynamics of sharing information, based on what you learn as you go along. Thus, sticking to rather straightforward and understated strategies is a safer approach at the pregame stage. After all, the goal is not so much to create an Academy Award-worthy imprint. Rather, your objective right now is to squeak; this is what ultimately gets the grease. There are three ways to ensure this lube job.

The Privileged Express

The "good ol' boy" network is alive and well; don't apologize if you're on the receiving end of this bastion of privilege. If you know someone who has an in with the company, see if that person is willing to open doors for you with a well-placed call or e-mail.

There are two caveats, however. First, the in must truly be of a compelling nature, and not just someone who kind of knows the VP or is a friend of a friend's cousin. The relationship must be meaningful to both parties. And only one person within the organization should be contacted. This is not a campaign to mobilize with great fanfare and shove down the throats of many. Understand that the individual receiving information about you will likely forward the details to others involved in your interview process, and appropriate notations will generally be made in all the right places.

Second, your benefactor should not be in strong-arm mode. Rather, this is about giving your recruiter a heads-up and an endorsement indicating that you are someone worth considering. "I'm calling about Gena Andresen, Mark. I understand she's coming in for an interview in a week. I want to let you know that I've known Gena for over fifteen years and I couldn't think more highly of her or her family. She's very sharp and energetic, and I sense she'd be an asset to your organization. I was pleased to hear about the meeting and hope it goes well."

While it's tempting to take the initiative and toot this horn yourself, it isn't appropriate. Don't say or write, "I just want to let you know that I've been acquainted with George Fulbright for the past ten years. Mr. Fulbright, who I understand is a good friend of yours, has been close to our family and thinks very highly of me—and anyone in the McAllister clan, for that matter." A less self-ingratiating approach along these lines, however, can work (see above, "Personal Tidbits").

Snail Mail

Chapter 9 reviews the critical fundamentals behind your communications with prospective employers—including writing letters the old-fashioned, postage-stamped way. These rules all apply here as you use the U.S. mail to deliver pregame buzz before your interview.

While black and white isn't necessarily an exciting game plan, it is a very effective way to converse at this stage. With a hard copy letter, you're noticeable these days. Snail mail is increasingly a thing of the past, so it is often a refreshing, new-age strategy. Additionally, stationery allows you to succinctly solidify your important message and present it in an auspicious way.

Having chosen your message, you may execute on one page of formal letterhead along the lines of these examples:

A Letter Expressing Heartfelt Desire

Dear Ms. Torrence:

I'm looking forward to our upcoming meeting next week. Thank you for the opportunity to talk further about a career at Sullivan Brothers and your "one company, one team" approach.

My experiences throughout college have taught me a lot about which jobs are appealing and also afford me an opportunity to excel as a material contributor. Because I tend to be very people-oriented and creative, I believe that Sullivan Brothers is an organization where I fit and where I can bring value. I look forward to sharing and learning more along these lines next week.

Thank you again, and I'll see you on May 22.

Sincerely,

Kelly Pointer

A Letter Conveying College Experiences

Dear Mr. Henderson:

I'm looking forward to our upcoming meeting next week. Thank you for the opportunity to talk further about a career at Newton Inc. and to learn more about your team of "passionate innovators."

In preparation for my interview, I came across a paper that was recently graded by my Latin American literature studies professor. He wrote, "Your insights are compelling, and you have an uncanny way of drawing the reader in to keep turning the page. Outstanding."

I would like to share this project with you. I believe the writing is representative of my abilities and my sensitivity to the reading audience. I hope to discuss this and more on February 24.
Sincerely,
Luvean Solomon

Another Letter Conveying College Experiences
Dear Mr. McKinven:

I'm looking forward to meeting you next week when you interview on Elon's campus. I've signed up for the 1:00 time slot on November 19, and I welcome this opportunity to talk about career possibilities at Highland Bank and your "customer-custodian" approach.

I recently returned from a campus retreat where we explored current trends with local leaders in commerce. This experience provided very interesting perspectives and solidified my desire to use my business-administration degree in the financial world.

Highland Bank offers the full breadth of services critical to meeting the needs of today's market. I feel that my experiences, along with my attention to detail and my leadership capabilities, are compatible with your mission. In essence, I'm very excited about the potential fit.

I hope your trip to North Carolina is a good one, and I will see you next Thursday.
Sincerely,
Yuki Kobayashi

A Letter Sharing Personal Tidbits
Dear Ms. Boggs:

I hope to meet with you at the Pathways to Education Job Expo in Chicago on February 24. I will graduate from the University of Illinois with a degree in special education in May and would like to teach elementary or middle school students starting this fall.

Because I grew up in the Chicago area and have always been committed to helping populations with developmental disabilities, I know the community well. I would embrace a chance to continue working with the organizations and families I am close to and have assisted over the years. I believe that my upbeat approach and team orientation would be an asset to your school district.

I most recently assisted with the Special Olympics qualifying events in Chicago and ended up spearheading a neighborhood sponsorship for one of the athletes. We will be cheering on our track star in just a few short months.

I look forward to seeing you on February 24 and hope we have a chance to talk further at that time.

Sincerely,

Herbert Belk

A Letter Imparting Work-Related Particulars

Dear Mr. Bender:

Thank you for inviting me in to meet more of the team at Lettuce Dine You Enterprises. I'm very excited about this opportunity and look forward to learning more about the organization and your mission "to be at the forefront of America's taste buds." I'm also anxious to fill you in on the contributions I am capable of making following my graduation from the University of Denver.

I would like to reiterate that while employed by Keifer's Cafe and Grill, I was handpicked to complete a comprehensive supervisory training program last year. I ended up capitalizing on the coursework immediately, since the restaurant added a lunch offering in addition to its dinner menu. Despite a sudden doubling of staff and customers, we were successful from day one.

I believe this experience was meaningful and further prepared me for more challenging opportunities, such as those you spearhead at LDU Enterprises.

I look forward to seeing you again on January 17, and I hope your trip to San Diego was enjoyable over the holidays.

Sincerely,

Katherine Abdul

E-mail

There is little question that e-mail is a contender. But before you log on to get wired to all the interviewers on your calendar, take a moment to review chapter 9. Once you're comfortable with the dos and don'ts surrounding online communication as it pertains to your interviewing process, carefully consider the feasibility of this tactic to convey your pregame buzz.

While it doesn't make as much of a statement as crisp linen

stationery, e-mail has a few advantages. Since time may be of the essence, a cyberchat might be the ticket in this instance. Additionally, some people simply prefer electronic correspondence over anything else these days. Your instincts will help you discern which individuals are partial to connections via a keyboard and a mouse.

Whether delivered by virtual mail or snail mail, pregame correspondence to prospective employers follows the same tack. These communications are essentially identical: short, filled with heartfelt desire, professional, and all about fit ... in other words, similarly squeaky.

Learn from Misfires that Replaced Advantage

The stories below are from innovative and exuberant recent college grads who did the unthinkable, yet survived to dish about pregame execution that backfired. Yep, this is a blooper reel, of sorts. These insights, along with what's known about a successful interviewing process, show that it's best—even in very creative fields such as advertising, event planning, entertainment, marketing, and public relations—to keep the warm-up short and simple. Learn from these misfires that replaced advantage.

A DVD Misfire

Bret decided to show his enthusiasm and creativity in one fell swoop. He got his band pals together to record an original song: a tune all about Bret's upcoming interview. Bret sang the chorus solo, in perfect pitch, and then shipped off a DVD chronicling the entire creative process from composition to performance. He made sure the cadre of managers he was about to meet received his melodic pregame buzz. Despite Bret's tremendous production effort, the DVD wasn't viewed by anyone at the interviewing company. Instead, it was frequently referenced in conversations with Bret: "What was that CD you sent us, anyway?" Too much of each interview was spent explaining the DVD, as opposed to the more pertinent, salable features of Bret's candidacy.

A Web Misfire

Lauren designed her own Web site to detail her fit and desire for one specific job in an unparalleled way. She was gunning for an opportunity at an elite IT company. But Lauren sent the wrong link to her site in an e-mail to members of the management team. She provided the link in such a way that the address was highlighted in her sentence within a set of parentheses. As each of the recipients clicked on the link, an error message popped up, indicating there was no domain by that name. When the third interviewer pointed out the mishap to Lauren, she realized she probably wasn't going to be hired by the elite IT company.

A Flowery Misfire

Braiden grew up with flowers in her household. They were given as a way to celebrate, make up, or simply say, "Have a nice day." No matter what, flowers always delivered a feel-good moment. It's no surprise that Braiden's thoughts went to carnations and Gerber daisies with baby's breath as she approached her interview with Clindamon Pharmaceuticals. While she was profusely thanked for the gesture, the interviewer pointed out that her office is in a lab, where it's impossible to enjoy flowers due to a highly controlled environment. She thought Braiden would have known ...

A T-shirt Misfire

About a week before his on-premise interview, Pat had a T-shirt designed and delivered to his prospective employer, whom he had met and understood to be an avid golfer. The front of the shirt read, "Interview Goal? Perfect Par." The back of the tee advertised: "Zero Handicaps. No Slices. No Balls. Out of the Rough." Unfortunately, the T-shirt was delivered by Pat's roommate, sight unseen by Pat ... who claims he would have caught that "Water" was missing between "No" and "Balls."

A Singing-Telegram Misfire

Colette wanted to shout from the rooftops when she got the interview for an internship at the ad agency. She did what she thought was the next best thing, especially since she knew karaoke had a following in the office. There were several problems with her attempt to convey unbridled enthusiasm ... but the standout complication was her choice of the wrong place and time.

On the day the telegram arrived, a major client was being wined and dined as a way to make up for an unfortunate customer-service snafu of great magnitude. All employees were on their very best behavior, having been ordered to exude austerity over anything else. The six-foot clown holding the dozen multicolored balloons and belting out, "I've Got My Mind Set On You," was not a welcome distraction.

Chapter 5

Spend More Than Chump Change

"A few years ago, the women's national lacrosse champs
wore flip-flops to visit the president of the United States and later
sold their 'if these suede puppies could talk' Birkenstocks on eBay.
"Count on the fact that the average collegiate Joe will never cash
in on such a brazen fashion faux pas as graduation rolls around.
"The reason for this is simple: the White House has nothing on
us tightly-wound HR managers."
—VP, Human Resources, Fortune 100 Company

His goal: "Launch my own consulting business within the next two years."

WHEN YOU WALK INTO an interview, it's not wise to evoke the words "eye candy." As a matter of fact, you're striving for an unremarkable appearance—your outfit should blend into the background, not stand out as the reason you are memorable. And by the way, you can't be frumpy or boring either. Smart, fresh, and suitable are the yardstick measurements.

You're likely getting the idea that this is tricky. After all, clothes, hair, and makeup choices are about as subjective as they come. Factor in the culture of the workplace, and you hopefully get the picture that the morning of isn't the time to sift through do-rag dynamics or your closet.

The "what to wear?" question is a quagmire, but there are guidelines to help you maneuver through stilettos, piercings, and belted or not.

From Spandex to Wool and Everything In Between

The game of dressing for work is played by a set of rules you've only visited occasionally, if at all. You can't even count on church or dinner-with-the-grandparents attire to be the white knight in this instance. But factoring in three considerations usually gets the interview outfit right; your clothes should be appropriate, professional and comfortable.

Appropriate

You're really hoping to fit in rather than stand out. An age-old suggestion is to scope out the target office by positioning yourself on a corner with eyes peeled to ascertain the best combination of clothes to wear. This game plan might work and it might not. You could inadvertently zero in on someone making a delivery or working in the penthouse suite of offices for a different company.

Your safest bet is to adhere to what is expected in most situations. Even though internal dress codes may be more casual these days, the interviewing runway hasn't been similarly relaxed. Unless you are specifically told to dress a certain way, or you are absolutely certain of an alternative style, follow the guidelines below.

Appropriate Attire for Males
- Conservative gray, dark blue, or other subdued color two-piece, single-breasted business suit
- Conservative long-sleeved white or pastel shirt
- White T-shirt (this helps with perspiration, and you will be thankful if you are invited to remove your jacket during the interview)
- Subdued tie that complements your shirt and suit
- Dress belt
- Dress socks
- Conservative dress shoes

Appropriate Attire for Females
- Conservative two-piece business suit, preferably a skirt instead of pants (women have a bit more leeway than men in terms of color, but should still stick to a subdued palette)
- Conservative blouse or other top in a restrained color or pattern

- A belt, if needed or desired, to stylishly tie together the outfit
- Pantyhose, instead of tights or bare legs
- Conservative dress shoes (preferably close-toed, or open-toed with a very professional leaning)

Professional

You have to pay attention to the details that punch up the professionalism quotient of your garb. These accents say you're ready to be a player in the sophisticated business milieu.

There are a few ways to accomplish a crisp fashionista look while maintaining your conservative, subdued presence. Men don't have as many wardrobe choices, and the precision by which their outfit is judged is similarly black and white. Females, on the other hand, must be ever diligent within an arena that boasts broad fashion boundaries.

And regardless of your gender, a two-hundred-dollar suit and a five-thousand-dollar Armani look equally shabby with a mustard stain on the pocket. Clothes—expensive or otherwise—are only as attractive as the care they receive. This is a good time to start your collection of those flimsy plastic bags from your corner dry cleaners. Most of these establishments have an "early in, out the same day" deal, and you should be a frequent flier during interview season.

A Professional Look for Males

- Opt for a short-sleeved, crewneck T-shirt. If you choose a V-neck, a triangle of bare skin might show through your shirt and look odd. If you wear a sleeveless tank, you run into the same appearance issue as with a V-neck, while also defeating the pit-shield purpose of a tee with sleeves.
- Wear your underwear so that it is not visible above the waistband of your pants. Colorful boxers may show through the material of a white shirt, even when the shirt is tucked in.
- Fasten all the buttons of your shirt, including the very top one and the sleeves.
- Allow your shirtsleeves to show slightly below your suit-jacket sleeves.
- Tailor the sleeves of your suit jacket to end around your

wrist.

- Fasten the top buttons or the middle button (but never the bottom button) of your jacket as you enter an interview. Once you sit down, you should unbutton the jacket, but keep it on.
- Bring your outfit together in a subtle but sharp style through your tie. Draw in colors from your shirt and suit, and choose striped, geometric or dot patterns.
- Your tie should be carefully knotted, so it is even and compact. The back flap of the tie should not be longer than the front flap. The bottom point of your tie should hit at your waist, around the top of your belt.
- Smoothly cover your tie all the way around your neck with the shirt collar. If there are buttons on the collar of your shirt, fasten these to affix the collar to the shirt.
- Neatly tuck your shirt into your pants, so there isn't a lot of excess material blousing over the belt.
- Wear slacks that are long enough to break slightly where pant hits shoe as you stand up straight.
- Use a belt and shoes in the same color family to bring your look together. If wearing a blue or gray suit, use a black belt and black shoes or a deep, rich burgundy color for both.
- Fit your belt around your waist, not your hips.
- The belt should be fed through the pant loops and, after you fasten the buckle, the end of the belt should be tucked neatly away, around your waist.
- Avoid droopy socks so no bare leg shows when you are seated.
- With a gray or dark blue suit, wear black dress socks. Use a dark brown pair with a similarly colored suit.

A Professional Look for Females

- Wear unobtrusive underwear. This means that straps and other peekaboos are off-limits, as is a black bra under a white blouse.
- Opt for flesh-colored pantyhose, without patterns and without runs.
- Avoid tops that might fit, but are snug, see-through, or low cut. Cleavage should not be a part of your "you" brand,

although it might make some employers salivate.

- Allow your shirtsleeves (if wearing a long-sleeved blouse) to show slightly below your suit-jacket sleeves.
- Tailor the sleeves of your suit jacket to end around your wrist.
- Make sure your skirt balances the professional look of your outfit. Maintain the length so you don't go shorter than two inches above the knee. Your skirt should also be miles away from skin tight, and without deep slits.
- Wear a belt that isn't flashy or noisy. It's important not to jingle-jangle your way into a room with beads, sequins, or metal.
- Keep your shoes in a single neutral color, with a heel that is no more than about two inches high.
- If wearing an open-toed shoe, use sandal-foot pantyhose with the seam tucked under your toes, out of view.

Comfortable

It's vitally important to feel at home in your interview outfit. Once you ace advanced shirts and shoes, you exude confidence, because your clothes are "right." Comfort—and ultimately the most flattering style—comes from all of the above and by paying attention to the following.

Fit

There's no question that you come across as a more professional, polished candidate when your clothes are neither too big nor too small. But the illusion of fit isn't the whole story. Many people can look pristine while still suffering in silence. Fastening a garment together with safety pins or vowing to eat a light lunch aren't smart wardrobe tactics during interviews. Imagine yanking up droopy pantyhose or tugging on your collar to negotiate an open airway while fielding questions about your greatest weakness and what it has taught you throughout the years. Essentially, a snug or ample fit, even when it may not necessarily show, is a bothersome diversion you don't want and can't afford.

And while a trendy look may be comfortable, and very much in style, with a suit jacket that technically "fits" as a short, figure-hugging number, it doesn't work for job interviews. When it comes to dressing for recruiters, a good fit avoids too tight, too short, or too baggy.

Fabric

Linen crinkles very easily, and you look crumpled before you know it. It's hard to be a refreshing answer to a corporation's hiring dilemma when you are a wrinkled mess. Similarly, wool can be a beautiful, breathable fabric, but some varieties are also heavy and uncomfortable, especially in the fifth hour under fluorescent bulbs.

Some fabrics are more economical and therefore kinder to your wallet. If you can get professionalism and everything else you need for a steal, by all means go for it. But be aware that this is hard to accomplish. Less expensive fabrics often wrinkle easily, are not as durable, are sometimes shinier, and often pill. Suddenly, you've lost your luster (despite the "glow" of poly), and you have to go back to the drawing board—and the ATM—all too soon.

Certain fabrics simply hold up under lights, camera, and action better than others, and in the climate you're interviewing in. Since clothing is an important and significant investment, you're wise to understand this ahead of time and calculate it into the purchase of your outfit.

Season

Some say you can wear white before Memorial Day without worrying about the fashion police and jail time. But it would be just your luck to end up with an interviewer who marks the calendar with Miss Manners's precision, donning white Nubucks like clockwork.

It's best to be sensitive to the seasons when putting together your interview outfit. This way, you'll avoid looking like yesterday's news or next quarter's forecast. Your presentation is simply and gloriously correct when you wear a bold, rich striped tie in winter, and a lighter pastel version in the spring.

Personal Panache

In all of this, remember that you are the mainstay—the one constant that will rule the day. As such, you should gravitate toward styles and colors that you know look and feel good on your body. Confidence emanates from the inside out, even when it comes to belts and socks. If you feel good about what you're wearing, you will exude an attractive presence.

Head-to-Toe Nitty-Gritty

Your immaculate set of clothing deserves nothing less than a meticulously orchestrated total package. You can't let down your guard when it comes to hair, general grooming, makeup, scent, and accessories.

Hair

Here's that *c*-word again. The more conservative you can get your hair (including mustache, beard, and sideburns) to appear, without changing your overall look or the age appropriateness and attractiveness of it, the more likely the locks on your head will be an asset as opposed to a liability. A few basic considerations accomplish this goal rather nicely and are detailed below.

Clean and Fresh

You might think it goes without saying that a head of hair recently shampooed and combed is the order of the day. Surprisingly, many candidates forego this basic detail and show up with oily strands in clumps. In addition to making sure that your hair shines and is neat, pay attention to how recently you visited the barber or salon. An exuberant pair of scissors does wonders for split ends, vision-impairing bangs, fuzzy necks, and overgrown facial hair.

Color Dynamics

Subtle highlights enhance. Thick, random streaks of burnt orange steal the show ... and don't usually command a standing ovation during most job interviews. While you might take it on the chin where your individuality is concerned, you make the right choice for your interview strategy when you tone down to a mellow, more middle-of-the-road color scheme.

Style and Control

Just as serving a new dinner recipe to company is risky, so is trying out a new hairdo on a job interview. While meeting with a prospective boss, you want your hair to be a nonissue. Assuming you have a style that passes in the professional arena (Mohawks, reverse Mohawks, dreadlocks, severely spiked hair, and overpowering sideburns are a few not making the grade), you'll do your nerves and your stylist (that's you) a favor if you stick to the tried-and-true. Opting for a hairstyle off the beaten path usually involves too much mousse ("plastic head") and eleventh-hour angst.

General Grooming

Speaking of oily ... this is not the way to get noticed in your interviews. A few general grooming habits that may have gone by the wayside during your years in college are decidedly vital now. Chances are, most of you know your marching orders here and only need a brief refresher course. Still, HR managers scratch their heads wondering why all college grads aren't as squeaky clean as this list when it comes to their appearance in a job interview. Take the information below and use it to fit your situation. You know best if—and where—there's work to be done.

Clean Behind the Ears

And in them. There's nothing quite as disarming as a sideways glance into someone's yellow, waxy ear.

Trim Fingernails (and Toenails, if visible)

Clean and groomed nails (as in, not raw or tattered from a lot of biting over four or five years of final exams) are noticeable and a detail rarely missed by recruiters. Women's fingernails can be longer and should be tastefully manicured.

Scrub Your Face

Washing away that shiny layer that makes you appear to be more nervous than you are gives you a healthy looking complexion. You also remove the unattractive crustiness of sleep from your eyes.

Shower

Showering is the best wake-up call around and is also an activity that handily removes a variety of smelly sins.

Shave

Clean shaven equals fresh. Females wearing a sleeveless top under a suit should shave under their arms in the event the jacket comes off during an interview (even if you don't plan on this, stranger things than air-conditioning giving out have happened).

Pluck/Wax

Streamlining brows to take away that haphazard, unibrow, or menacing look is a good idea.

Deodorize

Even in the dead of winter, you'll need an antiperspirant and not just deodorant.

Brush and Gargle

Since smiles and rapport are a focal point of your interview, get your pearly whites dazzling and make sure your breath is its minty best.

Control Static Cling

While not a matter of cleanliness, skirts and pants creeping up on your legs is assuredly a grooming issue. The more you try to solve the problem, the worse it gets. Keep a can of Static Guard in your bathroom, and you'll be gloriously clingfree.

Makeup

Less is more. You've heard this since you were ten years old, and it's still good advice. Makeup, like anything else about your appearance during a job interview, shouldn't be the focal point of your meeting. Bright colors and heavy application cause interviewers to concentrate on your lips and eyelids more than on your candidacy. Staying with softer shades, applied with a light touch, brings out your best features in a subtle, professionally perfect way.

Scent

Again, less is more. Think of how torturous it is to sit next to someone in the movie theater who reeks of cologne. This is not the reaction you're aiming for in a job interview. Spraying one brief mist of cologne into the air for you to walk through on your way out the door affords just enough allure.

Accessories

You will have baubles and bangles of all sorts that qualify as accessories. These essentially fall into one of two categories: fashion statements and interview necessities. The former are embellishments that you choose to complete your look. Interview necessities include supplies you should take along to your upcoming meetings.

Fashion Statements

Jewelry, purses, and accessory clothing are fashion statements. There are a few miscellaneous forms of expression, such as tattoos, to consider as well. Inappropriateness revolves around the overall glitz factor, any unprofessional message you send (overtly or otherwise), and manageability/distractibility aspects. Basically, you must smack of professionalism, you don't want to be particularly glamorous, and you shouldn't introduce variables that are unwieldy or attention grabbing.

The following recommendations have been gathered from a number of HR heads who underscore that traditional is still the standard. While some of this advice might hit you where it hurts the most, the pointers are meant to steer you toward the side of caution. Below are thumbs-up and thumbs-down guidelines when it comes to fashion statements and their appropriateness in most job interviews.

Thumbs-Up for Females
- Tasteful, conservative jewelry (this includes a watch; earrings; necklace; elegant, neutral bracelet; and up to two rings)
- Trim and conservative scarf
- Slim purse to neatly fit into your carryall (see "Interview Necessities" below)
- Tasteful headband, barrettes, and other hair accessories to complete a style or for control

Thumbs-Up for Males
- Tasteful, conservative jewelry (this includes a watch, tie bar/clasp, and one ring)
- A slim wallet to fit unobtrusively into your suit coat or pants pocket

Thumbs Waffling for Males
These are not really offensive, but potentially problematic in that you may look out of your element, because the following are too

stylized for most recent college grads.

- Cufflinks with French cuffs
- Handkerchief (pocket square) in suit breast pocket
- Double-breasted suit jacket

Thumbs-Down for Females
- More than one earring in each earlobe (an earring in cartilage is acceptable to some HR managers)
- Earrings in nose, tongue, chin or eyebrow (a pierced belly button is all right if you don't talk about it)
- Hat or scarf covering your head
- Hair accessories that are overly obvious or gaudy
- Flamboyant scarf, shawl, or poncho
- Noisy, large, flashy jewelry and belts
- Large or statement-making purse
- Any prominent branding or logo information
- Any visible tattoos
- Bold or overpowering nail colors or designs

Thumbs-Down for Males
- Earring visible anywhere on your body
- Noisy, large, flashy jewelry
- Necklaces or bracelets of any kind
- Hat or scarf covering your head
- Any prominent branding or logo information
- Any visible tattoos
- Any color nail polish

Interview Necessities

Your presentation is further enhanced—or not—by how you look when managing the fundamentals of the interview process. Appearing sleek and clean, but fumbling with a bunch of papers and hunting for a pen, peels away at your professionalism, and probably your composure.

The final consideration impacting your appearance has to do with organizing the business details of your meeting. How will you juggle your résumé, KISS, purse, and so on, while coming across as client savvy and worthy of a corner desk?

You start with one carryall and add from here. You can opt for a briefcase, a portfolio, a padfolio, or a zippered binder, but never a backpack. Any one of these should be emptied of all other contents and should be brown or black leather, vinyl, or canvas. The carryall should be relatively new and without scuff marks. Overly fancy or gimmicky closure or locking mechanisms should be avoided at all costs.

Most portfolios and binders are compact and have a light and breezy style about them. You look unencumbered, yet professional. However, they might not be large enough. On the other hand, a briefcase is sufficiently sized, has the advantage of a handle, and is often easy to get papers in and out of. Understanding that you will usually not bring your laptop to an interview, you should make a personal decision regarding a carryall based on what suits your taste, style, and needs.

Because it's important to compactly organize your materials and operate from this one carryall during your interviews, add the following to your binder, briefcase, or portfolio, and then restock as needed for each meeting:

- Your HOP arsenal (see chapter 6, "Nutshelling")
- Personal-details summary: On one sheet of paper (consider a color noticeably different from your résumé and KISS), summarize very specific dates, names, titles, telephone numbers, and addresses pertaining to an emergency contact, a primary physician, your place of residence and where you can be reached, colleges attended and degrees earned, and previous employers. You may be asked to provide this information on an employment application during your interviews; it's convenient, and impressive, to have the information at your fingertips. Just be sure that the specifics are consistent with your résumé.
- Fresh pad of paper and at least three pens
- Ten to twenty copies of your résumé in a blue folder or fastened together with a blue paper clip (blue=résumé): Include ten copies for interviews and twenty copies for job fairs.
- Ten to twenty copies of your reference packet in a yellow folder or fastened together with a yellow paper clip (yellow=references): Include ten copies for interviews and twenty copies for job fairs.

- Ten to twenty copies of your KISS in a red folder or fastened together with a red paper clip (red=KISS): Include ten copies for interviews and twenty copies for job fairs.
- For females, a slim purse to hold your personal essentials: your purse should slip into the carryall, so you don't have two separate satchels to juggle. If you need to excuse yourself to go to the ladies' room, simply remove your purse and make a smooth exit to the restroom.

Chapter 6

Ooze "the Right Stuff"

*"It was manageable for the first few weeks. But then the names
and times inundated me from all directions ... people I
networked with, others I met at job fairs, my dad's friends,
even a prospective boss or two. I was collecting phone numbers,
e-mail addresses, and appointment times every day.
"I found a couple of business cards in my back pocket,
but I don't know where the rest are at this point.
"I'm in trouble. I'm supposed to get in touch with
some of these guys because they've got leads for me
to follow up on.
"I have no idea which end is up right now."*
—Graduate, Communications Major, Southern Methodist University

*His goal: "A career in advertising with clients
who prefer to strategize on the golf course."*

IT'S PROBABLY NO SURPRISE to learn that candidates in the right place
at the right moment, saying all the right things, are the ones getting
job offers. These are focused interviewees with time and energy to
dedicate to details that make a difference. They don't find themselves
spinning their wheels or apologizing for arriving ten minutes late.

Organizing interviewing's who, where, when, and what hinges on
an up-to-date record-keeping system that makes you better, not busier.
This chapter outlines a simple, yet effective approach for staying on
top of the onslaught of facts and figures bombarding you from left
to right.

Setting up the system and condensing the information—filtering, streamlining and nutshelling—may take an hour when you use the guidelines here. Maintenance will only require a few minutes of your day if you do it on an as-you-go basis. In addition to the immediate benefit to your interviews, this approach provides opportunity-laden information for years to come.

Filtering

Keep or pitch? This question is the bane of anyone responsible for make-or-break specifics. After all, too much extraneous information is as detrimental as too few of the important particulars.

As an example, in chapter 2, you researched a great deal about the employer, market, and the upcoming interview. All of this analysis supplied an important backdrop for your familiarity and understanding; it was definitely worthwhile reading. At this point, however, you should extract the most pertinent information with a ruthless highlighter. When you go to the trouble of distilling, organizing, and documenting, the data should be of the utmost importance to your candidacy, and your current and future job prospects. At the same time, however, use a level head and consider that your dream job is on the line; thoughtless shortcuts can hurt your chances.

By answering five key questions, you'll know which information to hang onto and which details you can let go of. If you answer yes to any of the following questions as you evaluate the worthiness of the data at your fingertips, you know that the tidbit is worth keeping. If, however, your answer is no, you shouldn't crowd your personal records with information that doesn't make this critical cut.

Question 1
Is this piece of information about meeting specifics, contact details, or insights pertaining to the employer important to my interviews and immediate job search?

This question scrutinizes the staying power of the following type of information:

- The exact, complete name of the organization, along with addresses and phone or fax numbers
- Buzzwords or signature phrases used by the company when

defining their mission and primary focus

- Current marketing and sales profile (market/industry classification, products and services, geographical scope, customer definition, annual revenues, competitor profile, and so on)
- Other key facts or insights about the organization (headline items, key slogans, promotions, and so on)
- Date, time, and exact location of your interview
- Names and titles of your interviewers and their contact information, including telephone numbers, fax numbers, and addresses
- Key interviewer facts or insights
- Key interviewee facts or insights
- Details about the specific job, including title, responsibilities, reporting relationships, location, pay and benefits, future expectations and opportunities, start date, and so on
- Very specific follow-up information regarding your next steps

Question 2

Is this piece of information about meeting specifics, contact details, or insights pertaining to the employer potentially important to me in the future?

This question similarly examines the same type of information listed above, but asks you to consider a longer time frame. With the immediate horizon as your prime focus right now, it might be tempting to quickly answer no all the way down the list. But it's often worth considering that a rainy day or change of heart isn't all that unlikely at some point in your career. When the clouds roll in, or you're simply itching to move on, you will have a bonanza at your fingertips. With some minor updating, this foundation of reliable facts can be used to jump-start a job search relatively quickly.

Additionally, the world is all about contacts. Even if you don't use this type of information for a future career move, you might pull up a file and, for example, contact a former recruiter while you're employed elsewhere. Just when you need a good resource, your copious notes might verify that you've got the guy who can help.

Question 3

Is this piece of feedback specific, insightful, and important to my interview process and job search—and possibly to my future endeavors?

It's important to catalog feedback of a specific, professional nature. Criticism (positive or negative) gives insight into what might make you better. This input comes from recruiters, your campus career office, confidant, friends, and so on. Recording that someone said, "Good job," can be helpful, because you'll be reminded that you knocked 'em dead that day. However, "You really grabbed the marketing director with your clear and complete answers, but it unnerved him that you rarely made eye contact," is more likely to be useful as you prepare to ace your next interview.

Question 4

Is this piece of information about the market, the economy, or other extraneous factors important to my interview process and job search, either now or into the future?

This question scrutinizes the staying power of the following type of information:

- Key market factors (competitive overview, details about the health of the industry, past and future growth, technological innovations, etc.)
- Key economic factors influencing the growth of the market and the organization's business (fiscal policy, foreign trade, etc.)
- Key extraneous factors influencing the growth of the market and the organization's business (politics, Mother Nature, etc.)

Question 5

Is this piece of information simply interesting or fun to know?

Because it's important to inject personal interest and even levity into your interview process, be sure to take note of tidbits that are intriguing, for whatever reason. You might need the giggle, a feel-good moment to bolster your fraying nerves, or the ticket broker's name you spoke about at lunch the other day.

Streamlining

"Garbage in" translates to "garbage out." Your record-keeping instrument should be dependable, providing up-to-date, organized information. Routinely slotting the above filtered specifics into three streamlined categories—Interview Lineup, Market Stats, and Personal Bytes—transforms what might otherwise be odiferous trash into eau de interview.

The key to streamlining all of this information is your trusty computer. Create a new folder and three separate files within it. You can manage most of this information as a spreadsheet, or you can use a simple text format.

Interview Lineup

This file—the most important one by far right now—consolidates all the information you distilled after answering questions 1, 2 and 3 above. Through this document, you access key facts about the employer, specific meetings, strategy, and follow-up.

Organize your file by organization name, along the lines shown below, understanding that as you continue to interview with the same entity, you will update the information to reflect current status. Additionally, many candidates find it helpful to make note of meetings and other due dates on a separate day calendar as a crosscheck and to give a complete overview at a glance. If you don't use a calendar through your computer or a PDA phone, consider this as a good time to start. Or use an old-fashioned paper version to remind you of the critical days and times ahead.

Set up the Interview Lineup file as follows:

- Type in each interviewing organization's name as a heading.
- Then, include the following for each organization as you gather and filter information and proceed through the interview process:

1. General Contact and Background Info
   Addresses
   Phone/fax numbers
   Start-up particulars
   Market/industry classification

Marketing/sales detail
Revenue information and growth overview
Buzzwords/phrases
Key facts/insights

2. Job Details
Title
Responsibilities
Reporting relationships
Location
Pay/benefits
Start-up particulars
Other

3. Interview Specifics
Basics
    Date
    Time (note Pacific, Mountain, Central, or Eastern)
    Location
    This information is registered onto another calendar—Y/N
    Other
Interviewer info
    Name
    Title
    Contact particulars
    Key facts/insights
        1.
        2.
        3.
Other interviewee info
    Who
    How many
    Other

4. Feedback
Who
When
What, specifically

5. Follow-Up/Next Steps
   Documents provided (to whom) and dates
       Résumé
       References
       KISS
   Additional
       Who
       What
       When
   This follow-up information is registered onto another calendar—Y/N

6. Other Notes and Details

Market Stats

Your Market Stats file makes information readily accessible to enhance your knowledge, and ultimately your presence, during interviews. As you learned in chapter 2, understanding more about the world at large—and the specific arena upon which your career will hopefully center—adds meat to your professional chops.

The details you catalog here are based on the distillation you did after answering question 4 above. Consider that you might be tracking a few different industries. Your job search could involve interviewing across a number of markets. If you're looking for a financial-trainee position, your path might lead to very diverse niches—information technology, personal banking, women's retail, sports marketing, entertainment, and so on. Separate records on each one of these industries, as an example, would be pulled up and reviewed as you prepare for your respective meetings. This affords you the most streamlined, manageable system.

Set up the Market Stats file as follows:

- Type in each market/industry classification as a heading.
- Then, include the following for each classification as you gather and filter information and proceed through the interview process:

1. Brief Description of the Market

2. Key Market Factors and Competitive Profile
    1.
    2.
    3.
    4.
    5.

3. Key Economic Influences
    1.
    2.

4. Key Extraneous Influences
    1.
    2.

5. Other Notes and Details

Personal Bytes

Your peers strongly suggest answering question 5 above and then recording the most pertinent tidbits in this file. This is your freewheeling record in which you can note anything of interest to you. Some candidates structure the information as a diary, citing dates and players by name and graphic description. Others are more eclipsed, numbering details that strike a personal or professional chord in list form. However you go about organizing and using this file, be sure to include specifics. Candidates who were stingy on the particulars later expressed dismay.

Nutshelling

Guidelines for creating handy, take-along summary notes for your interview are included in this section. By focusing on the insights you recently filtered and streamlined—key, hot-off-the-press (HOP) information—you create an essential security blanket. With these HOP details organized and packaged as compactly as a nutshell, you'll be calm, cool and collected in your recruiter's reception area and beyond.

Despite your laptop's status as a nearly grafted appendage, it usually isn't necessary, or wise, to tote your computer to an interview. You're aiming for a crisp, unburdened look, and keeping it light accomplishes this best. Instead, consider the following as a way to make sure the reminders you need are with you on interview day.

First, pull out summary information from your Interview Lineup and Market Stats records. Add in a few reminders about effective interviewing. Then organize these specifics onto compact index cards. When your interviewer shows up in the doorway, your 3 x 5 HOP arsenal can be surreptitiously slipped into your jacket pocket and out of sight in the blink of an eye. (But keep in mind that being caught red-handed with notes for the day's meeting is simply impressive and nothing less.)

If you have a poor memory or an unusual case of stage fright and feel that you need an information crutch during your meetings, build in one more step as you distill your facts. Put the most critical points from your index cards (or those which you have the hardest time remembering, or are most nervous about) onto the pad of paper you will use for taking interview notes. In this way, you can maintain a smooth veneer; no one need be the wiser about the cue card right in front of you.

The additional advantage to consolidating key facts is that it is another way to learn the information. By thinking about the details, sorting through them, and then transferring the particulars to an organized system of index cards, you instill the data into your head and onto the tip of your tongue in a logical way. As a result, you handle yourself in an informed, easy-to-follow style in the interview.

Following are thorough and manageable guidelines for establishing your HOP note cards. In other words, the system is right up a new college grad's alley.

1. Index card 1
   Title this card as, "Remember This Above All Else Today!"
   This is a reminder to do, show, drop off, refer to, or not do something that you feel is especially important.

2. Index card 2

   Title this card as, "[The organization's name], Interviewer Info"

   Then fill in this information:

         Interviewers' names and titles

         Key facts/insights about interviewers

           1.

           2.

           3.

3. Index card 3

   Title this card as, "[The organization's name], Sales and Marketing"

   Then fill in this information:

         Annual revenues

         Market/industry classification

         Main products/services

         Target markets

4. Index card 4

   Title this card as, "[The organization's name], Key Insights and Buzz"

   Then fill in this information:

         Other key facts/insights/buzzwords and significant phrases

           1.

           2.

           3.

5. Index card 5

   Title this card as, "[The organization's name], Start-up and Growth"

   Then fill in this information:

         Start-up date

         Start-up details

         Growth details

6. Index card 6
   Title this card as, "[The organization's name], Competitors & Key Influences"
   Then fill in this information:
   > Key competitor detail
   > Key market and economic influences
   > Key extraneous influences

7. Index card 7
   Title this card as, "[The organization's name], Questions to Ask"
   Then write out four potential questions to ask during this interview (see chapter 11).

8. Index card 8
   Title this card as, "[The organization's name], Wrap-up"
   This is a summation of your parting-shot wrap-up (see chapter 10).

9. Index card 9
   Title this card as, "Smile!"
   Remembering that a sunny disposition counts for a lot, jot down something that will cause you to smile.

The only "note" of caution is to relay what happened to one candidate who lost a few of his index cards while at an interview. Unfortunately, a recruiter picked up the strays. Rather than coming across as diligent, the interviewee wound up pegged as immature and inappropriate for the dirty joke he included on his "Smile!" card. The moral of this story is the principle to use for your entire interview process: Keep it professional. Everything. Always.

Chapter 7

Sweat Simple Around the Clock

"Yes, Mom, I shaved."
"Yes, Mom, my shirt was clean."
"No, Mom, I didn't wear brown shoes with my gray suit and black belt."
"Yes, Mom, I combed my hair."
"Uh, well ... "
"Um ... kind of purplish, maybe ... "
"No, I can't remember. It was yesterday morning at six-thirty!"
"What do you mean, 'That's awful'"?
"Oh, they'll get over it. If they noticed, that is."
"Well, that's just wrong. Thanks a lot. Good-bye, Mother."
"Oh, crap."
—*Graduate, Economics Major, Kenyon College*

*His goal: "A lucrative investment banking opportunity, and
quick, personal success in the financial markets."*

YOU CAN SPEND COUNTLESS hours fussing and fidgeting as you prepare overtime for your in-person job interviews. It only takes an ugly coffee stain on your suit, just pulled from a closet at the crack of dawn, to trip you up.

New college grad interviewees who took the wrong bus, mismatched shoes, mixed up company names, or showed up a week early all underscore the importance of sweating the simple details ahead of time.

Twenty-Four Hours and Counting

As much preparation as you can accomplish the day before your meeting (early in the day, not just shy of the stroke of midnight), the more relaxed tomorrow will unfold—just when you need a dose of tranquility. If your interview is out of town, consider the day before as the one preceding travel.

A foolproof checklist focuses on clothes, supplies, paperwork, schedule specifics, travel particulars, bedtime and wake-up details, and—last, but definitely not least—your trustworthy confidant. If there is a glitch with any of these details, it's up to you to find a remedy, using all the resources and creativity you can muster. In a moment of crisis, you will be glad that you cut yourself some slack and introduced at least twenty-four hours into the prep.

✔ Locate and set aside all clothing items you intend to wear tomorrow. Fill in the blanks, if there are any.

✔ Check all clothing for dirt, ring around the collar, lint, scuffs, loose threads, holes, runs, or wrinkles. Fix or replace as needed.

✔ Check the fit of your clothing and fix or replace as needed.

✔ For your personal benefit, infuse your outfit with pizzazz.

✔ Crosscheck your computer's Interview Lineup file with your calendar to verify the date, place, and time of your appointment. Check e-mail and voicemail for messages. Adjust accordingly.

✔ Research travel times and directions assiduously, being sure to handle all the car or public transportation details completely.

✔ Stock your carryall with personal salvation, and notes summarizing meeting specifics, travel directions, and transportation schedules, along with the interview necessities spelled out in chapter 5.

✔ Avoid partying and a late bedtime. Charge your cell phone, locate your keys and wallet, and set two alarm clocks, giving yourself more than ample time to get ready.

✔ Touch base with your confidant.

Clothes

Recent degree holders admit that clothing snafus foul them up more than anything else come interview day. If you don't yet believe this, read on. You're lucky that others have walked in your squeaky, new dress shoes before you. The most common trip-ups include clothing that is missing, poorly maintained, ill fitting, and boring. Fortunately, with time and ingenuity on your side, you can sidestep most of these hazards. The earlier in the day you take inventory and perform a quality-assurance inspection, the easier it is to carry on looking like a pro.

Clothing Snafus from the Trenches

As you contemplate delaying the inevitable, it might help to know how other recent college grads struggled when they didn't bother with the clothing checklist a day before their interviews.

Caroline's Snafu

Caroline was interviewing in downstate Illinois at a large critical-care hospital. She packed her bags and drove south from Chicago, arriving at the hotel midevening for an 8:00 AM curtain call the next morning. When Caroline unloaded her suitcase, she realized that the skirt completing her suit was nowhere to be found. Pantyhose … check. Jacket … check. Skirt … definitely not in any of the pockets or flaps of her luggage.

Caroline was now six hours away from home and her gray skirt with pinstripe detail. That translated to another twelve hours on the road, taking into account the round-trip distance. Not an attractive or smart alternative, despite the fact that jeans were her only backup.

Caroline whipped out the yellow pages to locate department stores that might be open in downtown Springfield on a Thursday night. After several phone calls, she broke out into a cold sweat. She next tried the front desk of the hotel and was informed that Wal-Mart was her best—and probably her only—shot.

For $8.99 (winter clearance), with fifteen minutes to spare before closing, Caroline snagged a black skirt that worked with her gray jacket.

The view from outside Caroline's trench: The interviewer never suspected that Caroline's outfit wasn't as picture perfect as she had intended, and this is the best outcome of all. It's wonderful that

Caroline bothered to unpack the day before her interview and another bonanza that retail hours, however scant, were still on her side. However, imagine how relaxed Caroline's evening could have been had she taken inventory as she packed, back at home. And the fact that Caroline is female is nothing less than over-the-top lucky; guys would have a much harder time pulling together this last-minute suit disaster.

Heath's Snafu

An hour before his interview, Heath couldn't locate dry boxers. His roommate had a robust night of partying and, upon entering the apartment, had promptly vomited on to Health's pile of laundry. In an effort to reduce the stench and to "tidy up," the inebriated roommate had poured a bucket of water all over the clothing heap.

This rank mess greeted Heath at 7:30 AM just as he was preparing to sift through and unearth the cleanest pair of boxers he could find. This was Heath's typical ritual, and it usually didn't fail him.

Since Heath slept in sweatpants, he couldn't easily use the clothes off his back to pinch hit. His roommate's underwear? Not happening.

As a result, Heath ended up going bare bottomed to meet and greet his interviewers.

The view from outside Heath's trench: The interviewer was technically never brought into the complication, which is especially wonderful, given the focal point of the problem. But Heath was plagued with a nuance that probably coaxed him a step or two off dead center. Heath admits to being uncomfortable throughout the seven-hour day since his new blue suit was made from a fine wool blend. While all of this doesn't sound particularly onerous, Heath also admits to not getting a callback from that company. Perhaps his squirm quotient was, in fact, too much for the interviewer to endure. The question is, is Heath "itching" to get organized the next time around?

Daniel's Snafu

Daniel met with a Human-Resources associate to start off his morning of interviews. The associate was particularly plucky, and the banter back and forth was lively and spirited. As the meeting drew to a close, the recruiter suggested that Daniel was looking somewhat "iron deficient."

Daniel apologized, saying that the lighting probably made him appear less than robust. He assured his interviewer that he was the picture of health. The associate unabashedly told Daniel that she was referring to his wrinkled shirt when she made this observation.

Daniel's self-confidence and poise took a major hit just as he had to face two additional interviewers at the same company that day.

The view from outside Daniel's trench: The interviewer was clearly brought into the problem, and this had dire consequences. The associate, on one hand, can be ignored as being rude. On the other hand, she can be thanked for providing a wake-up call. Pressed, immaculate clothing was clearly required. If Daniel wasn't particularly handy with an iron, he should have paid a dry-cleaner to shore up his dress shirts. And that is exactly what Daniel did from this point forward.

Claire's Snafu

Claire decided to go all out, purchasing new underwear to complete her interview ensemble. No chump-change charge would be levied here. However, the silky new bra straps kept slipping off her shoulders.

Claire kept pushing up the delicate straps, often poking her fingers inside her suit jacket and blouse to take care of the annoyance. As a matter of fact, Claire persisted in this vein rather unconsciously—and like clockwork—every few minutes.

Fortunately, her campus career counselor witnessed the problem as Claire waited to be called for an interview. This seasoned professional pulled Claire aside and shared her observation, suggesting that Claire keep a pen and paper in her hands as a way to exert control over the dilemma for the moment.

Claire took the advice, even swapping her new underwear for the remainder of her interviews.

The view from outside Claire's trench: The interviewer was blessedly spared the ill-fitting distraction. The campus counselor was a pro of the first order, and Claire hung in there with a viable plan, despite the temporary setback.

Ill-fitting clothing, no matter how beautiful or pristine, can end up being the distraction that leads to a lost opportunity. What a waste. While it's wonderful that Claire got a heads-up, we're all not so lucky. It makes sense to check out such details ahead of time and then make sensible, comfortable corrections.

Missing Clothes

✔ Locate and set aside all clothing items you intend to wear
tomorrow. Fill in the blanks, if there are any.

You're certain you put the shirt in the closet, but it's just not
there. Chances are, it's at the dry cleaners, and you forgot to pick it
up. Or, the once-starched beauty is perhaps buried under your sweaty
gym clothes on the bedroom floor. Could it be that a roommate is
looking very *GQ* as you scratch your head? Ouch.

First of all, don't panic. The clock is on your side right now. Do
a methodical search of the premises, and take a minute to backtrack.
Actually, this is a good time to reconstruct your entire clothing
ensemble for tomorrow. Lay your head-to-toe outfit on the bed,
checking to make sure that all pieces are present.

Second, if you can't locate an article of clothing despite having
looked up and down and all around, either call or visit the dry cleaners.
Once at the dry cleaners, make sure the bundle they hand off to you
is actually your stuff. If this all fails to produce, you should probably
make a beeline for the mall before it's too late.

Yes, AWOL suit jackets and pants/skirts pose a dicey, pricey
conundrum. But before you try to do it on the cheap, understand
that you (especially males) can't easily mix and match these pieces
of your ensemble. You simply run the risk of looking all wrong when
appearance matters the most. Obviously, if you're going to lose
something, make sure it isn't the suit you use for interviews.

Poorly Maintained Clothes

✔ Check all clothing for dirt, ring around the collar, lint,
scuffs, loose threads, holes, runs, or wrinkles. Fix or replace
as needed.

Careful scrutiny takes a moment or two, an eagle eye, and good light.
Consider this a white glove effort to unearth any and all imperfections.
In other words, give your ensemble a top-to-bottom Scotland Yard
would be envious of.

Then, when you've isolated a culprit, attack with a long-range
perspective. Using tape to fix a fraying hem works in a pinch, but
doesn't necessarily hold the answer for long. You might trip sooner

than you think ... while trailing strips of well-intentioned masking tape onto your interviewer's carpet.

A professional-looking repair is just as important as a repair with staying power. A patch used to cover up a hole certainly delivers a solution, but it also creates an issue appearance-wise. If you're not particularly handy with a needle and thread, this probably isn't the time to take up Sewing 101. You're better off calling in a favor or paying a pro to get out of the jam.

Even if you don't necessarily amass dirt as a matter of course, you should adopt a routine regarding clothing care. Cleaning a shirt or blouse after each wearing simply bullies away any signs of wilting. You'll avoid wrinkles by hanging up a suit right when you return home. In essence, a little bit of effort and attention go a very long way.

Ill-Fitting Clothes
   ✔ Check the fit of your clothing and fix or replace as needed.

There will be a period of time when you're in dark blue or gray more than you're out. As such, you and your interview outfit quickly learn to understand one another's foibles. For the most part, the coupling works. But you can end up with a skirt that doesn't quite zip up. Or a collar that simply won't button come Monday morning. (Or the opposite: a pair of pants that bunch up and hang on for dear life around your now-slender waist.)

Perhaps it was all the burritos and beer from spring break. Or maybe you grabbed a two-for-one-sale right after the holidays, never suspecting the strange-fit reason these pants remained on the rack. Whatever the explanation, check the fit of your clothing by donning pieces you're even slightly suspicious about. The biggest offenders are typically collars and waistbands.

If a fit problem insinuates itself, your first strategy is to make it work, by hook or by crook. This is only an option, however, if the solution doesn't materially impact your comfort or the professionalism of your appearance. An unobtrusive safety pin is fine as long as "inconspicuous" isn't simply wishful thinking.

An overly loose fit is manageable if all it takes is another notch up on the ol' belt. On the other hand, if your clothes are clearly wearing *you*, you've got another challenge on your plate.

Your best—and perhaps only—alternative might be to replace

the guilty party. This is not a solution you're likely happy about, but one that is realistically strategic. After referencing chapter 5 and the importance of your interview outfit to the ultimate brokering of the deal, you shouldn't easily talk yourself out of *Vogue* contention now.

Boring Clothes

   ✔ For your personal benefit, infuse your outfit with pizzazz.

If you've paid attention, making sure your clothing boasts sharpness and professionalism, your clothes will rarely bore an interviewer. This is true even if they see you in the same outfit two or three times. The reason for this is that most recruiters simply don't bother to notice or remember. Despite all your poking and prodding, you've been aiming for your attire to become a piece of the background, not stand out for all the wrong reasons. If you accomplish this, it's a guarantee your interviewers won't yawn when you make an entrance.

That said, interviewees, who have to live in their interview uniform day in and day out, cry, "Borrrrrrrring!" Since clothes are often said to make the person, it might not be a bad idea to infuse your outfit—and hence your demeanor—with some get up and go. After all, variety is the spice of life; some wardrobe fun might be the chili powder you need to get jazzed for your fifth interview this month.

The caveat is to maintain that professional reserve you're coming to appreciate. A different tie often does the trick, as does changing up the shirt color. Going with a burgundy combo for belt and shoes instead of black just might be the ticket. Women can add a belt or a unique piece of jewelry, swap tops and shoes, play with their makeup, or layer on a demure scarf.

Schedule Specifics

   ✔ Crosscheck your computer's Interview Lineup file with
      your calendar to verify the date, place, and time of your
      appointment. Check e-mail and voicemail for messages.
      Adjust accordingly.

The wrong day, wrong place, or wrong time are also the wrong foot. While it's unlikely you will swing and miss on all three counts, any variation on this theme is ugly.

Recording information about the upcoming appointment in

two different places (computer and other calendar) at the time you establish the meeting catches most mistakes. Also, checking your e-mail and voicemail for last-minute changes is often helpful.

Make sure you fully understand where your meeting is taking place. This confuses more candidates than any other schedule detail. Rob went to the corporate office, but spent thirty minutes (making him late *and* sweaty) tracking down Mr. Detmer in the twenty-two-floor complex. Instead of recording a name, Linda jotted down "lobby restaurant," only to find there were three of these eateries.

If you missed your meeting or are posed with a similarly undoable schedule circumstance, you have to fess up. The sooner you set the record straight, the better. While a fabrication about a near-death experience in the emergency room sounds glamorously tragic, this tactic should remain a figment of your imagination; it always comes across as lame and fictitious. You're far better off laying it out on the table: "Mr. Conant, I apologize. I apparently made a mistake, originally recording our meeting for tomorrow. As I was getting organized today, I noticed a discrepancy in my record keeping. I immediately phoned your office and was informed that I missed my nine o'clock appointment with you. This is my fault, and I am very sorry that it happened and for any inconvenience I caused. I don't usually operate in this manner, and I sincerely hope we can reschedule our meeting."

If you discern a problem ahead of time and orchestrate a fix without involving the prospective employer, this is ideal. You get close to the ideal by using resources at the company other than the boss. This means calling on receptionists, telephone operators, personnel assistants, and so on.

But if you must, go directly to the top for clarification as opposed to not verifying sketchy schedule specifics. While you might come across as someone who is slightly disorganized, an offensive strategy is far more advisable than a defensive one. "I apologize for bothering you, but I note a discrepancy regarding the time I recorded for my interview tomorrow. Would you please confirm that we are meeting at ten-thirty in the Brookburn office complex, in suite 12A?" In this way, you stay in the game and have a chance to put all your best characteristics forward when it matters most.

Travel Particulars

✔ Research travel times and directions assiduously, being
   sure to handle all the car or public transportation details
   completely.

Just when you think you'll have no problem getting fifty bucks out
of the ATM, it's down for servicing ... and so is the one two blocks
away. It's easier to manage this situation—or any other travel-related
complication—twenty-four hours ahead rather than as the last morning
train speeds away from your empty pockets on interview day. Advance
planning, when it comes to getting you where you need to be, is simply
smart. This is true whether you are driving to your meetings or using
public transportation.

Driving

True, it's not usually complicated to hop in the car and get from
point A to point B. But the dynamics of unfamiliar territory are more
daunting. Point B might be in a neck of the woods you've never visited,
and rush-hour traffic might be a bumper-to-bumper headache you
don't know much about.

If you adhere to the following dos and don'ts, you're more likely to
coast into your interviews, as opposed to breathlessly careening into
the receptionist's desk. This makes it far easier to maintain the driver's
seat once you're face-to-face with a prospective boss.

1. Directions
   Destination
   Don't just familiarize yourself with how to get there; learn
   the route. It's actually a very good idea to drive yourself to
   the destination ahead of time to learn the lay of the land.
   Slip these directions into your carryall.

   Parking
   You want to know where you will park and how much (if
   anything) it will cost. On your test-run drive, locate a first
   choice and an alternative in case the lot is full tomorrow, or
   you suddenly discover your vehicle doesn't meet the height
   restrictions in the garage.

2. Time
   Logical
   A reasonable calculation determines how long it will take to
   travel the distance based on mileage.

   Realistic
   While a mileage calculation is helpful, never use distance
   as your sole determining factor regarding driving time.
   Consider time of day (rush hour) and construction or
   detour factors, then add on thirty minutes for the occasional
   traffic jam. Again, a trial run the day before at the same
   time of day is the best way to estimate (assuming you're
   comparing apples to apples—comparing weekday to
   weekday and not weekend to weekday).

3. Gas
   Fill up the day before to make sure it's done and to avoid
   a gasoline smell that comes from an inadvertent spill on to
   your hands—or, perish the thought, your clothes.

4. Money
   Get cash to pay for parking tomorrow (note: city and airport
   parking can be expensive, often running over twenty-five
   dollars).

Public Transportation

Public transportation is often the most reliable option for getting
to your meetings on time. Not subject to traffic backups, trains are
typically your safest bet. This, of course, assumes you've done your
homework as far as public transportation is concerned. Moseying
down to the station the morning of, expecting the train to arrive at
your beck and call, is a recipe for tardiness. Similar to testing out the
trip by car, taking a public-transportation trial run is sensible.

1. Logistics
   If you have a choice between grabbing a bus or a train,
   decide which option is the most efficient for tomorrow's
   purpose. Consider location (where is the meeting relative
   to where you get off?); schedule details (is there even a

bus or train that is conveniently departing and returning to suit your timing?); and reliability (what is the general dependability of the bus or train in this town?). Then, figure out which bus or train line will get you to your destination, and specifically locate the exact spot where you catch this mode of transportation. Directions, as well as schedules and fares, can usually be researched online or via customer-service hotlines. Slip these specific instructions into your carryall.

2. Schedules
    Most buses and trains run on tight schedules. During rush hour, there are more options available than during the middle of the day. It isn't advisable to take the bus or train that gets you to the interview with only seconds to spare. Give yourself ample breathing room in this regard. Also research the schedule for your return trip in a general way, understanding that it's hard to pinpoint specifics ahead of time.

3. Fare
    You may need exact change to ride public transportation. Research the fares and make sure you understand how much you'll need, and in what form.

4. Money
    Get cash to pay for any fares tomorrow.

Your Carryall or Briefcase
    ✔ Stock your carryall with personal salvation, and notes summarizing meeting specifics, travel directions, and transportation schedules, along with the interview necessities spelled out in chapter 5.

This part of the checklist boils down to making sure you have what you need at your fingertips to get through tomorrow's meeting without a hitch. Stocking up on headache relief and other personal salvation is an order of business in its own right, and you should address this just as seriously as any 8.5 x 11 piece of paper.

Personal Salvation

It's perfectly all right to tuck in a few bosom-buddy essentials. Don't make the same mistake Lucy committed, however, when she threw in her bottle of cologne. The top came loose and, not only did the contents of her carryall reek, but there was an overpowering smell of lilies of the valley trailing Lucy wherever she went that day.

Basically, pack smart and judiciously. You don't want to weigh yourself down in any way. Nor do you want to clang and bang as you move from one office to the next. If you'd like to carry breath mints and headache medication, choose varieties that are noiseless in their packaging (a roll of mints as opposed to those in "curious" metal containers or rattling around in plastic boxes, a small paper packet of two Tylenol or Motrin tablets, and so on).

Successful interviewees share that they routinely stash the following personal items in their carryall:

- Purse
- Keys
- Cell phone
- Compact umbrella
- Compact can of Static Guard
- Lip gloss
- Hairbrush or comb
- Individual packets of Saltines
- Lip balm
- Bandages (for blisters)
- Individually packaged moist towelettes
- Small packet of tissues
- Breath mints (to use on your way to the interview and never during)
- Cough drops (to use on your way to the interview and never during)
- Personal hygiene items
- Spare pair of pantyhose

Important Notes

The essentials of the day should be in your carryall for easy reference. This includes all the information about the interview, including names, phone numbers, and detailed location and travel particulars. You'll be amazed at how often you pull up this set of facts and figures.

Interview Necessities

Make sure the interview necessities noted in chapter 5 are organized and ready for tomorrow. As a reminder, and because of their importance to your meeting, the specifics are again detailed below.

- **HOP arsenal**. As you learned in chapter 6, this tidy refresher course does wonders for last-minute jitters. Your HOP index cards keep the interview essentials straight and your knowledge fresh. First, carefully finish the note cards for tomorrow's interview, if you haven't done so already. Then, neatly pack the arsenal into your carryall, keeping the small stack organized and readily accessible.

- **Personal-detail summary.** You may be asked to complete an employment application as part of your interview process. To prepare, you will need to collect and provide information (think exact dates, names, titles, phone numbers, and e-mail or street addresses) regarding an emergency contact; a primary physician; a place of residence and where you can be reached; colleges attended and degrees earned; and previous employer specifics. Organize these details (and make sure they are in sync with your résumé, by the way) onto one piece of paper, so you can finish required paperwork efficiently during your meetings.

- **Pens and pad.** Taking notes during your interview is a wise move. You therefore need three pens (the hope is that in packing three, you'll end up with at least one that writes and isn't lost or left behind somewhere) and a pad of paper. The pens should have caps to keep them from marking up anything else in your carryall. The pad of paper should look as crisp and fresh as you do, rather than replete with doodles, frayed edges, or notes from yesterday's interview.

- **Paperwork.** The crown jewels of your carryall. Your personal paperwork—résumé, reference packet, and KISS—should be afforded the place of highest honor (and protection) in your satchel. Pack ten of each (twenty if heading to a job fair), because candidates continually lament they "never have enough" and end up apologizing and making excuses to interviewers. Additionally, make sure these pages are easily accessible and distinguishable (chapter 5 laid out a color-coded folder scheme). As a result, you will be poised and smooth as you hand out these important sales pieces during your interviews.

Bedtime and Wake-up Details

✔ Avoid partying and a late night. Charge your cell phone, locate your keys and wallet, and set two alarm clocks, giving yourself more than ample time to get ready.

You might think that by locating your keys and money-laden wallet the night before, you can dream through a few more precious minutes of shut-eye in the morning. While it's true that you will likely have time to spare somewhere along the way before your interview, it makes more sense to take a breather once you've arrived in the general vicinity of your destination. Getting up and out is job one and should be timed to afford you a generous amount of leeway. After all, ten minutes early to an interview is on time.

If you're an unusually sound sleeper and have nerves of steel, call in the cavalry to help get you out of bed tomorrow. Enlist a friend or relative to make a persistent "rise and shine" appeal. While you're organizing these details at the end of the day, charge your cell phone. Not only will you want to call your best buddy the minute you step out of the interview, but your phone might come in handy if you somehow find yourself in a pickle tomorrow.

Your Trustworthy Confidant

✔ Touch base with your confidant.

At some time during the day, make contact with your confidant. This is a chance to calm your nerves, clarify details, or just shoot the breeze about tomorrow's interview in general. If you've chosen well, this individual is your rock, and you will be fortified by touching base.

Ten, Nine, Eight ...

Blast off! In easy-to-follow black and white, your interview-day checklist clears the fog by taking the pressure off your back. This up-front and personal inventory won't let you down and guarantees to get you where you need to be, looking and smelling like a "pick me first" rose:

- ✔ Eat early.
- ✔ Check e-mail and voicemail.
- ✔ Play your favorite music while getting ready.
- ✔ Put your "pants" on one leg at a time.
- ✔ Scrutinize yourself in the mirror.
- ✔ Delight in what the mirror shows.
- ✔ If you haven't put an umbrella into your carryall, add one.
- ✔ Add keys, wallet, and cell phone to your carryall or a suit pocket.
- ✔ Don't speed if you're driving.
- ✔ Drink and eat very carefully and avoid smoking.
- ✔ Review your HOP arsenal.
- ✔ Freshen up before you head into the fray.
- ✔ Smile!

Fortify
- ✔ Eat early.

Getting something into your belly is important. Carol learned this lesson the hard way when her tummy kept growling. Her famished state ultimately became the butt of a recruiter's joke and his parting shot: "I'll get back to you and your stomach in about a week." On a less acidic note, Jerry became dizzy and felt faint from lack of sustenance four hours into the meeting.

So make sure to eat ... and chowing down *before* you get dressed is simply spill savvy.

Tune In
- ✔ Check e-mail and voicemail.

Just to be sure, check e-mail and voicemail one last time for any late-breaking messages or instructions regarding your interview. Meetings are occasionally canceled and locations and times are often changed at the last minute.

Dance
✔ Play your favorite music while getting ready.

Get yourself into a happy, mellow frame of mind. Most recent grads claim that their music is the fastest, most effective way to put a spring into their step and a lilt into their voice.

Dress with Care
✔ Put your "pants" on one leg at a time.

The care with which you planned your outfit deserves your continued attention until the last button is fastened. Take the time to make it straight, tucked in, and perfectly collared.

Look Hard
✔ Scrutinize yourself in the mirror.

This advice might seem far too anal for you to consider, but it's probably sound. Yes, check the nose area for visible odds and ends. A discharge saga actually happened to one grad, Ben, who nodded vigorously at one point and ... well, the rest is history. Highly unattractive, green history.

If you won't go there, get close by giving yourself a very diligent once-over. The most common last-minute hiccups include:

- Open fly
- Random button left open
- Too few buttons fastened (cleavage alert!)
- Visible dirt, pet hair, scuffs, deodorant marks, and so on
- Shirt not tucked in properly
- Bad hair day (flyaway strands, a stubborn cowlick, and so on)
- Static, causing pants or skirt to ride up on your leg
- Crooked tie
- Lipstick smudge on the teeth

- Poorly blended, blotchy makeup
- Shiny forehead or nose
- Stray facial hair that should have been shaved or plucked off

Look Again
   ✔ Delight in what the mirror shows.

Glance back over your shoulder and take note of how great you look. If you haven't felt confident up to this point, this should convince you that you're ready to tackle the day.

Stay Dry
   ✔ If you haven't put an umbrella into your carryall, add one.

True, you're not used to toting along an umbrella. But can you imagine how you'll look if the skies open up and drench you without mercy? An umbrella is a no-brainer lifesaver, and fairly unobtrusive if you choose one of the compact models. Neal was caught in a torrential downpour and actually started packing a plastic poncho as a backup from that soggy moment on.

Pack Up
   ✔ Add keys, wallet, and cell phone to your carryall or a suit
      pocket.

Since you generally need these items until the very last minute before your departure, your keys, wallet, and cell phone are easily left behind. Remember that consolidating your paraphernalia into one carryall enhances your efficiency and sleek style. This exudes composure and professionalism.

Obey
   ✔ Don't speed if you're driving.

The last thing you need (really!) is a moving violation on your way to the interview. Not only will it trip you up time-wise, but it will do a number on your confidence quotient. Observe the traffic laws religiously.

Stay Clean
✔ Drink and eat very carefully and avoid smoking.

If you indulge after you're dressed and before your interview, do so very cautiously to avoid any last-minute disasters (the most common offender is a grande coffee filled to the brim). If you smoke, be aware that your clothes will carry the aroma of tobacco into the meeting. This is a turnoff of the greatest magnitude.

Study
✔ Review your HOP arsenal.

If you're early to the meeting and find yourself in a corner coffee shop, take a few minutes and pull out your HOP arsenal. Or, review these notes while in the reception area … or even the company restroom.

Spruce Up
✔ Freshen up before you head into the fray.

When you arrive at your destination, make a beeline for the washroom and check your hair and outfit one last time. Chew a piece of gum or a breath mint and then pitch it so your mouth is empty when you head back out. Make sure your cell phone is off.

Nail It
✔ Smile!

In the Nick of Time

Sometimes you need the cavalry. All the planning and prep can't possibly manage those instances that are unplanned, fall through the cracks, or sit squarely in a gray zone. Fortunately, seasoned interviewees have insightful words of wisdom when it comes to last minute SOS.

- Lightly spray Static Guard onto your hairbrush or comb before tackling an out- of-control, flyaway mane.
- Use Carmex to soothe chapped lips. This lip balm isn't shiny and therefore does the repair while being unobtrusive.

- Ice down (at two-minute intervals over a half hour) a new pimple rather than popping it. You avoid redness and swelling and possibly reduce the blemish to an invisible size.
- Apply cucumber slices; damp, chilled tea bags; or a wet, cold cloth to get rid of puffy eyes.
- Ease hangover pain by consuming any one of these home remedies: water, Gatorade, bread spread with honey, juice (tomato, orange, or grapefruit), or bouillon. Aspirin also helps, as does avoiding caffeine.
- Wipe away deodorant marks from your clothes with a sheet of laundry softener.
- Hang a garment in an enclosed bathroom during a shower to diminish wrinkles.
- Remove lint from clothes by wrapping several fingers with masking or cellophane tape (sticky side facing outward) and then pat the clothing with your sticky fingers.
- Act quickly to fix a run in pantyhose if you don't have a spare pair. Apply clear nail polish or any kind of soap to all sides of the run.
- If tape is your only option, use duct tape to repair a ripped hem. Duct tape has more staying power with fabrics than masking or scotch tape.
- Since garment lining is usually the reason behind a stuck zipper, stop tugging, yanking, and wrestling. Gently pull the lining away from the zipper (making sure to pull the lining and not the zipper).
- Rub a No. 2 pencil or a candle along the teeth of an old, worn zipper that is stuck. Graphite or wax will smooth out the rough spots.
- Pour club soda onto a fresh stain to treat the problem. Blot dry.
- Rub white toothpaste (non-gel) or baking soda onto your just-soiled clothing and rinse thoroughly with water to remove food or drink stains. Some fabrics—silk being one— may be left with a slight watermark after drying, but this is perhaps better than petunia-pink lipstick on a white blouse.
- Realize that many dry cleaning establishments have a tailor on the premises who can perform clothing repairs.
- Leave your car with a hotel or restaurant valet if all the

parking lots are filled because the Shriners rolled in overnight.

- Approach hotel doormen and concierge staff if you're lost and need help.
- Keep your head relatively dry in a downpour with a newspaper. Yes, it works.
- Don't use Magic Marker to paint your legs black when you can't find your dress socks. Try your next-door neighbor instead.

CONNECT

CONNECT

YOU'VE SO FAR PERSEVERED to establish a rock-solid foundation. You diligently researched facts and figures, gingerly stepped outside the box, and even ditched the flip-flops for sleek footwear with a high polish.

But in one fell swoop, "I can't friggin' believe what those bogus Bears did in overtime last night" can strip away much of your hard work.

As you meet with prospective employers, you garner positive impressions by remaining sensitive to the circumstances and your interviewers. If you communicate professionally, with passion and persistence, you continue raising the bar. Ultimately, your ongoing effort will forge dynamic connections. In this way, you maximize, differentiate, and become memorable for all the right reasons.

Chapter 8

Bring Along an Entourage

"As a corporate recruiter, I clearly understand
that seasoning hones a person's ability to interview.
Despite a lack of work experience, however, even the greenest
of the green make me sit up and take notice when they have
an air of maturity and attentiveness about them."
—*Senior Associate, HR,*
Worldwide Pharmaceuticals Organization

Her goal: "Catapulting over two other employees
to become the Director of HR here."

THE OBNOXIOUS GUY IN the Escalade just took your parking space—
robbed it with a smirk, actually. The text message from your former
roommate clearly spells out plans for the weekend: p-a-r-t-y. You
weren't dreaming when you got a callback yesterday after last week's
appointment with J.P. Hey, when you're good, you're good.

Life is gloriously complicated ... until the minute you start today's
meeting, that is. At least that's the way it's supposed to play out. But
even though your personal frenzy should not muscle through the door
to take a seat alongside you, you're guilty as charged. HR managers
lament that far too many new grads are "all over the board" and even
display a "shocking" demeanor during interviews. These insiders
suggest using this revelation as a keen opportunity to differentiate
yourself.

As such, bring along an entourage of VIP stature. Just be sure that
it comprises your two new best friends: balance and focus. Embodying
these qualities is essential as you strive to stand out from all the other

candidates. This chapter addresses the issue head-on, helping you master the necessary, seasoned composure sought by recruiters.

Balance

There are distinct ways to display a steady evenhandedness that smacks of maturity and plainly says, "Hire me." If you're slightly squeamish at the thought of somehow selling yourself short or muffling your larger than life personality, you needn't be concerned. Reining in the extremes basically entails keeping the highs and lows in close check. Balance is a smart approach to your interviewing sales pitch and an advisable way to negotiate the professional arena throughout your life.

The most likable individuals are often even-keeled. They're not the loudest or the quietest of the bunch. Generally, they don't have much to say when gossip goes full throttle, nor do they reveal "too much information" on a regular basis. These steady Eddies are simply likable because they are easy to be around, without a lot of drama at either end of the spectrum. In other words, they have balance.

Perhaps you can imagine why someone like this is appealing to have around the office water cooler. Not only are these employees more productive, but they infuse the work culture with a cooperative, respectful demeanor. Assuming that their skills are sufficient, these workers are like catnip for most organizations.

Accomplishing a balanced composure during your interviews makes a desirable, immediate impression and indicates that you hold promise regarding long-term attractiveness and fit. Thus, adhering to the following is worthwhile, because these characteristics evoke images of levelheaded, responsible and congenial employees—also known as hiring material:

1. Think before you speak.
2. Use professional and positive words, phrases, tone of voice, and mannerisms.

Think Before You Speak

We're all guilty of inserting a foot into our mouths every so often. Minimizing this circumstance during your job interviews is key. If there is any doubt about the validity of this advice, consider how you would have reacted had you been the recruiter saddled with these actual new-grad slipups:

"I'm absolutely blown away. My friend just called to tell me she didn't get a job she thought was in the bag. She's devastated; I need a minute here to collect myself." —Dee

"I thought the President was a total buffoon last night in his State of the Union address." —Kevin

"I don't really like getting up early in the morning. Actually, I can't think before eleven." —Sean

"This would be my second-choice job, to be quite honest. Well … even my third." —Becca

"Oh, sorry. I didn't mean to write that. My girlfriend filled out the application for me while I dictated, and she must have made a mistake." —Hank

"My boss was such a loser last summer. All of us thought this." —Marshon

"I can't stand born-again Christian types." —Cyndi

True, your honest observations might be refreshing, your passion infectious, and so on. However, many of your habits and opinions are simply controversial outside the campus bubble. You say "po-tay-toe," and someone twenty years your senior says "po-tah-toe." While much of college life is about embracing diversity and speaking your mind, the workplace is more about weighted contributions and guarded insights. It's a tough transitional pill for many to swallow.

If you remember that the rules have changed on you overnight and that you basically know nothing about the person you are talking to in your interview (even if you feel a warm, cozy connection), you can make important headway. Your goal is to build in a measured approach, keeping in check any "first thing that comes to mind" blurtings. Essentially, steer clear of these conversational minefields:

- Complaints
- Criticisms
- Political opinions
- Religious judgments
- Graphic or unattractive personal insights
- Anything that portrays you in a less than capable, committed light

Adhering to these guidelines, the candidates noted above would have phrased their comments differently or simply chosen to omit their remarks all together. The tweaking below demonstrates that thinking before speaking is advantageous:

"I'm fine, thank you. How are you?" —Dee

"Yes, I did watch the State of the Union address last night. I thought some issues were handled better than others, and it was interesting to watch the audience's response throughout the night." —Kevin

"I understand that college and work are on different schedules, and I'm ready and willing to do whatever it takes." —Sean

"Yes, I am interviewing elsewhere, but am most excited about the opportunity we're discussing today." —Becca

"I'm sorry about the mix-up. How can I clarify?" —Hank

"I was independent and reliable—a summer employee who contributed without requiring maintenance. As a result, I didn't have a lot of one-on-one interaction with my boss, but I am confident he would be very complimentary." —Marshon

"I've had an opportunity to interface with people from all sorts of religious backgrounds, and I respect that this is a very private, and sometimes passionate, matter for most." —Cyndi

Use Professional and Positive Words, Phrases, Tone of Voice, and Mannerisms

Certain trigger words evoke extremism or immaturity for most recruiters' attuned ears. Your tone of voice and mannerisms also have a lot to do with how pathologically or apathetically your message comes across. Concentrate on the middle of the road all the way around, with an upbeat leaning.

Words and Phrases to Avoid	Better Words
"hate"	"dislike"; "am concerned about"; or point out what you like instead
"love"	"like"; "enjoy"; "embrace"; "prefer"
"to die for ..."	"impressive"; "meaningful"; "worthwhile"
"loser"	"could have been better in this way ..."; "perhaps a more effective approach ..."; "While he made many meaningful contributions, I would have handled this particular situation as follows ..."
"suck-up"	When talking about yourself: "diligent"; "responsive"; "reliable"; "tuned in" When talking about the other guy: well, just don't talk about the other guy in this way.
"sucks"	"concerning"; "unfortunate"; "inappropriate"
"really upsetting"	"somewhat bothersome"; "troubling"; "concerning"
"totally!"	"I agree"; "good point"

"brilliant"	"quick"; "sharp"; "fast learner"; "eager to learn"
"bummer"	"that's unfortunate"; "I'm sorry"; "that's a shame"; "that's too bad"
"huh?" or "what?"	"pardon me"; "excuse me"; "I didn't hear what you said"; "I'm sorry"; "I didn't catch what you said"
"yeah"	"yes"; "that works"; "I'd like to"
"nah"	"no"; "I'm sorry, that won't work"; "perhaps this might work instead"
"'kay"	"yes"; "OK"; "all right"; "I understand"

profanity of any sort

And while on the subject, "supposably," "eggspecially," "expecially," "ax" and "pitcher" are not the correct terms to use when you mean "supposedly," "especially," "ask," and "picture." Three out of five of the former words are not even in the dictionary. Still, these are used with alarming consistency—and to your disadvantage. Correct pronunciation is worth your effort.

Also use words and phrases that are bridgelike—those that ease conversation into more neutral, safe territory, including "perhaps," "sometimes," "a bit," "occasionally," "maybe," "may," "slightly," "somewhat," "while," "despite," "prefer," "suggest," "probably," "I hope," and "possibly." These terms are used in professional arenas by individuals who regularly command respect and attention.

Tones to Avoid	A Better Overall Tone
Monotone	Composed enthusiasm with measured intensity, using a conversational level that is forthright and respectful
Bored, ho-hum	
Hyper, mile-a-minute	

Brash, loud

Coy, demure

Mannerisms to Avoid	Better Overall Mannerisms
Pounding fist onto desk or table	Focusing eyes on interviewers
Saluting	Thoughtfully taking notes, making understated hand gestures without pointing fingers or banging fists
Making a peace sign	
Yawning	Subtly nodding the head to show agreement or interest
Rolling eyes	Offering a slight smile rather than a too-serious frown
Pretending to gag	
Hugging	Restricting touch to shaking hands
Backslapping	
Pointing fingers	
Overly contrived gestures	

Focus

Once you've embraced a balanced communication style, you can concentrate on cozying up to your other new best friend: focus. Keeping the agenda crisp and well-defined allows you to maximize communication without rambling or talking from out of left field. Strategies to achieve this dead-center comportment while in the hot seat are included here.

Focused individuals are usually far more compelling than those who have a tough time getting to the point or those who get easily sidetracked. If you've had a professor who didn't follow an outline and talked about whatever came to mind, you probably know how painful this circumstance can be. It impacted you on a day-to-day basis—and also as final exams rolled around. Make it your personal goal to be as unlike this instructor as possible when it comes to the sharpness with which you conduct yourself in interviews.

Your professor clearly failed to develop some qualities that would have made all the difference to your interest, the notes you took, and your desire to take a class with this guy next term. By concentrating on the following, you won't make the same mistakes and end up being dismissed by recruiters:

1. Snap to.
2. Highlight appropriate material.
3. Listen and respond accordingly.

While you've already been introduced to the importance of each of these attributes, you may not yet realize that the combination of these three is what creates the sharp, accomplished style sought by recruiters. Take the information below to glean new insights as you revisit advice spelled out in previous chapters. Through this review, you should begin to comfortably mesh three tendencies into one pivotal habit. Focus.

Snap To

While simply showing up reportedly defines much of your success throughout life, your enthusiastic investment in the moment counts in equal measure. You've learned to achieve a tuned-in style in the following ways during your interviews:

- **Know your material**. Familiarity with the subject matter allows you to stay a step ahead of, instead of a step behind, the conversation.
- **Streamline your paraphernalia**. Keeping your personal distractions to a minimum and key information at your fingertips allows you to pay attention to the significant facets of your meeting.

- **Understand your audience**. Personalization adds definition and creates a direct link to the person you are talking with.
- **Maintain eye contact**. By looking the recruiter in the eye, you are less likely to lose the gist of the conversation.
- **Keep your head in the game**. While the office, technology, panoramic view out the window, and artwork may be intriguing, make a very conscious effort to postpone self-indulgence until the very end of your meeting, if at all.

Highlight Appropriate Material

By now, you know that this is a time to avoid the Technicolor version of your life, from baby steps through college. Your personal experiences are only intriguing to a point, and your most heartfelt wishes and desires are simply not interesting to recruiters. This is a brutal reality byte for far too many interviewees, who claim there is no better way to love them than to know them. Your "to know me is to love me" approach should only include juicy tidbits that make you right for the job.

Listen and Respond Accordingly

George had a terrible habit of interrupting. He was so anxious to respond to the interviewer that he completed the recruiter's sentences and forged ahead to supply his well-rehearsed answers. Unfortunately, this was annoying and impolite. Very quickly, George alienated even the most good-natured corporate recruiter.

Kendra confounded her interviewer by answering very astutely … but to the wrong questions. Kendra was apparently following an agenda—her own, versus that of the recruiter.

Both of these instances reinforce how very important it is to recognize your recruiter as a person who deserves your respect and consideration every step of the way. The interviewer sets the agenda, not you. This is true no matter how fervently you pray that she requests the one answer you can't wait to deliver. Since you will generally be invited to seize control of the interview at some point, don't take the liberty at the wrong time—and at the expense of ignoring the key person sitting across from you.

It shouldn't be a surprise that the best listening comes from:

- Being prepared and tuned in
- Respecting the importance of other people and the meeting
- Understanding that your interaction matters tremendously to the outcome

Chapter 9

Assume the Versatile Chat Position

*"I was so embarrassed when the recruiter called and got my voicemail message.
At this point, I can only hope that someone over there has a sense of humor and
appreciates clever innuendo ... set to explicit rap."*
—*Senior, Hospitality Major, University of Denver*

His goal: "To successfully manage a five-star hotel in Hawaii."

YOU MIGHT BE INVITED to break bread with the purchasing manager,
or you might be asked to hobnob in cyberspace. Perhaps you're
given one shot to demonstrate how well you manage in front of a no-
nonsense group of head honchos. And while you dismissed yesterday's
note as "only an e-mail," it made you look like a rookie. Spelling
"appreciate" correctly was important to that recruiter.

Basically, interviewing's diverse communication demands keep you
on your toes. Understanding what you're up against, and learning how
to navigate the complex, ever-changing arena, is critical.

Online

Online exchanges involve videoconferencing, personnel
assessments, and e-mail. Both videoconferencing and personnel
assessments (usually screening measures or profile building) are
highly structured with the employer setting the tone and mapping
out the course. E-mail communication is ongoing and often in the
hands of the candidate, who is typically making independent choices
about what to say, how to say it, and when.

Because your computer is like an old, trusted friend, backing you up 24-7 and making no demands on your appearance or decorum, you have a comfort level with this medium unlike any other generation before you. On one hand, technical savvy that is second nature is bankable. On the other hand, being unusually relaxed isn't necessarily a good thing in this instance. You'll probably have to rewire your own internal processor to successfully confront the new links and attachments inundating you during online interviewing.

Videoconferencing

In the past, online videoconferencing (VC) was largely reserved for high-level executives and very specific technical jobs. But VC is an increasing possibility as time and technology march on. Because organizations save recruitment time and money with this screening process, the format may capture the future of interviewing.

VC takes place at the employer's request in videoconferencing rooms found in campus career offices, airports, corporate offices, hotels, staffing organizations, local businesses (such as FedEx Kinko's), and at job fairs. Because the sophistication of the technology varies, it's difficult to predict what you might be asked to do during an online video interview.

For example, some systems are set up so you can display your résumé and other pertinent documents as part of the exchange. PowerPoint capability is available in certain situations, allowing you to enhance your presentation and focus the spotlight. Expectations regarding bells and whistles will typically be reviewed beforehand, so you are clear about what to bring and in what format.

In general, most VC involves a "face-to-face" exchange between you and another person(s) who is in a remote location. You engage in an interview visible on a computer monitor as you talk into a microphone and create your presence in front of a camera. You're seated in a private room or convenient space created for this purpose.

Sounds simple enough, and strangely like the tête-à-tête you've been expecting all along, doesn't it? Until you've been there and done it, however, it's hard to put this format's few uncomfortable, unnatural elements into words. Suddenly, you're overly focused on your movements, eye contact, and expressiveness. And potential time delays toss conversational flow into a stilted zone that's far more awkward than you bargained for.

Therefore, a few insider tips regarding VC are invaluable to someone who hasn't experienced this new-age path to getting a job. You don't want to learn the quirky details cold turkey once you're broadcasting live. The key to coming across as a darling of the camera boils down to understanding and following these insights:

- **Understand that you're ready for a videoconference interview.** With a few tweaks here and there, everything you've prepared makes perfect sense for VC.
- **Ask pertinent questions of the person setting up the interview, so you're less likely to be surprised at the last minute.** "How many people will be interviewing?" "How long will the interview last?" "Should I bring along any materials and in what format?" "Do you have any other guidelines regarding the videoconference?"
- **Contain your physical movements, and don't lean toward the camera.** You're far better off to sit back comfortably, but smartly, in the chair provided.
- **Look at the camera, rather than the monitor, and speak in a conversational tone.** If there are time delays during conversation, wait them out. This is an instance where you should go with the flow and remain composed rather than making comments about how awkward the situation is. Try to ascertain the pacing early on and configure it into your interview, finding an even rhythm.
- **Don't take notes during a VC.** The top of your head would be on camera far too often and this would distort the interview, making you appear awkward.
- **Leave jewelry at home that has the potential to be noisy or overpowering.** While you have heard this guideline mentioned before, it is especially sage advice during a VC.
- **Consider using a personal computer with an online video option for VC rehearsal purposes.** Compared to even a few years ago, installing this capability costs little more than pocket change. With your own camera setup, you have a chance to practice the real deal beforehand. This naturally works best if the person on the other end assumes the interviewer role and is experienced enough to give

meaningful feedback and provide a rousing go at a realistic give-and-take.

Personnel Assessments

Personnel assessments are reminiscent of test taking—or of those online college applications you completed years ago. A Personnel battery lends insight into the validity of your candidacy, sometimes pinpoints your niche within an organization, and often determines whether you're invited to the next round of interviewing. In other words, there may be a clear "score" that makes the cut and another that sends you packing. If you are fortunate and go to the next round, this profile will follow you throughout your interview process. Multiple sets of eyes will ultimately scrutinize the information you include here.

When interviewing with larger organizations, you will encounter a virtual screening more times than you will not. An online assessment is a variation on the old-fashioned hard-copy employment application. For the type of job you are seeking, you will be asked to pony up more than dog-tag specifics when an organization uses this tool in its interviewing arsenal.

You complete an online screening when a potential employer asks you to do so. You might be directed to a specific section of the company's Web site, or you might be given instructions to navigate to an independent address. You then complete the assessment as directed and submit it electronically according to rather straightforward instructions. If the organization is interested, you might be asked to complete yet another series of online assessments to further define your suitability and acumen before scheduling a face-to-face interview.

The measurements are often of the multiple-choice variety (instantaneously graded by the computer), but these assessments are increasingly designed with space for written responses. The questions are diverse, but share the same aim: the organization is looking to find out more about you, such as factual background details, your integrity quotient, and specific skills you possess.

Trying to outsmart the system usually doesn't work; many of the questions are phrased in such a way that there is no right or wrong answer on the surface. Consider this example:

How do you classify yourself in group work/study situations?

1. As a leader
2. As a follower who works hard
3. Depending on the circumstances, sometimes a leader and sometimes a follower
4. As someone willing to take risks and step outside the box, even if it means going it alone

Depending on the organization and the job, any one of these answers might be suitable. It's unlikely you'd know enough at this stage to provide the answer you believe the company is seeking.

Other questions might be more obvious, but be careful. The wording and intent can still be tricky.

- Are you hard on yourself at work?
- Should quality take a back seat when the work is needed quickly?
- Are there instances where it is OK to break the company rules?
- Do procedures sometimes get in the way of getting the work done?

Since you are usually required to answer these questions as yes or no, without being given the opportunity to explain more, your responses should reflect personal attitudes regarding everyday circumstances—not extreme, unlikely situations. And yes, be honest … but consider that organizations are looking for individuals who toe the line, are quality oriented to a fault, and who have a solid work ethic through and through.

You might also encounter an increasingly popular assessment, the Predictive Index® (PI), or a variation of this measurement. At first glance, the PI is a simple adjective checklist that you apply to yourself and then apply in relation to how others perceive you. The PI takes a short amount of time to complete (although this survey is usually untimed), and you respond by indicating your choices according to very straightforward directions.

For all its apparent simplicity, however, the PI is a sophisticated instrument that professionals in the field count on for its outstanding ability to predict work-related behavior. As with any of the other online assessments, you can't outguess the PI assessment, and you shouldn't try; be honest.

Additionally, keep in mind these important reminders when completing any online personnel screening:

- **Read all the instructions very carefully.**
- **Don't rush.** You should concentrate on getting the details perfect; typically there isn't a time limit. You are often allowed to save your work and reenter the site to complete the assessment according to your schedule.
- **Record your username and password in a place you can readily access.** You will probably have to refer back to the application at some point and will need these identifiers at your fingertips.
- **Be sure to hit "Save" when prompted to do so (often on a page-by-page basis); otherwise you could lose all of your input so far.** Be forewarned that some programs may not allow you to go back to change previously saved responses. Yes, it's lousy, but another reason to be very diligent from the start.
- **Look through the instructions to figure out if the default value to insert is "O" or "NA" or another alphanumeric combination.** Use this designation when you don't know an answer, or if the question does not pertain to your circumstances.
- **Review the guidelines for e-mail and letter communications in this chapter and, where fitting, apply them to online personnel assessments that require written replies.**
- **Ask the person who directed you to complete the online assessment which position or job title you should enter if asked for this information.** "Does the online screening require that I note a specific position or job title that I am applying for, and if so, what should I designate?" Your choices are usually tied to a pull-down menu for a response. If it boils down to making a decision on your own, review the list very carefully because your selection might dictate how your résumé gets routed and evaluated within the organization.

- **Be honest when providing answers that ask you to pinpoint your location preference and the amount of travel that is agreeable to you.**
- **Be realistic when designating a desired salary.** Your campus career center will have up-to-date data on current average salaries by industry, and these should be your guide for what is acceptable.
- **Keep your résumé, cover letter, transcript and references ready to go in Word format.** You may be asked to provide attachments or to copy and paste these specific documents into your online profile. There will probably be a limit to the number of documents you can attach. As a result, you can consolidate your three recommendation letters into one file, with clear page breaks. Also make sure that you have carefully formatted your résumé and cover letter so that neither exceeds one page.
- **Think twice and review your work before hitting "Submit" or "Send."**

E-mail

aamof   otoh   cu   lol   afk   brb   eod   JM2C   @@@@:-)   dqydj

You're likely well versed in lingo that's stingy on keystrokes and brazenly to the point. dqydj ("don't quit your day job") if you try this while communicating amid any phase of the interview process—online or otherwise.

While many professionals prefer Internet communication these days, your efforts in this medium are an adjunct to many other points of contact with prospective employers. E-mail is primarily used to establish an introduction, provide background information, firm up details, lay out follow-up particulars, and deliver brief closure specifics. A little bit here and a little bit there, which usually adds up to a lot over several weeks. As a format that can be overly casual, e-mail deserves your careful and thoughtful approach each and every time you hit "Send." Otherwise, "Delete" may well be in your immediate future.

You may tend to use the computer as much as possible, but it isn't always advisable. This is an area that requires your antennae be fully extended and tuned in to the organization and the people you're contacting. Signs that e-mail is an acceptable—possibly even preferred—form of communication include the following:

- A cyber thumbs-up answer to the question, "Do you prefer to be contacted over the phone or online?"
- Business cards that include a person's e-mail address.
- An e-mail response to your résumé and cover letter submissions.
- A request by the organization to submit your résumé and cover letter online.

Once you're confident about proceeding with your keyboard and mouse, the finer points of e-mail communication deserve more than a passing glance. After all, the rules are different than what you're used to, and an important someone is paying close attention. Thirteen guidelines can help steer you in the right direction when corresponding via e-mail during any phase of the interview process:

1. **Use e-mail versus instant messaging or text messaging.** This isn't the time or place for quick and dirty.
2. **Take a detour from funkytown.** Avoid unusual colors, sizes, fonts, nicknames, and so on. Incorporate black and white, legible, and conventional elements; pink script is not the way to differentiate during the interview process.
3. **Address and end formally.** "Dear" and "Sincerely" are not passé.
4. **Do not use abbreviations.**
5. **Keep your online communications short and to the point.**
6. **Proofread your communication twice, checking grammar, spelling, and word usage.** Specifically, consider the following:
   - Ask a reliable source to review the particulars of your writing for good measure.
   - Using the word "interview" four times in three sentences, as an example, gives your message a tedious tone. This error might be more easily caught by another proofreader.
   - Be especially vigilant about correctly spelling the contact person's name and the name of the organization.
   - Always include the full name of the business. If the business is legally Cambridge and Associates, don't ignore the minions by leaving out the associates.

- Address business contacts as Mr. or Mrs./Ms. until you are invited to refer to them by their first names. When in doubt between Mrs. and Ms., use Ms.

7. **Always include a specific subject heading that is brief, professional, and spelled correctly.** In this way, you improve the chance your communication won't inadvertently end up in the recipient's junk mail.

8. **Attach documents thoughtfully.** You're well aware that the world is wary about attachments due to viruses. You can always ask whether it's acceptable to send an attachment, or you can copy and paste your message into the main body of your e-mail. If you do forward an attachment (cover letters, résumés, and transcripts are typically sent as Word attachments), title it professionally and descriptively (j_valeresume.doc; j_valetranscript.doc; and so on).

9. **If you catch yourself copying another person on an e-mail, realize they are probably entitled to a separate, personal e-mail.** This is not a time to economize, even though the computer makes it seamless for us to do so.

10. **Keep a copy of your communications, so that you can refer to them in the future if needed.**

11. **Despite the user friendliness of our virtual world, step back and consider the appropriateness and purpose behind your e-mail communications.** If you are asking for clarification regarding a particular topic, wait a day to make sure you don't have another question. A string of e-mails is more bothersome than indicative of interest and commitment. Along the same lines, carefully weigh your comments and questions. Being politically correct, positive, and nonconfrontational is important. Once you've committed in black and white, it's a tough do-over.

12. **Substitute a straightforward and businesslike e-mail address for an edgy or cute one.** There are other, more appropriate ways to reinforce your individuality than 2much4u@hotmail.com.

13. **Don't cop out with e-mail.** Faceless, voiceless e-mail is an easier mode of communication for a lot of reasons. This is precisely why the Internet isn't always the most professional route to take when communicating with employers.

Declining an offer or negotiating particular facets of a job offer, for example, should usually be done in conversation (face-to-face or over the telephone) with the interviewer.

Consistently using these guidelines is the best way to ensure effective online communication that's noticed for its professionalism as opposed to any other reason. The examples below demonstrate how to use the advice when addressing a variety of topics throughout the interviewing process.

Examples of Effective E-mailing
Effective E-mailing 1
Dear Ms. Shelton:

Thank you for arranging my interview on Wednesday, May 10, at 10:00. I look forward to meeting you and Mr. Cairns. I understand that Mr. Cairns is traveling and out of the office at this time; I'm happy to provide a résumé to him via e-mail if this would be helpful, and if it is acceptable to send as an attachment.

Please let me know if I should proceed along these lines. Thank you again.

Sincerely,

Nicholas Stoyack

Effective E-mailing 2
Dear Mr. Vagt:

It was nice of you to take the time to meet with me the other morning. I learned a great deal about the not-for-profit sector and I'm excited about this as a career direction.

Your insights about work and graduate studies were also meaningful, and I will carefully consider this advice. As you suggested, I will follow up with Colleen Hemphill right away.

I wonder if you would be willing to meet again in a few weeks after I've had a chance to do additional homework and talk with more people. Your advice has pointed me in new, interesting directions and I would value another chance to touch base at your convenience.

Thank you very much.

Regards,

Jamie David

Effective E-mailing 3

Dear Mr. Conroy:

Thank you for letting me know about the change in location for our meeting next Friday. I look forward to seeing you at 725 Culpepper Drive, Suite 91, at 8:30.

Regards,

Michael Corbin

Effective E-mailing 4

Dear George,

Thank you for meeting with me earlier today. As you requested, I am assembling more design samples for your review. I should have these together by tomorrow and I will drop them off at your office, to your attention.

Please let me know if you need other information. I will follow up by Friday to see if I can answer any questions and to discuss next steps.

Regards,

Stephan Lacoste

Effective E-mailing 5

Dear Marie,

I'm really looking forward to starting work on July 9. I appreciate the opportunity and am excited to be the newest member of the team.

Thank you again.

Sincerely,

Laura Jo

Over the Phone

Andy's cell phone is rarely an afterthought, left behind for the day. Basically, if he wants to hear from you, you're golden. As recruiters verify, there isn't a more reliable way to get in touch with Andy and most other interviewees these days.

But there is a slight hitch. Andy was in Starbucks when he got "the call." Two frappucinos and one grande latte later, Andy still wasn't sure what the HR manager said to him. A coffee shop generates a lot of noise to drown out as you're offered the Omaha or Manhattan territory. You may inadvertently end up signing on for a year of Nebraska's blood-red beef as opposed to New York's bright lights and fusion pasta. Or vice versa.

Just like e-mail, the telephone is an integral piece of the interviewing pie, requiring a similar, meticulous attention to detail. Unless your aspiration is to sling hash at the corner diner, it's unlikely the entire interview will be conducted over your cell. But you will regularly use your phone during the screening process and beyond to touch base and firm up particulars.

Andy's all-too-familiar predicament, along with the importance of making a good impression at every turn, are good reasons to get religion where your phone is concerned. Add in the reality that a stellar telephone screening usually guarantees a straight shot to a face-to-face meeting, and it's clear that these suggestions should inch you closer to an offer of employment:

- If "kiss my ass" is the essence of your voicemail greeting, record a new "hello." Music, poetry, quotations, and slang should all step aside for a crisp greeting such as: "You've reached Andrew Franklin. I'm sorry I'm not available right now, but if you leave your name and number, I'll get back to you as soon as possible. Thank you."

- Let an employer's call go to voicemail instead of picking up while you are involved in another activity. You are simply not in a position to be scintillating while ensconced in the bottom of the seventh inning or while doing eighty on the expressway.

- Ask if it's all right to get back to an employer if you answer their call and are unable to comfortably talk or listen. Politely indicate your predicament and be sure to return the call as promised.

- Keep gum, mints, food, and the like anywhere but in your mouth.

- Make sure you're in an area that guarantees quiet for the duration of your phone call, and that you have pertinent information at your fingertips: résumé, KISS, HOP cards, calendar, notepad, and pen.

- Adjust the volume, speed, and inflection of your voice so that you are conversational, moderate, and upbeat (put a smile in your voice without sounding manic). Remember that heavy breathing sounds just like what it is.

- Apologize for any unusual interruptions (such as a cough attack, hiccups, or sneezing fit) and, if you think it's necessary, ask if it's all right to call back later to continue the conversation. In these instances, it is important to avoid coughing, hiccupping, or sneezing directly into the mouthpiece of the phone.

- Apply the rules you are coming to appreciate as standard where interviewing is concerned: be polite and professional, and render crisp, clear, and direct answers. Unlike face-to-face exchanges that grant some leeway, telephone conversations are very intolerant of extended discourses, long pauses, and a heavy dose of "um" or "uh."

- Record brief notes regarding points made, people mentioned, follow-up specifics, and so on.

- Take an unobtrusive swig of water to clear your throat while the interviewer is talking. Since nerves wreak havoc on saliva, a beverage (no ice) close at hand is often a lifesaver, keeping your speech flowing smoothly.

- Leave voicemail messages that are professional and complete when you can't reach a recruiter directly. "Yo, Andy here," gets the point across to your college suitemates, but this isn't enough for a potential employer. Instead, use these guidelines for your voicemail message:
    Address the employer by name, using surnames (Mr., Mrs., Ms.) unless you've been invited to be more informal.
    Leave your first and last names.
    Identify a generous window of time for the employer to reach you.
    Offer to take the return-call burden off the employer.
    Leave your phone number, even though you know the employer has your contact information.
    Say thank you.
    As with e-mail, never leave a string of voicemail messages.

- Consider these examples as the voicemail message standard to adopt:

"Mr. Talbot, this is Andy Franklin, returning your call. I'm sorry I wasn't here when you phoned. I'd like to talk with you and should be available between two and five this afternoon. Otherwise, I'm happy to phone you again if you let me know when you're free to touch base. My number is 847-555-1234. Thank you."

"Hello, this is Maggie Harding, Ms. Kruger. I'm calling to confirm our appointment on Thursday, May 9, at ten-thirty. As you requested, I've put together a portfolio of my designs. I'm happy that I was able to add two new projects that recently received awards of distinction. I appreciate the opportunity to meet with you, and I'm looking forward to it. If you need me for anything before Thursday, I can be reached at 703-555-6891. Thank you."

- Use direct conversation rather than voicemail to convey certain information. If you're accepting, declining, or negotiating an offer, as examples, it's usually best to take care of this sort of business by making contact.

- Close out a telephone screening the same way you do a face-to-face encounter. You must express your interest and desire to go to the next step, often asking what it is that you should do to get there: "I'm very interested in what we just talked about and would like to go to the next step, Ms. Garcia. What can I do to make this happen?"

In a Letter

A letter has a few advantages. It says you've gone the extra mile in a day and age when watermarked stationery is flirting with obsolescence. There's an opportunity to cover important details in a letter; weave in warm, yet professional, fuzzies; and instill near perfection in a way that isn't always possible during a brief conversation or eclipsed e-mail communication.

During the interview process, sending a letter to a prospective employer makes sense in these instances:

- As a way to communicate in the time frame between setting up the meeting and the actual interview date
- As a way to detail "stepping out of the box" buzz (chapter

4), or to provide additional information requested by the employer

- As a follow-up after the interview to express thanks and to underscore a few key points about your candidacy and fit with the organization
- As a follow-up after a job offer has been made or after you've been notified that the organization is not extending you an opportunity at this time

Review the rules for e-mail communications spelled out earlier in this chapter. Dust off those English 101 notes, factor in the following specifics as you write letters during the recruitment process, and study the example further below.

- Avoid handwritten letters. This goes for the envelope as well. While a nice personal touch, you've accomplished more harm than good when someone struggles to decipher your handwriting.
- Match the envelope and the paper and make sure that both are at least 20 lb. weight and (typically) white, ivory, or a pale pastel in color.
- Keep letters to one page or two pages, maximum.
- Follow the same guidelines regarding layout and mechanics used for the cover letter attached to your résumé.
- Personalize your communication and, when fitting, include these specifics (all-important thank-you letters are reviewed along these lines, and in more depth, in chapter 12):
  A brief reminder about who you are
  Your theme
  The organization's buzzwords or phrases
  An indication of how you fit and why you're the best
  An expression of interest in the employer and
  desire for the job
  The next steps, defined as explicitly as possible (who
  is following up by what date and how)
- Sign the letter with your first and last names, using a black or blue pen.
- Keep any enclosures similarly crisp and professional.
- Affix proper postage to the envelope. There's no need to

overnight your letter (this actually backfires sometimes, making you look flush with cash—or desperate). You can always deliver your letter by hand to the office reception area if there is a sound reason for unusual urgency.

- Be judicious. As the example below demonstrates, a single, well-written letter is compelling. Several hasty letters are a red flag.

An Example of an Impressive Letter

Liza Gould
42 Berkshire Drive
Sturgeon Bay, Wisconsin 54032
lgould@interconnect.com   920-555-5234

Today's Date

Mr. Gregory Fell
Senior Marketing Manager
Halliway Inc.
One Halliway Blvd.
Northbrook, Illinois 60062

Dear Mr. Fell:

Thank you for our meeting yesterday. I enjoyed getting to know you, Mr. Weiser, and Ms. Peterson and learning more about Halliway Inc. and your team of passionate innovators.

I was excited to hear about your plans to expand into China. While the marketing challenges appear great, I believe your instincts regarding print advertising make a lot of sense, given the market research you've done so far. I hope your upcoming trip is fruitful, and that your worries about the food are unfounded.

While talking with you and the other managers yesterday, I noted that your division operates under a very goal-directed structure. As we discussed, this is a culture that appeals to me. I readily embrace key targets from day one and don't look back until we're at the finish line. The two semesters I dedicated to intense, independent study programs are one example of how I effectively budget time, zero in on primary objectives, and consistently produce successful outcomes. These experiences also utilized my unique organizational and people skills as we developed new strategies for attracting focus-group participants to our market-research center.

I would very much like to be selected for your management-trainee program. In addition to my pertinent experiences, I've always been someone who can be counted on as an enthusiastic, hardworking contributor and am confident that I can step up to the passionate innovator plate. Please know that I would apply myself in this way as your employee. If there is anything else I can do to convince you of my fit with Halliway Inc., please let me know.

Thank you very much for your time and consideration. I am happy to provide more information if you need it, and I look forward to hearing from you when you return in two weeks.

Sincerely,
Liza Gould

Face-to-Face

It's reasonable to feel that everything you've been working on has to do with getting you to this time and place. While you've witnessed firsthand that interviewing is actually a series of equally important highways and destinations, there's no disputing the "yes!" moment of a face-to-face meeting. This is unquestionably the hour to bring your candidacy to life, transforming black and white into a rainbow of color and opportunity.

Before blasting onto the scene with all engines at full throttle, however, it's worth learning more about the milieu you're about to enter. Face-to-face interviewing is conducted in a variety of places, and you might be asked to participate both off- and on-site.

You'll talk with an assortment of people from Human Resources, rank-and-file personnel, and probably your potential boss. Most interaction is usually one-to-one but occasionally includes a group of interviewers. Your exchanges might be as basic as filling out an employment application or as involved as a behavioral assessment. A majority of the interviews will be dictated by screening and general questions.

All in all, these days promise to be head turners, requiring an on-your-pointiest-toes mentality and approach. To come across more like a prima ballerina than a street-corner hoofer, you must fully embrace the following as you come face-to-face with recruiters (you have been introduced to many of these already):

- Arrive on time ... which is ten minutes early.
- Use spare minutes in the reception area wisely: turn off your cell phone (even vibrate mode should be disabled), review your HOP cards, stash your gum and mints, throw back your shoulders to straighten up, and commit to a smile for the duration.
- Shake hands using that firm, but never numbing, handshake.
- Continue addressing your interviewers by surname, if you haven't yet been invited to use their first name.
- Grant first-name rights to an interviewer if you are addressed as Mr. or Ms. It's appropriate to say, "Please call me Steve."
- Personalize your opening lines as follows: "It's very nice to meet you. I've been looking forward to the opportunity, Mr. Kennedy" or "It's nice to see you again. I've been looking forward to our meeting, Ms. O'Malley."
- Wait to be seated until directed to do so or until the interviewer starts to sit down.
- Place your carryall on the floor next to your chair, within easy reach.
- Ask permission to take notes during the interview. "Is it all right if I make a few notations while we're talking?" Use this opportunity to jot down important names and key phrases, rather than recording each and every word uttered by your interviewers. This short list will be useful to you as you continue interviewing and in your follow-up correspondence.
- Use a balanced style, and keep your focus.
- End by asking what you can do to advance to another interview or an offer of employment.
- Understand the particulars about the various face-to-face scenarios you may encounter. (In other words, read on.)

Off-Site Interviews

Off-site meetings are conducted away from the hiring organization's place of business. In addition to videoconferencing centers, off-site venues include college counseling offices, hotels, airports, job fairs, and restaurants. Between locales, there are unique dos and don'ts worth understanding. In each instance, your goal is to get further along in the process; many of these interviews are screenings meant to define your stay-or-go quotient.

College Counseling Offices

Most schools provide a pleasant (albeit sterile and compact) space for your interviews. The upside is that you usually have closed-door privacy, so distractions are minimal.

Maximize your campus interviews by adhering to the following advice:

- If given the opportunity, choose an interview time slot to suit your needs. Candidates often ask whether early or late in the day is better for a job interview. While most recruiters are hesitant to admit that fatigue can result in a time-of-day bias, some insiders claim that a meeting after the lunch break, the midpoint in the day, is optimal. Aside from trying to outguess the system, book an appointment that supports putting your best foot forward. If you're not an early morning person, steer clear of the sunrise interview.
- Review and follow the interviewing guidelines and tips assiduously prepared for you by your counseling office.
- While the mojo of campus life is often defined by last-minute, hasty entrances, arrive early with the sleep removed from your eyes.

Hotels

You're not as unfamiliar with the hotel-meeting setup as you might think. When you were applying to colleges, it's a good bet you poked around your fair share of hotel lobbies looking for admissions reps. This is simply a variation on that other high-stakes moment. As a result, you probably realize that privacy might be at a premium if you interview in a public area as opposed to a separate room (often a "safer," more appropriate option for obvious reasons).

Additionally, consider the following tips:

- Understand that you might be heading into unfamiliar terrain; hotels are often in an area of town off your beaten path. You may need more time to locate the address, maneuver through rush hour, and locate parking that doesn't cost twenty-five dollars an hour (but, by all means, slam on the brakes here if it means being on time versus arriving late).
- If it isn't immediately clear where you're supposed to go for your interview upon entering the lobby and after checking the daily-events board, ask for assistance. Head to the front desk or the concierge and explain the purpose of your visit.
- If you're waiting to be called by the interviewer, stay in the vicinity and in the moment. While the coffee kiosk and various shops are appealing, you must be available and focused on the meeting. Similarly, this isn't a time to strike up a conversation on your cell phone that ends with the recruiter apologizing for interrupting your business.

Airports

Although security restrictions make them less attractive, airport locations are still used for recruitment purposes. Basically, follow the same guidelines noted for hotel interviewing, and you won't go wrong amid the friendly skies. Without a concierge, however, you'll need to look for officials in case you get lost. Get help based on the directions you were given. In extreme despair, there's always the airport paging system, which is better than a missed interview ... but not by much.

Job Fairs

Described by many as a meat market, a job fair is action and people packed. This is fast talking (not to mention fast thinking and fast doing) at its best. There is scant time to plan ahead. You may have the chance to learn which organizations plan to attend. But you rarely get an opportunity to know much about the positions being recruited, let alone schedule an interview.

You'll circulate through the venue—often a hotel or convention center—and notice organizations with booths or tables manned by recruiters. The jobs are usually entry-level, often inordinately stacked toward sales. Even if you're not interested in the positions offered, you can still learn a lot and possibly establish a connection that is worthwhile. "I'd like a chance to speak with someone at Bryce and Associates about a position in your finance division. If this is a possibility, who would you suggest I get in touch with?"

Most of the exchanges at job fairs are brief encounters. You might be lucky enough to orchestrate a one-to-one session but don't count on much privacy or in-depth discussion. Your goal is to get beyond this cattle rush and into the office for an interview. The best course is to focus on your GEAKE pitch, cut out most of the small talk, and simply ask for the opportunity: "I'd like to have more time to talk with you, because I'm very interested in the Long Beach Park District. Is it possible to arrange a meeting now?"

Staying mindful of your goals, maximize your time at a job fair with these tips:

- **Increase the number of KISS copies and résumés in your arsenal to twenty of each.** Although you may not have a chance to use many of these, it's wise to be prepared.
- **Bring along an ample carryall.** The amount of information you collect at job fairs (annual reports, sales brochures, career pamphlets, business cards, and so on) necessitates serious space.
- **Handle paperwork efficiently.** Neatly stash away the various glossies and business cards given out by organizations. Keep a fresh résumé, KISS, pen, and pad of paper (making sure to continually flip the front page to a fresh, blank one) organized and at the ready as you approach each employer.
- **Consider your timing.** Arriving an hour or so after the opening bell may help you avoid the initial, intense push. Your goal is to sidestep standing in lines in order to stay front and center as much as possible.
- **Construct a game plan.** Take a walk around the entire venue to get the lay of the land. Where are the longest lines? Where are your target organizations set up? Is the interviewing setup a booth or curtained-off area? Strategize your approach before looping around to zero in on your prey.
- **Stay fortified.** Job fairs have a strong wilting effect, and the lighting is usually unflattering. Thirty minutes to revive with liquids and food does wonders for your demeanor, attitude,

and appearance.

- **Remain focused.** When a potential employer asks why
  you're attending the job fair, astutely allude to the
  organization when you provide an answer. "I'd like to use my
  communications degree to concentrate on global consumer
  marketing, and I'm especially interested in talking to you
  because of your international presence and innovative
  strategies" grabs more attention than an uninspiring reply,
  such as, "I'm looking for a job."
- **Make a point of stopping back at organizations that are on
  your A-list before you leave the arena.** Don't expect to be
  remembered by name, but count on making a favorable,
  potentially lingering impression when you make the effort.
  "Hi, I'm Mac Talbot; we met earlier. I wanted to stop back to
  say good-bye and thank you again. I enjoyed our talk and am
  very interested in going to the next step. Is there anything
  else I can do to make sure this happens?"

Restaurants

Answering questions amid bread plates and pats of butter makes
restaurant interviews a unique beast. The good news is that you're
probably beyond the screening stage and into the selection phase,
where the pool is smaller and you're closer to the finish line. A
mealtime interview is meant to catch you at ease and in a more casual
mode. But regardless of how much fun this is all starting to seem,
remember that this is a business meeting with an agenda.

You might have been the cream of the crop up to this point, but a
misstep here can be huge. While the details are assuredly painstaking,
they are well worth your scrutiny; you make a statement when you chew
with your mouth open and another when your chops are clamped
shut. So sit back, don't relax, and enjoy.

- **Put the napkin in your lap when you are seated and place it
  on your chair if you excuse yourself during the course of the
  meal.** When you are done and leaving, it's appropriate to
  place your used napkin on the table.
- **Always push in your chair when getting up from the table.**
- **Strongly consider declining any type of alcoholic beverage.**
  If the interviewer is indulging and vociferously encouraging

you, however, stick to one glass of wine or beer (never hard liquor). Make the indulgence last throughout the meal as opposed to chugging it.

- **Be prepared to order first, since you are the guest.** If you are at a loss, it's all right to ask for a moment and encourage others to order before you. This way, you can actually take their lead and order similar dishes. You can also ask the interviewer if they have a recommendation regarding what is particularly tasty on the menu. The trick with this question, of course, is that it can be awkward if you don't like the suggestion.

- **Order foods and drinks that are medium-priced, easy to eat, and rarely controversial.** Spaghetti, olives with pits, triple-decker sandwiches, and barbecued ribs are therefore poor choices. If you deplore rare steak, it's wise to avoid sirloin, because you don't want to send it back—nor do you want to have a gag attack.

- **Be cognizant of the quantity of food you're ordering.** You will be doing a lot of the talking and may not have time to consume an appetizer, salad, entrée, and dessert.

- **Continue passing shared foods after you've helped yourself.** This includes bread, butter, crudité (vegetable) platters, etc.

- **Be aware that your bread plate is to your left, and your beverage glasses and cup and saucer are on your right.**

- **Begin eating each course when your host starts and not a second sooner.** Then, bring food to your mouth, not the other way around.

- **Use utensils from the outside in as the meal progresses.** As an example, if you have a salad before your entrée, use the outermost fork (the one farthest away from the plate). If you aren't eating a salad or an appetizer, and waitstaff haven't removed any utensils from the table, use the longer-pronged fork set at your place to eat your entrée.

- **When in doubt between fork and fingers, default to utensils.** You probably eat french fries and fried chicken with your hands when you are more casually engaged. But this isn't wise, even if your interviewer is happily up to his own armpits in grease.

- **Chew with your mouth closed, and don't talk with food in your mouth.** Aside from looking unpleasant, the last thing you need is to choke on a piece of pie.
- **Never use bread to sop up extra gravy or sauces.**
- **Do not smoke.** Period.
- **Never groom yourself at the table.** Lip gloss gets touched up in the ladies' room.
- **Do not complain about anything.**
- **Do not pick up the check or politely offer to chip in.** This is as free as it gets. Recognize that you are a guest and say thank you at the end of the meal, indicating what an enjoyable time you had.

On-Site Interviews

All the gears and pulleys are underfoot and operating before your very eyes. You're in the front door, and this is where futures are made. The next chapter of your life may very well begin here. Take a moment to absorb the journey up to this point, breathe deeply, throw back those shoulders, and bring it on home. You've got a job to get, and the opportunity is yours for the taking.

It's possible that you'll be involved in a variety of interviewing situations while on-site. Screening assessments are still a possibility. However, selecting the top candidate for the job is fast approaching. You're where you need to be if you want this offer.

There is a decent possibility you will meet with more than one person in separate interviews today. You might start out in Human Resources, where a schedule for the next several hours is mapped out. In this scenario, you'll be passed along on a rather strict timetable, so the team gets a look-see and a say. Your visit might include a tour of the facilities and a formal video presentation about the organization.

Or, you might meet one key individual who holds all the cards. In all scenarios, conversations will be held in someone's office or cubicle—or you may convene in a conference room or boardroom. There is usually privacy and a decent opportunity to focus on your interviewers and presenting yourself in the best possible light as someone who meshes.

For good measure, review the "Face-to-Face" introductory section in this chapter again and study chapter 10, "Seize the Moment." And know that without a doubt, you're ready to knock 'em dead right here on their own turf.

Human Resources

Not all organizations are large enough to have a separate Human-Resources (sometimes called Personnel) Department that is actively involved in the interview process. In this case, you'll be screened and selected by peers and departmental managers. However, if HR is in residence, you'll undoubtedly meet one or more from this faction, if you haven't already had the pleasure.

Good HR people are simply this—good. They make you feel welcome and comfortable as you complete rudimentary details such as a Personnel profile (if you haven't completed one online already). At the same time, they assess and catalog your every move to figure out what you're made of. Even though an associate from Personnel may have a demeanor suggesting kindred spirits, this is not someone to dish and bitch with.

Whatever the agenda with HR, remember that you can't outmaneuver a top-notch Personnel guy—or even a mediocre one. Tell it straight and professionally while continuing to sell yourself in all the ways you now know are important to secure a job offer.

Everyone Else Beyond Human Resources

Chances are good you'll be sitting across from your prospective boss in a few minutes. Along the way, you might be asked to spend time with peers (those in a position similar to the one you're interviewing for) and management personnel. You might even engage in a group interview as the day unfolds. In all of this, the goal for the organization is to decide whether you are their type, and if you outrank the other candidates.

Peers

Peers, like some of those clever HR types, might come across as symbiotic siblings. After all, they've been there (recently), done that (just), right? Not so fast. This is the very reason peers may have scrutiny dripping out of their pin-striped pockets. An attitude of, "I know what this is all about, and I'm not going to let anyone off easy," often prevails.

The best course is a professional one. Respect the business relationship of this meeting first and foremost, and save the bar-story swaps for your buddies back home.

Boss

It's true you want to like the guy sitting across from you as much as he wants to like you. But keep in mind that you're not in the power seat. You can quietly make your assessment and deal with it after the interview. Your job is to impress, not hold your prospective boss accountable for wowing you.

It's important to understand that you aren't always going to like your superiors. It's essential to embrace this fact of life sooner rather than later. At the very least, you should be able to respect him or her, giving your best work. This will rest at the crux of your ultimate decision about how a specific opportunity relates to your career path. But you can't make today's interview your moment of introspection.

Right now, you need to be likable to this top gun. Hang tight to what you know about face-to-face interviewing and how to bring it all together to make an effective imprint; this is particularly important when sitting across from the head honcho.

Groups

Group interviews are nerve-racking, even for interviewees who handle one-to-one meetings with seamless ease. Many individuals simply freeze up when confronted with a one-to-many format.

Group interviews are a time-saver for the organization, but they also give insight into your cool and collected personality within a stressful setting. The goal generally isn't to embarrass, but to challenge you to demonstrate your ability to adapt and effectively work a number of people simultaneously. This may be critical to the position you are applying for and something you'll be called upon to do with regularity. No time like the present to figure out if you've got what it takes.

When managing a roomful, consider these tips:

- Feel satisfied that you brought along more KISS copies and résumés than you thought you might need. One per person is preferable.
- Greet everyone individually by shaking each person's hand and looking them in the eye.
- Launch gracefully. Grab the moment, and thank everyone for attending and giving you this opportunity.
- Take in the various people all around you throughout the entire session. Focusing on one person, even when you know

someone is fabulous and famous, is inappropriate.

- Allow one of your recruiters to suggest that it's time to wind down and finish. This is never your call, since you're in the hot seat until informed otherwise. When an ending has been offered, thank everyone again for the opportunity and their time.

With a Bozo

You may end up with an interviewer who likes to talk, and perhaps another who doesn't have the foggiest idea which end is up. Then there's the associate who doesn't know the law and asks some of the most improper questions this side of the Mississippi. Now what?

Any out-of-bounds affront may be enough to convince you that you're not interested in this establishment anymore. Before deciding that this is a dead end, however, you're usually better off to quietly take it on the chin and move on with the meeting.

Most often, these instances of inappropriateness—and even illegality—occur due to isolated ignorance or a personal gamble, rather than to a bias supported by the organization. It's true that this isn't always the case, but you'll have to be the judge. Sort through the scenario and make a more calculated decision once back at home.

To keep the interview humming along, you can handle yourself in one of four ways if you are faced with particularly inappropriate questions. "Are you bisexual?" "Will you observe any holidays other than typical Christian ones?" "You look like you're younger than twenty-two ... just how old are you, anyway?" In any of these instances, it's important to remain composed, professional, and upbeat while steering the conversation toward the job and selling yourself.

1. **Answer honestly.** "I observe the standard holidays, but am always willing to pitch in when needed, no matter when."
2. **Redirect the question back to the interviewer by asking what this particular topic has to do with the job.** "Do you mind explaining a bit more about what you're driving at and how this relates to the job so I can be sure to answer appropriately?" Based on the response, you still may have a decision to make about which way to go.
3. **Draw a clear line in the sand by stating that you're**

uncomfortable with the question and are unable to see the relevance of the information. If you take this tack, it is helpful to redirect the discussion to pertinent topics you want to highlight. "I'm sorry, but I'm uncomfortable with how this information pertains to the job. What I can tell you is that I'm … "

4. **Acknowledge the question, but then ignore it by smoothly redirecting the conversation back to another, more appropriate agenda.** "I see what you're driving at, and I'd really like to review …" This strategy clearly takes a cue from experienced politicians who know how to mix it up and keep the focus where they want it.

While inappropriate isn't always illegal, it is just as uncomfortable—especially when delving into such topics as age; sexual proclivities; disability or health; marital or parental status; country of origin; and religion. But if you're committed to learning what the law specifically allows and doesn't, your local library is the best source. Right and wrong differ between many of the fifty states.

There are no laws against an interviewer being a dweeb by talking too much or listening too little. In these cases, you simply must hijack control and salvage what you can. Somehow, some way, you have to interject your strengths and demonstrate your suitability.

The best you may be able to come up with is when you say good-bye. Consider offering something along these lines: "I've been so interested in what you've shared about the job and the organization that I'm afraid I may not have let you know enough about myself. I hope you'll feel free to call me—or perhaps we can schedule another time to meet. At the very least I'd like you to know … [insert GEAKE]." In these last-ditch instances, be sure to concentrate on follow-up that ups the ante, as spelled out in chapter 12.

And despite your urge to shout "loser!" from the rooftops, it's often a dicey proposition to share the ugly details with other employees. If, however, you're in a position where you were given a raw deal of the first order, and you sense that doing nothing is the very worst option, you can proceed with HR or another associate who is involved in your interview process. "I'm concerned that my interview with Mr. Randolph wasn't as meaningful as I would have liked. While I learned a lot about Pinnacle, we ran out of time, and I wasn't able to provide much information about myself. I'd appreciate a chance to do this with Mr. Randolph again … or with someone else, if it's possible."

Your message is clear, but professional. And chances are that others already know Mr. Randolph is a tad on the pompous, puffed-up side.

As a Callback

Hold that sigh of relief. You may be asked to come back for another interview or a series of additional meetings. And then you might be asked to do this yet again. These guys are serious, and you're clearly in the running. You're not a shoo-in, however, and you need to persevere and be as scintillating and focused as ever. It costs far more to fire or lose someone than to hire them; being "sure" is becoming increasingly important.

You shouldn't adopt a new angle or pitch to your candidacy. After all, you're not entertainment, but an investment expected to provide a return. The organization is seeking affirmation, deeper insights, and greater understanding about your fit. The best way to elicit continued interest—and ultimately a job offer—is to stick to what you know and adhere to the following:

- Revisit the research you earlier filtered, streamlined, and put into a nutshell (chapter 6) to refresh your knowledge.
- Ask who will be interviewing and do the same type of fact-finding you did the first time around.
- While your overall pitch stays the same, call up new story material that underscores the same salient points that got you here.
- Use your notes from the last interview to establish a connection and come across as interested and on the ball: "Kirsten Sigalos mentioned that you are moving toward …"
- Ask what you can clarify to solidify your candidacy. If ever there were a time to pose this question, this is it. Then clarify, remembering that fit will determine whether interviewers open the door or press the eject button.

Chapter 10

Seize the Moment

"The three worst sins in my interviewing bible after
all these years of recruiting?
Hands down: mumbling, poor eye contact,
not knowing your stuff cold."
—VP, Human Resources, Management Consulting Firm

Her goal: "Partner in one year. Tops."

BECAUSE FACE-TO-FACE MEETINGS ARE generally where the ultimate deal is brokered or lost, this interview moment deserves additional attention and preparation. First and foremost, without any hesitation: seize the opportunity. Drive home a few key points to accelerate critical momentum and your candidacy. If you play your cards right here, all your hard work and diligence will pay off with a compelling, showstopping presence.

Deal with Your Nerves

Anxiety before and during interviews afflicts even the most seasoned job applicant. You shouldn't be alarmed if you find yourself with sweaty palms and a queasy stomach as you don your gray suit. It's only natural; there's a lot riding on this moment, and you're definitely standing center stage, with a bright spotlight shining down on you.

In most instances, nervousness will push you up and over so you hit your peak when you need it most. Jitters get the adrenaline pumping to fuel your internal reserves and sharpen your overall approach. In essence, a slight edginess and mild physical reminders of the upcoming moment are often your very best friends.

Conversely, dry heaves and diarrhea are not the enhancement you're looking for right now. There are situations where your skittishness simply paralyzes you. Recognizing when you've likely moved past giddy energy and toward an apprehension abyss is beneficial. With this understanding, you can move forward to figure out how to control what threatens to undermine your efforts.

Dealing with your nerves is decidedly easier said than done. However, conquering this relentless beast is manageable with a few tips from others who've been around the nail-biting block a few times and triumphed.

Apprehension Abyss

Marla didn't perspire as a rule of thumb. Sure, she "glowed," but she didn't pour buckets of sweat. This suddenly changed, however, when Marla began interviewing on campus and attending job fairs. As she approached a prized meeting at the corporate headquarters, everything about Marla—save her sweat glands—shut down. The closer the appointment got, the more Marla quaked at the thought of her glossy forehead, beaded upper lip, and stained armpits. Forget all those rehearsed questions and answers; Marla was in strict dry-survival mode.

Marla's situation is definitely an example of nerves gone awry. Below are other instances where butterflies are no longer your friend:

- Intense abdominal discomfort and activity
- Pounding, gnawing headache
- Crippling dry mouth
- Rapid, insistent heartbeat
- Excessive dizziness
- Persistent insomnia
- Extreme perspiration
- Sustained nausea

As if the physical torment weren't enough, candidates often can't hide their extreme discomfort and end up muttering, using poor posture, averting their eyes, and stumbling over their words.

If your nerves are clearly hindering more than augmenting your interview process and are a direct result of this high-stakes moment in your life, it's helpful to dig out the root of this evil. Figure out where all this anxiety comes from.

Typical Fear Inducers

Recent degree holders, who are now gainfully employed and better able to look back with a clear head and dry palms, concur that a number of causes prompt unusual interview anxiety. The following is a list summarizing their insights:

- Insufficient time dedicated to interviewing's 411
- Rehearsal took a far back seat
- Clothing hiccups or another appearance snafu
- Last-minute details nightmare (missing résumés, lack of cash, MIA keys, and so on)
- Getting lost or held up in traffic
- Arriving late or with scant time to spare
- Overwhelmed by all the *t*s to cross and *i*s to dot
- Fear of the unknown
- Habitual failure to remember names

Each and every one of these concerns is legitimate and worth your attention. These involve details that, when corrected, separate the men from the boys in today's interviews. Instead of despairing and throwing up your arms in total surrender, consider that this current state of affairs isn't all that hard to fix.

Strategies to Conquer the Beast

First, take the time to figure out what's causing your personal anxiety. Second, map out a strategy to remedy the offender. This will naturally take some time, and it's unlikely you can make headway the morning of your meeting. Chances are, you realized the problem after your last interview and have been living with the apprehension since. Give yourself a fighting chance this next time around by building in latitude to work through the challenge.

Uncover the Specific Offender(s)

Some rare situations are simply out of your control. You can't personally control an unprecedented three-hour traffic jam or a hurricane evacuation. As a result, don't even try to imagine that the impossible is something you should fix or prepare for on an overtime basis.

On the other hand, the list above details a number of individual responsibilities that cause anxiety when left unattended. These are assuredly worth taking a hard look at as you try to figure out what's eating you. Have you done your homework? Are you familiar with the types of questions you'll be asked in your interviews? Is rehearsal only a reminder, rather than a reality in your life? Have you thoughtfully concentrated on your appearance? Do you really know where you're going and how to get there in advance of the day?

Yes, this is the nitty-gritty of chapters 1 through 9 and represents the work you've been doing ... or not. If you missed a few key steps or slid some of the more uncomfortable tasks under the rug, you might wrestle with a migraine headache as a result. Only you can identify the specifics that were mislaid somewhere along the line and are now causing such angst. While being honest adds to your to-do list, it also provides the answer to what is a most unpleasant state of affairs.

If you've done all you can to prepare, then you might be struggling with anxiety regarding the interview process in general. Many new grads are overwhelmed by the magnitude of details and worry that they haven't mastered these well enough. Additionally, they're fearful of the unknown, having scant experience with interviewing and the notion of being bombarded with nonstop questions from left and right. Most are uncomfortable knowing they will have to remember a number of names in order to come across as charming and memorable. Only you can determine if such concerns are the sole reason, or part of other reasons, behind what's gnawing at you.

Apply a Remedy

Putting a stop to your stomachache might be as simple as rereading some of the earlier chapters and making a renewed commitment to handle the prep process from A to Z. Taking an advance trip to the meeting location, learning more about the competition, and keeping two clean white shirts in your closet are often all it takes to ease the panic for most new college grads. Suddenly, nervous energy is an enhancement rather than a crippler.

In addition, consider these tried-and-true remedies:

- **Talk.** Speak with others about interviewing to get their insights and suggestions. You can use certain people to listen to doubts or concerns you have. Allow your confidant, friends, family, and the professionals working in your campus career office to listen and help you through the uncertainties. Through these conversations, paint a picture of the interviewing process, sketching your place in it a little more boldly each day. The combination of better defining the details and sharing your fears may ease some of the pain.

- **Write.** All those journal entries in school had to be good for something. Why not use your educational experiences to relieve your stress? Many candidates indicate that getting it all out and onto paper is a release that helps to more explicitly identify the problem—and alleviate it.

- **Read.** Decent books are available to help you compose yourself in front of an audience. Consider skimming a few or hunkering down with one to learn more from the pros. While you're turning pages, recognize that you're clearly not alone.

  Coping With Anxiety: 10 Simple Ways to Relieve Anxiety, Fear and Worry, by Edmund J. Bourne
  I Can See You Naked: A Fearless Guide to Making Presentations, by Ron Hoff
  Do Not Go Naked into Your Next Presentation: Nifty Little Nuggets to Quiet the Nerves and Please the Crowd, also by Ron Hoff
  Presentations for Dummies, by Malcolm Kushner
  The Truth About Public Speaking: The 3 Keys to Great Presentations, by Ed Barks

- **Take care.** People who eat and sleep well, and who are in good physical and mental health, have an advantage when it comes to quelling the jitters. Take very good care of yourself as you approach your interviews and consider increasing your workouts for the next several months.

- **Remember.** Don't forget that you have a lot to offer and that interviewers want you to succeed. Recruiters fervently hope you're "the one."

- **Smile.** Not only does your sunny disposition speak volumes to recruiters but it also charges you up while calming you down.

Remember Your Manners

Exemplary manners add an exclamation point to your candidacy. You are noteworthy when you inject your interview with a natural, endearing politeness and use the rules of professional etiquette.

Since "How do you do?" is relatively uncharted territory for many new college grads, it's easiest to learn the protocol by taking one mannerly step at a time—starting at hello and ending with good-bye. While you learned some of the pointers in previous chapters, a few are repeated below in order to present Manners 101 as logically as possible. After all, as you've learned by now, a little refresher course never hurt anyone intent on acing a job interview.

Hello

"You had me from hello." While this is not typically where deals are made for new college grads (or anyone, really, in most interview situations), your "correct" entrance bestows a halo upon your candidacy. And the clock is actually running from the time you hit the premises. The courtesy with which you handle each and every person you meet is critical. Be sure to show consideration to receptionists, security personnel, and so on, because their scorn is rarely a well-kept secret.

1. **Shake hands using a firm, dry-as-can-be grip.**
2. **Look your interviewer in the eye, state your name (if the recruiter hasn't just called you by name), and indicate that it is nice to meet or see them again.** Use the recruiter's name in this exchange. "Cory Rendell. It's very nice to meet you, Mr. Levy."
3. **Wait to be offered a seat before you sit down. Say thank you in response to this invitation.** If the interviewer doesn't offer, wait until he or she starts to sit and then you may do the same.
4. **If offered a beverage, accept by saying, "Yes, thank you very much."** Be sure to ask where you might place your beverage once you have it in hand (you don't want to hold onto it for the duration of your meeting). Your goal is to avoid staining the mahogany—or anything else, for that matter. "Is there a

coaster or a napkin I can use, please?"

5. **If handed a business card, show respect for the person and briefly glance at the card before you put it away.** Express your thanks for the business card.

6. **Let the recruiter have the honor of launching into conversation.** But if the interviewer isn't particularly adept, and silence is filling the room like poisonous gas, by all means get chatty.

In the Thick of It

Once you're settled in and chugging along with the recruiter, it's easy to get caught up in the other aspects of your meeting. Try to remember that the subtlety of manners—or lack of—speaks loud and clear all through your interview.

1. **Wait for a natural break or pause in the action to use the bathroom.** Asking to be excused is appropriate, and this eventuality deserves rehearsal time so you avoid, "Uh, I've gotta go. Where to?" The appropriate request is, "Will you please excuse me for a minute? Where is the nearest restroom?" Then say, "Thank you" before you leave. When you return, you might say, "I'm sorry for the interruption." Never reveal any more about the gory details by announcing, "Whoa, just in the nick of time. I wouldn't go into that bathroom right now if I were you."

2. **Stand to greet someone who comes into your meeting.** This is true whether the person coming in to the room is male or female, and whether you are male or female.

3. **Ask permission if in doubt about how to proceed at any point in time.** As long as you don't overdo it, you're generally on solid ground when you politely ask whether you may take action. "Would it be all right if I shared work from my portfolio now?" "I'd like to point out a few additional experiences on my résumé. May I give you another copy while I go over some of the details?"

4. **Never correct another person's bad manners.** "Excuse me, but you've just interrupted me." "Fellas, we're supposed to stand when a lady enters the room." These are inappropriate reprimands on your part. Instead, ignore the infraction.

5. **Never badmouth or complain about anyone or anything.**
   This not only is rude, but it makes you appear petty and
   insecure.

Good-bye

Your parting shot is a time to keep the dream alive, rather than
crushing it with poor manners. The latter happens, sometimes, when
candidates get comfy with their recruiters during interviews (especially
when they've been on the premises all day, or if this is a second,
third, or fourth meeting). While being relaxed is certainly desirable,
it shouldn't translate into an overly familiar, less than professional
manner. Remember the following guidelines:

- The interviewer calls an end to the meeting. You never
  suggest that the appointment has reached its conclusion.
- You generally stand up after the recruiter starts to stand.
- Ask where you can put your empty, now dirty glass or cup.
  "May I take this somewhere to get it out of the way?"
- Look the interviewer in the eye, shake his or her hand using
  that same firm grip, and thank them for the opportunity.

The Handoff

You might be passed from one recruiter to another throughout
the day. As you take leave of one to greet another, you have to be
ambidextrous, using your best hello and most professional farewell
almost simultaneously. When someone introduces you, it's appropriate
to greet the new guy first. Then say good-bye and thank you to the
person who is moving you along in the process.

No Matter When or Where

These mannerly tips are useful, regardless of the when and where
of your job interview:

1. Turn off all electronics.
2. Stay focused (showing interest is as polite as it gets).
3. Don't allow your manners to seem like an afterthought.
   "OK, it was good to be here today. And, oh yeah, thank you."
   Rather, be as naturally polite as possible: "Thank you for
   inviting me in today."

4. Don't interrupt while another person is talking.

5. Use "please" and "thank you" regularly.

6. Use the best words, tone of voice, and mannerisms (chapter 8, "Balance").

7. Remember that "excuse me" is a request and not a command. "Will you please excuse me?" is preferable to "Excuse me."

8. Use proper names when referring to people in your interviewing moments. "That lady I just spoke with" or "The head of Human Resources said" aren't as hard-hitting as "Mr. Ripa mentioned a new territory opening up on the West Coast."

There are a few other instances where the devil is in the details as far as your manners are concerned. Mealtime etiquette was reviewed in chapter 9, under the "Face-to-Face" section, and is worth studying, should lunch or dinner be on your meeting's menu. And for the very rare interview that might take place out of the country for a job overseas, imposing unique formalities, go to www.executiveplanet.com. This site highlights appropriate conduct to follow in forty-five different countries.

Talk Turkey

This section includes essential words that denote succulence and preparation. Since you first began writing your résumé, you've likely been hammered over the head with advice regarding the use of active terms to sell yourself. This recommendation was never more salient than now, when you're seated in front of a prospective boss. Remember that this is an opportunity to make your candidacy come to life. If you underscore the thoughtfulness and energy that got you here in the first place, you won't be pegged as a flash in the pan.

You can't possibly use the entire list below—nor should you. You'll sound like *Webster's* on terminology overdrive and will annoy the heck out of your interviewers. Rather, scan the list and choose a few terms that make sense for your personal conversational style. Also consider words that expressly fit the job you're seeking and are compatible with your theme and branding advantage.

Candidates looking to make the grade in a creative field are most likely to do so by using words such as "fashioned," "revitalized," and "conceptualized." "Adapted," "clarified," and "enabled" make sense for someone seeking a teaching position. While these are fine lines, it should be obvious that you're far better off anywhere in this action-oriented neck of the woods than when you use words like "did," "made," "worked," "was," "said," "told," "started," "tried," and so on.

A

accomplished	achieved	adapted
addressed	advanced	advocated
applied	attained	augmented

B

boosted	broadened	budgeted
built		

C

calculated	captured	centralized
chaired	clarified	coached
communicated	compared	compiled
completed	composed	conceived
conceptualized	conducted	consolidated
consulted	continued	contributed
controlled	converted	conveyed
convinced	coordinated	counseled
created	cultivated	customized

D

debugged	decided	defined
delegated	delivered	demonstrated
designated	determined	developed
discovered	displayed	dissected
drafted		

E

earned	edited	eliminated
emphasized	employed	enabled
encouraged	enforced	engineered
enhanced	enlarged	enlisted

ensured   established   estimated
evaluated   examined   executed
exhibited   expanded   expedited
experimented   explored   expressed

F
facilitated   fashioned   finalized
fixed   focused   forecasted
forged   formed   formulated
fostered   fulfilled   furnished
fused

G
gained   gathered   generated
governed   guided

H
heightened   honed

I
identified   illustrated   implemented
improved   incorporated   increased
influenced   initiated   inspired
installed   instituted   integrated
interacted   introduced   involved

L
launched   led   lifted
located

M
maintained   managed   manipulated
maximized   merged   mobilized
motivated

N
navigated   negotiated   netted

O

observed	obtained	orchestrated
organized	originated	outlined
overcame	overhauled	oversaw

P

performed	persuaded	pinpointed
piloted	pioneered	predicted
prevented	prioritized	produced
programmed	projected	promoted
proposed	proved	publicized

Q

qualified	quantified

R

raised	reached	realized
reasoned	recommended	reconciled
reduced	regulated	rehabilitated
rendered	reshaped	resolved
responded	restored	retrieved
revitalized		

S

saved	secured	served
shaped	sharpened	simplified
sold	solved	spearheaded
specialized	sponsored	standardized
stimulated	streamlined	strengthened
strived	structured	summarized
supervised	supplied	supported
surpassed	sustained	synthesized
systematized		

T

targeted	tightened	transformed

U

uncovered	undertook	unified
united	updated	upgraded
utilized		

V

validated	verified	vitalized

W

widened

Maximizing your message extends beyond action verbs. It's important to remember an employer's interview mission. Recruiters are furtively looking to siphon out candidates who are able, suitable, willing, professional team players, and capable of solving problems. Fit. It simply makes sense to use these exact words, with stories to back up your claims, when talking about yourself.

Establish Rapport

"Sixty seconds" sells some books, but rarely the new-grad interviewee. True, you don't have a lot of time to be wildly intriguing, but there is a way to resonate more strongly than most while in the hot seat. Since no one is as engaging as the candidate who knows his or her way around skillful conversation, useful tips about the gift of gab and on-the-fly relationship building steer your meeting where it needs to go.

First and foremost, establishing rapport is key to your efforts. Secondarily and beyond the rudimentary, there are very specific ways to enhance your conversation skills, so the recruiter is sad to see you go.

General Rapport Builders

Preparation is at the heart of meaty connections; this book will greatly fortify your rapport-building strategy. Approaching your interviews positively, and with enough urgency to learn, focus, and rehearse—sharpening and fine-tuning in a balanced style—are at the core of being genuine and captivating. You'll avoid flapping your tongue in the wind, sounding empty and frantic during your interviews, when you diligently review important details.

Specific Conversation Skills

There are a number of conversation dos and don'ts that push your candidacy head and shoulders above the crowd. There's nothing tricky or particularly complicated here. Rather, what separates interesting from ho-hum boils down to understanding and accepting that you have a responsibility to be both proactive and sensitive. You know the importance of being a good listener; using comfortable language in a clear, audible voice; and asking tuned-in questions. Additionally, remember to do the following:

1. **Figure out your interviewer.** As accurately as you can, determine the recruiter's style, and adapt some of these nuances into your demeanor. Since people gravitate to those who are most like them, this is usually a winning (albeit sophisticated) strategy.
2. **Reference common ground.** If possible, refer to previous meetings, points made by the interviewer or other people in the organization, mutual acquaintances or interests, and so on. Familiarity and recognition create and solidify feel-good bonds. This is where the organization's buzzwords or significant phrases can be useful.
3. **Be complimentary.** We generally like people who like us. Without pouring on the sap too heavily, find a way to lend your sincere approval to something—the company's Web site, the organization's ad campaign, and so on.

Pace Yourself

There's a difference between a pause and a black hole; the former represents a tempo that is thoughtful and respected in an interview. Additionally, there is a rhythm to shoot for that makes sense in terms of logical flow and ease of conversation. Instilling beneficial pacing into your interviews is within your control.

Pause

Confidence bolsters your ability to take time, without worry or guilt, to collect your thoughts and put your best foot forward. Use brief silences to mentally pull up information from your personal reserves and archives. When candidates aren't prepared, they tend to rush into an explanation and hope their momentum will either cover up or miraculously generate the best response.

The bottom line, then, is to take a few seconds to collect yourself, whether you're prepared or not. You'll simply position yourself as being more in the game if you aren't hasty, and are instead composed and thoughtful. While this isn't enough, it's something, and most worthwhile for the candidate who comes to the table having done his or her homework.

Rhythm

Walking in to an interview throwing your résumé, reference packet, and KISS onto the table while boisterously spouting off your GEAKE pitch and asking for the job would amount to a rude introduction, hitting the climax before the plot has a chance to thicken. Similarly, if your responses and general chitchat are continually out of step, you've created discord.

Remember that the best, most memorable stories, meetings, and encounters are those with a clear beginning, middle, and end. Hooking in your audience, filling them up with substance, and closing with a bang has been good practice since you learned it in your fourth-grade English class. In the same, logical way, your interviews have indelible cadence when you carefully build in tempo and timing.

End with a One-Two Punch

Finish your interview with as much energy as you invested into the start of the meeting. Not only do final impressions usually linger the longest, but you also have an opportunity to alter and enhance opinions that have been formed. The clincher is that a hard-hitting finale takes guts. Given that your parting shot is a critical one-two punch, however, it's important to garner some pluck.

First, find out if there are any concerns before you leave the room. Chapter 11 outlines ways to figure out where damage control might be needed. This approach will quell objections that occasionally fester and possibly remove you from contention when you're not around to clarify.

You might believe that recruiters should and will take responsibility for addressing any gray areas before the meeting is over. While this makes sense, it just doesn't happen with regularity. Chalk it up to human nature, time constraints, or HR's game plan, but digging deep comes from the candidate more often than from the interviewer. Since you have the most to lose by not going here, prepare to run this offensive strategy.

Second, as the very last contribution you make to the meeting, run down your attributes (and hand over your KISS if you are using this document), provide your reference packet and tell the recruiter you want the job. Like any good story, you should supply a conclusion that highlights the salient points. Yes, this is redundant, and precisely the reason to do it.

Your best features will be memorable because you've mentioned them the most often. While you obviously can't be annoying in this regard, keep with the crisp and concise theme and use your instincts. Your summation will deliver.

> "Thank you for having me in today. I learned a lot, and am now even more confident that I would enjoy being a part of this organization, working for you. I believe I'm an excellent fit because of my work ethic, creativity, ability to communicate effectively and my desire to be part of a dynamic team. You can count on me to be an enthusiastic and solid contributor. Here is a brief summary of what I bring to the organization (KISS), and these are my references (reference packet), of which I'm particularly proud. Thank you again, and please know that I would like this job."

Chapter 11

Turn the Tables

"The interview was winding down and I'd been there since nine.
I really and truly knew everything about everybody in the industry, the company,
and the division after six hours, lunch, and meetings
with four good corporate soldiers.
"When my final interviewer of the day asked if I had any questions,
all I could do was shrug my shoulders, say thanks, and utter that I
pretty much understood it all. Besides, her squinty eyes weren't
exactly welcoming me into any extended chitchat.
"Boy, was I wrong; she was stunned. She expressed 'great surprise'
at my lack of curiosity. Those steely blue eyes were mere slits
by the time I got up to go."
—Graduate, Philosophy Major and Spanish Studies Minor,
Santa Clara University

Her goal: "An opportunity with international interface."

THE QUESTIONS YOU ASK, and when you pose them, are as important as the answers you have so far crafted and practiced into the wee hours. Yes, you're expected to be nosy during your interviews. Recruiters hope to learn more about the depth you bring to the mix through the way in which you manage tidbits of information, and yourself, on the spot.

As such, you raise safe questions that put your candidacy on parade before an offer is extended. The following first two sections, "Timing *Is* Everything" and "Right, Polite, and Knock-Your-Socks-Off Questions to Ask" address the inquiries you make while you are a job seeker. "Show me the money" grilling is fair game following an offer of employment and is reviewed in the "Hot and Heavy Inquisition" section further below.

Timing *Is* Everything

Your sensitivity to the various people and stages involved in the interview process should guide you as you craft the art of inquisition. This section clues you into particulars relating to who and when, so you are always on the mark with your questions.

Inquiries you pose on campus, in job fairs, and with HR associates address more general aspects relating to the job, the organization, and the interview process. While you will encounter informational overlap, meetings with managers and potential bosses delve into more specifics about the players, your role, the business, and specific responsibilities and goals.

As you ease into the interview after "Hello," no matter who you are meeting or where the interview takes place, your questions are generally rudimentary. You're taking care of business, establishing your professionalism, and extending certain courtesies. These may seem like small details, but collectively they set a noticeable tone while everyone gets their bearings early in the interview.

One or two questions you "spontaneously" initiate later, during the heart of the interview and based on what is being said by the recruiter, demonstrate your listening skills, ability to think on your feet, and interest in what is being discussed. This says loud and clear, "I'm capable of give-and-take."

Then, count on recruiters asking whether you have any questions. This almost always occurs at the conclusion of your interview. In a grand finale featuring your curiosity, you have a chance to wow your audience, add definition, and map out important next steps.

Dubbed by many young candidates as too much, too soon, some aggressive interrogation is simply a necessary, appropriate close. As the "End with a One-Two Punch" section in chapter 10 pointed out, however, much of this takes nerves of steel. Not everyone is a born salesperson embodying the adage, "If you don't ask for the sale, you'll never get it." Some candidates worry that any pushiness is too confrontational and almost hinges on desperation.

HR managers largely concur, however, that they are impressed when a new college grad has the poise and backbone to take charge and finish with an exit strategy that underlines earnest desire. Your questions here stand out, because you're willing to go out on a limb while keeping it professional. You suddenly become the tough act to follow.

These end-of-the-interview questions (two to four, depending on time) consist of a combination of inquiries you have already formulated and those that emerge from the meeting you've just had. There is often a great deal of overlap between the two, which is a good reason to do the work ahead of time. Based on your research and preparation, your top questions should be in your hip pocket as a part of your HOP arsenal.

Replying that you don't have any questions or trying to drum up scintillating and compelling queries while standing on the finish line aren't wise strategies. Even if you politely indicate how thorough the recruiter has been and that you are completely satiated, you are squarely in back-to-the-classifieds territory when you wrap up too early or in lame fashion.

Right, Polite, and
Knock-Your-Socks-Off Questions to Ask

With the sky as your limit, it's important to diligently choose questions that put you in the best professional light and give additional insight into your confidence, intelligence, and enthusiasm. This is clearly another chance to tell a recruiter more about you and to clinch the offer; take this opportunity and run with it. Formulate questions that meet the following criteria:

- **Logical in terms of timing.** Don't ask your most riveting question as you walk in the door and before you are seated. As outlined above, you typically and methodically move from polite to invested and ultimately to hard-hitting as you span the beginning, middle, and end of your interviews.
- **Reasonable in terms of quantity.** You're allowed curiosity, as long as you use good, measured sense and are thoughtful about your questions.
- **More open-ended than of the yes-or-no variety.** You infuse energy into the meeting when you add to the conversational

opportunities in a substantial way. However, yes-or-no questions that advertise your knowledge and insights are fine, as long as you don't overdo.

- **Considered.** It is not your goal to trip up the interviewer. It's amazing how many new grads believe they are on the right track when they stump the recruiter. You remember this scenario, right? The kid who asks a buddy to spell "antidisestablishmentarianism" during an impromptu spelling bee in the school yard. Basically, no one likes a smarty-pants, or egg on their face.
- **Not condescending.** Questions that start with "why" are sometimes construed as being demanding or haughty.
- **Nonthreatening.** Insinuating that you are a hot commodity with a number of other potential jobs waiting in the wings is inappropriate.
- **Dignified.** Begging for a job—"I really, really need this to come through for me. Can you help me, please?"—is never pretty. Desperation is pathetic.
- **Pertinent.** You should ask only about business-related topics and address subjects that parallel the recruiter's conversation.
- **Compelling.** Any old inquiry off the top of your head isn't enough. Your well-conceived questions will affirmatively answer *their* questions about your knowledge and fit.
- **Useful.** The more you can learn from the questions you ask, the better positioned you are to make advantageous personal and career choices.

Your questions, before you own a job offer, should avoid any discussion about what perks might be coming your way. Additionally, steer clear of probing personal matters ("You look awfully young to be a brand manager; how old are you anyway?" "Do you like to party?"); making whiny inquiries ("Is it always so hot in here?"); or concentrating on anything negative or accusatory ("How long do you think this will take today?" "Am I wrong, or did you guys miss the boat with that weird Web design?").

Questions to Ask at the Beginning of an Interview

Remember: Small talk matters, and mechanics count.

Goal: Establish yourself as polite, pleasant, and professional.

Examples:
- "It's nice to be here. How are you?"
- "Yes, thank you, I would like coffee. May I get it?"
- "Where would you like me to sit?"
- "May I give you a copy of my résumé?"
- "Is it all right if I take a few notes during our meeting?"

Questions to Ask in the Middle of an Interview

Remember: You're in the hot seat and doing most of the answering, not asking, right now. But mixing it up (ever so slightly) is refreshing and noticeable when you react to specific points made by your prospective employer. Many a hearty conversation has been spawned from an interviewee's insightful intrigue.

Goal: Underscore your dynamic, invested style.

Examples:
- "That's an interesting point. When did the market first show signs of shifting?"
- "I didn't realize that parents were so involved in the classroom here; this sounds exciting. What has been the greatest advantage of their participation?"
- "I can see how this customer-service model makes sense. What are the main changes to the former way of doing business?"
- "You earlier talked about improving customer awareness. What specific projects are in the works to accomplish this goal?"
- "From what you just said, it seems that the technological upgrade to your internal communications has streamlined business overall. What is the next step in terms of technological upgrades to other areas of the operation?"

Questions to Ask at the End of an Interview

Remember: You are expected to ask compelling questions, and it's smart to probe for useful information. If you generate a second question or make an observation based on an interviewer's response, you move into a conversational realm that is more robust than an asked-and-answered onesie. And for more technical, specific inquisition, make sure you have a general idea about the answer. The interviewer might throw your question right back to you for your take on the subject matter.

Goal: Leave nothing on the table. Show what you know, express interest, demonstrate intelligence, resolve concerns, define next steps, and ask for the job.

Examples of Compelling Questions:
(One recent college grad likened these questions to those you and your parents posed while on campus tours/interviews as you were choosing a college to attend.)

- "I made a few notes before I came in today. Is it all right if I refer to these? There are a few questions I would like to ask."
- "Will you please describe a typical day for someone in this position?"
- "What is the top priority of the person who accepts this job?"
- "What are the day-to-day expectations and responsibilities of this job?"
- "What are the reporting relationships for this position?"
- "What advice would you give to someone who is in this position?"
- "What are the initial projects I'd tackle?"
- "Is there a specific training program, or is it more learn by doing?"
- "How is performance measured?"
- "Will you please describe more about the makeup of the team and the dynamics of working collaboratively within this division?"
- "What are the traits and skills of people who are the most successful within the organization?"
- "Will you please describe the overall work culture here?"

- "What convinced you to come work here? What keeps you here?"
- "What does this company value the most?"
- "What do you think is the greatest opportunity facing the organization in the future?"
- "What do you think is the greatest challenge facing the organization in the future?"
- "In what ways is the relationship between sales and manufacturing collaborative?"
- "My research indicates that Fullerton Industries is a major competitor. What is your main differentiation strategy?"
- "From what I understand, you differentiate your products from the competition in three ways: twenty-four-hour customer service; money-back satisfaction guarantee; and simplified start-up. Is this analysis correct? What are the most vulnerable aspects of this differentiation strategy?"
- "Your approach to driving sales through unique channels of distribution has been written about a lot. What are competitors doing in response? And what will you do as a result?"
- "Your organization was founded on three strategic principles. How do these tenets drive the operation now, some fifty years later?"
- "Mr. Cartwright, your CEO, was recently quoted as saying, 'Customers and employees share equal status and require management's around-the-clock nurturing. Without the robustness of one, you don't have the robustness of the other.' How does this posture impact the culture here?"
- "The overseas expansion of the market has been explosive. You mentioned that you have looked into these opportunities. What will impact a decision to expand into Asia?"
- "Despite some market volatility these past few years, this organization has managed to stay ahead of the pack. What are the main reasons for this unique success?"
- "As I read about your company, I understood that your salespeople are responsible for servicing accounts in addition to cultivating new territories. How has this strategy made a difference to your growth in the past, and how do

you see it impacting growth into the future?"
- "From what you've said, fundraising is key to your budget. I read that not-for-profits are increasingly investigating unique revenue-producing avenues. Is it possible to branch out without deterring from your mission?"
- "At the school where I worked as a student teacher, we successfully enlisted parents to assist in the classroom by asking them to tutor one-on-one. Would an initiative of this sort help alleviate the strain from growing classroom size here? I've had some experience in this area and would be happy to get involved with the particulars."

Examples of Questions that Lead to Useful Information:
(The interviewer's answers to these questions should be your cue as to appropriate follow-up.)

- "Based on everything we've talked about, are there any concerns you have about my ability to do the job or regarding my fit with the organization?"
- "Do you believe I can do the job?"
- "What is the next step in your interview process?"
- "What can I do to further the process along?"
- "Is there any additional information I can provide that would be helpful as you make a decision?"
- "May I ask how I stand relative to my competition?"
- "What is your timing like regarding this decision (or next steps)?"
- "When can I expect to hear from you?"
- "Will I be hearing back from you or someone else in the organization?"
- "Is it all right if I take the initiative to call back on a date you specify regarding your decision?"
- "May I please have one of your business cards?"
- "Based on everything I've learned, I think I'd be great in this job and would really like the opportunity."(While this is not a question, it is indirectly, but definitely, asking for the job. More experienced candidates, or those who are highly sought after, may add one of the following: "Are you able to make me an offer?" "Can we come to an agreement today?")

Questions that Shouldn't Be Asked

Sometimes, you just can't go there. For whatever reason, the information you crave isn't appropriate for someone in your position. Use your good judgment and what you learned in chapter 2 about touchy subjects to understand this distinction. For questions that can be asked, but should be rephrased, use better, more appropriate words, such as those suggested in chapter 8. Below are actual questions that were asked but shouldn't have been. Note how a slight rework gets you the same information and keeps your approach professional.

- "Is the boss a guy who breathes down your neck or will he cut me some slack every now and then?"
  (Better: "How would you describe the management style of the boss?")
- "Is training sequestered and boring, or do I get to see the light of day every so often?"
  (Better: "What is the training program like?")
- "If I got fired, how much pay would I get?"
  (Better: After an offer is made, you can investigate topics such as this one by asking about benefits for employees who leave the company for any reason.)
- "Do you really need me to fill out this job app? I already gave you my résumé and the information is redundant."
  (They know what they're doing, so just do it—no questions asked.)
- "My goal is to make money. Fast. What are my chances for rapid, upward movement in the company?"
  (Better: "I'm very motivated to succeed and willing to do what it takes to move up in the organization. Would you please tell me more about advancement opportunities?")
- "I read about the threat of a harsh climate to your business and, from what I know about tsunamis and hurricanes, there seems to be a real danger to your viability in the future with global warming. Is this true?"
  (Better: "My understanding is that conditions relating to climate may have an impact on business in the long term. If this analysis is correct, how is weather being factored into the company's overall strategy?")
- "I ran out of time and didn't get around to studying your

competition, but I thought of a cool idea that might work. Do you want to hear it?"
(Better: "Can you please give me more insight into your competitors?" After the interviewer's response, and if it makes sense, you can proceed with, "Given the competitive picture, I had an idea and wonder what you think …")

- "You said I'd hear in two weeks. Is this real, or am I going to have to hound you for an answer?"
(Better: "What is your most realistic guess about when I might hear something concrete from you?")

- "Won't you just give me a try? I promise I'll do a great job. I'm not sure why no one believes me, but I swear you won't be sorry."
(Better: "I'd really like this opportunity and feel strongly that I would be an asset to this organization. Are there any concerns I can address right now?")

Hot and Heavy Inquisition

After an offer has been made, new college grads learn more about the spice and sizzle. While most of your questions will generally be answered in a formal letter, this isn't always the case. But you now have relatively free rein to inquire about all the specifics that make your world go around and those that help you decide if this is the place for you. And even though you have the offer in your hot little hands, remember that this is now your potential employer; continue to be polite and respectful as you clarify.

Questions About the Essentials

If you don't receive an offer in writing (which is rare), you should ask for this before you give your decision. If you meet with resistance, simply respond by indicating that you are more comfortable evaluating important details in writing and would appreciate the chance to do so now. If the offer is not specific enough, HR is usually the place to go for answers regarding responsibilities, pay, vacation, benefits, and legal matters. You won't require answers to all of these questions before making a decision about an offer, but you're better off knowing as much as possible sooner rather than later.

Responsibilities

- "May I see a written job description?"
- "Are you able to provide information about my reporting relationships?"
- "Am I directly compensated on meeting specific objectives as outlined in the job description?"

Pay

- "How much is the salary and on what schedule are paychecks provided?"
- "Are there any unusual payroll deductions?"
  These might include charitable contributions, dues, and so on.
- "What is the company policy regarding overtime compensation?"
- "How are pay raises achieved and in what time frame?"
- "Is there an opportunity to receive any other type of compensation?"
  Additional compensation might include a bonus, merchandise discount, reimbursement for tuition, company-owned vehicle, and stock or stock options.

Travel and Expense (T&E) Reimbursement

- "How are requests for travel and expense reimbursement handled?"
- "What is typically covered through T&Es?"

Days Off

- "What are the company's paid holidays?"
- "How many sick days, if any, are compensated each year?"
- "How many personal days, if any, are compensated each year?"
- "How is vacation eligibility determined?"
  If the stated vacation policy is not explicit, the following questions still need to be answered:
- "What happens to unused vacation days?"
- "Are vacation days earned in any other way than through time on the job?"

Insurance

- "What insurance coverage am I entitled to, at what deductibles, and when am I eligible?"
- "Is insurance participation mandatory or voluntary?"
- "What percentage of the insurance premium is picked up by the employer?"
- "How is dependent coverage handled and at what cost?"

Relocation

- "What are the specifics surrounding a geographic relocation?"
- "Is there a stipulation surrounding length of employment and ultimate responsibility for relocation expenses?" Ask about reimbursement for the following:
- Buyout of an existing apartment lease
- Transporting furniture, a vehicle, and personal belongings (Is there a restriction on how much can be shipped and by which carrier?)
- Temporary living arrangements until a permanent residence can be found (how long and where?)
- Travel to locate housing (how many trips and does this include all travel, hotels, and meals?)

Other Benefits

- "Is there a stock-purchase plan, and how are contributions made?" You may be interested to know if the employer makes contributions.
- "Is there a retirement plan, and what are the funding particulars?" You may want to know what is used to fund the plan and what is the benefit.
- "If there is a 401(k) plan, what are the specifics?"
- "Is there a charitable gift-matching program?" This might include contributions to your alma mater.
- "Do airline miles earned for business travel belong to the company or to the employee?"

Other Matters

- "In the event of a separation from the company, what does the company offer in terms of compensation and for how long?"
  This should be defined for a lay-off, firing, or disability circumstance.
- "Are there any legal restrictions or stipulations surrounding employment?"
  Some organizations may require you to sign a contract or a noncompete agreement, as examples.

Questions About the Inside Scoop

You might need more insight and a different perspective in order to make a decision about the job offer. Though talking to HR will clarify most of the issues above, head to the rank and file for a better sense of the organization. "Can I please get in touch with a few more people on the team? I'm interested to learn more and want to get a better idea about the culture and the dynamics here."

In some instances, candidates have even spent a day in the field with a sales rep or on the job with an associate. No matter where or when, getting the lowdown from the organization's employees should focus on information gathering that is professional and helpful to your decision making. Below are questions you might pose at this stage:

- "What are the three best things about working here?"
- "What are the three worst things about working here?"
- "How would you describe the company's culture?"
- "What convinced you to come here and what keeps you here?"
- "Will you please give me insight into one or two people who have worked here but who decided to leave?"
- "Will you please list the strengths and weaknesses of my potential boss? How about her boss?"
- "Is there a collaborative culture here? Would you please give me some examples?"
- "What is the fastest track to promotions within the organization?"
- "Is there a prevalent sense of fairness and open communication here? Do any examples stick out in your

mind?"

Questions About the Down and Dirty

As you organized your research, you learned that management has been charged with sexual harassment twice in the past year. Or, a friend of the family whispered in your ear that minorities are consistently bypassed for promotions here. A few online news clips suggested that financial matters are circumspect. Basically, while you were dying to know more, you had to remain relatively tight-lipped during your interviews, so you could concentrate on your sales pitch. As a result, and appropriately so, you likely haven't broached these subjects yet.

Once you have a job offer in hand, you may clarify these burning issues. HR is generally a good starting point, as is your potential boss. The problem with talking to any old person or the guy you really hit it off with in purchasing is that details aren't always available to the masses—or even carefully reviewed when provided. Unfortunately, this doesn't stop most people from weighing in to lend drama and give a boisterous opinion. You might end up with a skewed version of reality that can't possibly be helpful.

Since HR is on the front line, they are often clued in to the whole story. The downside is that you might get a version that is severely watered-down or full of PR spin. All you can do is ask the questions, without accusation, do more research, and use your gut instincts.

- "I noticed in the news there are a few mentions of sexual harassment within the organization. Would you please tell me more about what happened, and what the company is doing about this issue now?"
- "Will you please review your policy regarding equal-employment-opportunity practices? If you can, I'd appreciate learning more about the minority makeup of the management ranks. Will you please give me a rundown of the people and any minority representation?"
- "Reuters highlighted information about third-quarter sales results and indicated that an independent agency has been hired to review accounting practices here. I'm wondering if this is something to worry about. Would you please shed some light on this news story?"

POWER UP

POWER UP

WHAT YOU STARTED REQUIRES your attention into a homestretch that has a few more last-minute detours. In some cases, your diligence will take you up and over. In other circumstances, continued initiative might be validation of a favorable choice made long ago. Or your perseverance might even cause regret for a decision gone against you. All in all, your actions count when you're down to the wire.

No matter what the other players in the process end up doing, how well the journey turns out has a lot to do with the way in which you proceed now. You gain short- and long-term benefits when you manage finish-line particulars with dogged determination, integrity, and thoughtfulness.

Chapter 12

Up the Ante

"I received the nicest letter from one of the candidates
I interviewed the other day. After meeting with four of us,
I was unusually touched that she recalled the account
I cut my teeth on when I started here.
"And it was actually refreshing to get correspondence on attractive stationery,
through regular mail."
—Senior Account Manager, Security Systems Provider

His goal: "To land the nation's leading fast food franchise
account by the end of the year."

MANY HR MANAGERS ACKNOWLEDGE the fine line between make or break for many interviewees. These professionals confirm that you have an opportunity to tip the scales, reverse mindsets, and solidify decisions after you leave the building. Essentially, a majority of candidates miss or ignore interview follow-up strategies—to their hiring disadvantage.

Since this is as clear a marching order as you'll ever get, it's worth upping the ante now. Basically, *mañana* isn't an option. And "giving it the old college try" just took on new meaning.

Don't Miss a Beat

Possibly bordering on cavalier following your "successful" face-to-face moment, you might be tempted to get sloppy regarding habits and practices that got you here, so euphoric and self-satisfied. But this isn't smart. Your continuing attention to the record keeping you started (chapter 6) is imperative. This is a time to document specific insider information and follow-up details so you don't miss a beat in the homestretch.

Each one of the files you previously set up—Interview Lineup, Market Stats, and Personal Bytes—should be updated following your interview. Scan the documents, change anything that is already obsolete or incorrect based on information gathered from your meetings, and fill in any blanks. Very meticulously record when you anticipate hearing back from the potential employer and any follow-up you promised (or are planning). If you also have a separate calendar as a crosscheck, register upcoming dates there as well. Tackle the organization of these details as soon as possible; the information is most fresh the day of—or, at the latest, the day after—your meeting.

Stand Out

Just about anyone can be the sultan of perfunctory. It's far better to be the king of stand-out perfection when it comes to thank-you letters. This correspondence, like the door-opening cover letter you sweated over with your résumé, requires your specific attention and diligence. An exemplary note reminds a prospective boss why you were welcome in the first place, and why you deserve to stay.

The question quickly confronting you is, "Cyberspace or stationery?" As spelled out previously, e-mail certainly has time on its side and gets the job done, often being the most preferred form of communication these days. On the other hand, hard copy boasts a better look. The paper color and weight, and the font and layout you use are all marketing tools, boosting your appeal.

If your instincts aren't taking you in one clear direction over another, you can use both mediums as long as you don't overwhelm your audience with two lengthy discourses. This strategy uses a short e-mail followed by snail mail. Your online communication, delivered early the day after your interview or late the same day, might read as follows:

Dear Ms. Constant,

While I have followed up with a letter in the mail, I also want to express a brief, immediate thank-you for our meeting. I enjoyed learning more about Avenues Ltd. and the dynamic ways in which you inspire your team and approach the market as customer custodians.

I would like an opportunity to work for you and very much hope you will consider me for the associate position. You can count on me to be an enthusiastic, solid contributor.

Sincerely,

Cal Turin

By mentioning that he has already sent a letter, as opposed to, "I'll also be putting a letter in the mail today," Cal avoids a hasty reply suggesting that he needn't bother.

If you decide that e-mail is the only way to go, follow the suggestions spelled out below for writing a thank-you letter put through the U.S. mail. At this point, whether using the Internet or 20 lb. paper, you have to thoughtfully convey certain information and an earnest vibe to keep the "choose me" ball rolling. Factor in these ten considerations as you craft this superlative gem of gratitude, expressed to each person you interviewed with:

1. Say thank you.
2. Include a brief reminder about who you are.
3. Weave in your theme and the organization's buzzwords and significant phrases.
4. Emphasize that you're the best.
5. Ask for the job.
6. Be concise.
7. Adhere to stringent guidelines for letter writing as detailed in chapter 9.
8. Through and through, exude desire and enthusiasm.
9. Pinpoint a time frame regarding next steps.
10. Strategize delivery.

Say Thank You

You can get so caught up in continuing your sales pitch that you forget to mention the reason it's acceptable to contact the employer yet one more time. By starting off your letter saying thanks, you validate the intrusion and politely set the stage for yet more feel-good fodder.

- "Thank you very much for our meeting yesterday."
- "Thank you for talking with me and introducing me to the

other members of your team yesterday."

- "Thank you for the chance to learn more about Goldstein Partners; I very much appreciated talking to you and came away with an overwhelming sense that this is definitely the place for me."

Include a Brief Reminder About Who You Are

Even though you were just there, remember that recruiters see a lot of people, read countless résumés, and lead personal lives. While this job opportunity is priority one for you, it is a small part of the interviewer's workday—an item on their never-ending to-do list. It's a good idea to spark the interviewer's memory about who you are. You can accomplish this by using one, or a combination, of these tactics:

- Mention who else you met during the day.
- Recall a personal aside the two of you discussed.
- Reference a specific point made or story told by the interviewer.
- Briefly revisit a unique experience, job, award, or distinction you brought up during your meeting.
- Mention your alma mater. Recruiters suggest that since college occupies a good deal of the conversation during new-grad interviews, your alma mater is one way you are mentally cataloged.

Weave in Your Theme and the Organization's Buzzwords and Significant Phrases

Since you found (in chapter 1) common ground between what makes you tick and what makes employers salivate, emphasize your juicy theme and highlight what you're made of. While you're at it, link your branding advantage to the organization by cleverly using their language to describe yourself.

Emphasize that You're the Best

Tell the interviewer you're the best. It's hard for many new college grads to say this face-to-face; it's easier to accomplish this "king of the world" pronouncement in writing. If you do it well, you might end up with a recruiter who believes what he reads. At the very least, it shouldn't hurt your chances.

- "Unlike many other candidates my age, I bring a lot to the mix that is meaningful to the trainee position we discussed yesterday. I've worked full time and, as my references show, I was very successful in this arena. I was frequently commended for my reliability and enthusiasm."
- "While I recognize that it's often hard to distinguish between college graduates at the interviewing stage, I believe that I stand out in this crowd. For years, I have committed to helping disadvantaged populations, and I've embraced many opportunities to build support for a cause from the ground up."
- "I don't believe you'll find another candidate who is as enthusiastic and committed to achieving your goals while also embodying the dynamic teamwork that is your hallmark."
- "Because of my track record and enthusiasm, I believe I can excel, and I would embrace every challenge of the opportunity."

Ask for the Job

By now, you know it is appropriate to hit your interviewer between the eyes with the fact that you want this job. Underscore this desire in your letter.

- "I would like to have this job, and I know you won't be disappointed."
- "After our meeting, I can only sum up my feelings by saying that I hope the job is mine. I would like to work for you very much."

Be Concise

A letter limited to one page is usually best, but as with everything in your interview process, it's more the thoughtfulness and pertinence of what you have to say that is important. Still, one and one half pages is about as compelling as you can get before losing your reader to other correspondence in his or her inbox. Stick to the points outlined here, and you won't stray from your concise message.

Adhere to Stringent Guidelines for Letter Writing

There are HR managers who freely admit that a typo blows your chances. As in, you're done. You might rationalize that you don't want to work for someone who is so rigid, but why bother being controversial in the first place?

Simply make the letter perfect. This includes spelling, grammar, punctuation, and formatting. Chapter 9 maps out the dos and don'ts, and these are worth your scrutiny before you express your thanks in writing. Avoid the most common mistakes new college grads make on their thank-you letters when it comes to the fundamentals:

- Incorrect form for a business letter
- Misspelled words or names
- No title for the person you are contacting
- Missed words: "Thank you very much the opportunity to meet with you."

Through and Through, Exude Desire and Enthusiasm

Just as a smile on your face set a tone and sent a message, a similar upbeat posture infuses your letter with magnetic seduction. A careful choice of words, rather than underlining or exclamation marks, is the best way to radiate passion. Refer to chapter 10 for words that are optimistic and reassuringly confident. Use these dynamic terms considerately throughout your letter.

Pinpoint a Time Frame Regarding Next Steps

You want to mention a date that you hope to hear back from the prospective employer. Either reference the time frame you discussed as you parted company or suggest one in your letter. This sets the stage for important follow-up and professionally underscores any commitments. It's discouraging how many people are flip about assiduous follow-up. But understand this, and try to be helpful regarding the details.

Strategize Delivery

You want your letter to get there as soon as possible without making you look desperate or flush with cash. Generally, priority mail (delivered in two to three days) is good enough. If you feel there is greater urgency, use the "e-mail plus hard copy letter" strategy outlined above, but still use priority mail—or hand deliver the letter. Drop off the envelope to reception rather than carrying it in to the addressee yourself.

Examples of Letters that Say Thanks with a Capital T

Using the guidelines above, there are a variety of ways to get your message across as you express your thanks to each person who interviewed you earlier today or yesterday.

Thank-You Letter 1

CHLOE HATHAWAY

10277 WESTSHORE DRIVE	**1025 ASHLAND AVENUE**
DALLAS, TEXAS 75275	**EVANSTON, ILLINOIS 60202**
chhath@smu.edu	**847-555-3232**

Today's Date

Ms. Gaye Merrill
Director of Development
Over the Rainbow Foundation
268 North First Street, Suite 2B
Fort Worth, Texas 76110

Dear Ms. Merrill:

Thank you very much for meeting with me yesterday. I enjoyed learning more about the Foundation and the new directions you plan for your development efforts. Pablo's impromptu midmorning recital was an unexpected bonus, and I found myself humming "New York, New York" well into the night.

When you mentioned that the assistant position requires creativity and a never-say-die mentality, I knew that Over the Rainbow is a place where I could make a material impact. You might remember that I shared information about my background and the opportunities I've taken to work with populations that are disadvantaged. Our school's annual weekend dance marathon event (Dance Because You Can) is one example of successful fundraising where I worked on the front line, orchestrating vendors, sponsors and participants.

In the three marathons I helped organize at Southern Methodist University, we surpassed each previous year's donations and involvement by at least ten percent. We accomplished this objective by increasing participation. I used my creativity to promote the event, and I worked tirelessly, refusing to accept anything less than "yes." We definitely hustled to keep our name and our cause at the top of the list, and we succeeded through sheer determination.

While my communications degree is certainly an asset to the position, it is my drive and intense desire to promote your mission that makes me the best candidate. I am as enthusiastic and earnest as they come, and "customer custodian" is similarly what I'm all about.

I would very much like to work for you and hope that you will consider me for the assistant position. Please let me know if there is anything else you need; I am anxious to answer questions you might have. As we discussed, I will be in touch at the beginning of next week.

Thank you again, and please say hello to Pablo, who said it best: I would like to "make a brand new start of it." In Fort Worth, Texas, at Over the Rainbow Foundation.

Sincerely,
Chloe Hathaway

Thank-You Letter 2

Barry Thomas Gleason
42 Riverside Lane
Denver, Colorado 80204
barrygl3@gotomail.com   303-555-3456

Today's Date

Mr. Albert Pecham
Director of Athletics
Denver Country Day School
6 Oak Street
Denver, Colorado 80220

Dear Mr. Pecham,

Thank you for fitting me into your schedule before heading out of town to the state championship game. I appreciate the time you took, and I enjoyed hearing about the progress you've made since you took over as director two years ago.

As a graduate of the University of Denver, you understand the very dynamic education I've received these past four years. You are also aware of the superb coaching I've been provided throughout college. These are both experiences that have shaped me and strongly influence what I bring to a teaching position.

What you may not yet fully understand are the personal attributes I bring to the table and which promote your goals. I am very organized, and I welcome the opportunity to be a full-time kinetic-wellness teacher, as well as an after-school coach for each of the three sports seasons, during the academic year. Additionally, I am anxious to help expand the use of your on-campus fitness facility, so all students embrace this aspect of their well-being.

I understand the importance of wearing many different hats in a smaller, private school and actually enjoy the opportunity to participate in different endeavors. My attention to detail makes it easy for me to tackle several different projects and remain focused and highly productive. Additionally, I believe that my enthusiasm for sports and fitness is contagious and would be instrumental in encouraging students to push themselves and test the waters on a few other teams. In essence, I guarantee that my presence and commitment to the school's motto—"Live and Serve"—would make the positive, long-term impact you are seeking on campus.

Thank you again, for the opportunity to interview for the teaching position at Denver Country Day School. There is no other job I want more, and I hope that you will extend an offer. In a separate mailing later this week, I will provide an outline of suggestions for expanding use of the campus fitness center.

Please let me know if there are any other questions I can answer as you make the decision. As we discussed, I look forward to talking with you next week.

I wish you and the Warriors all the very best this weekend.

Sincerely,
Barry T. Gleason

Thank-You Letter 3

Alexander Wetsel

96 Ashburton   41824 Sharon Road
Boston, Massachusetts 02108   Charlotte, North Carolina 28206
alexw@suffolk.edu   617-555-8889

Today's Date

Ms. Hollis Berger
Vice President, Human Resources
Affirm Inc.
297 East 60th Street
New York, New York 10022

Dear Ms. Berger:

Thank you for talking with me about your business and the associate merchandiser position. Even though our meeting was unexpectedly cut short, I came away feeling very enthusiastic about the possibilities. I sincerely hope you consider me for the next step in Affirm's interview process. I am anxious to let you know more about what I bring to further your "one company, one team" approach.

As you and I briefly discussed, I have had experience with merchandising in a midsize retail establishment. Through Suffolk University, I interned at Wannabes for two summers during my undergraduate studies. This compact general store for teens fits the target profile you are looking to for expansion.

I worked under a very dynamic professor who was hired as a consultant by corporate Wannabes. Our goal was to create an overall merchandising strategy that could be implemented by floor personnel on a routine basis. The regional chain hoped to upgrade the impact of its floor space to encourage purchasing behavior and to create an overall hip and slightly edgy feel. I learned a great deal through this experience and was also instrumental in devising a merchandising plan that is now used across the Wannabes organization.

I am confident that my unique ability to think outside the box was useful at Wannabes and would be to Affirm Inc. Additionally, I was often called upon to talk with Wannabes' employees about their customers and buying habits. I am typically a person who is asked to make meaningful connections with people, and I was successful along these lines during my internship. Several floor supervisors would attest to my professionalism, my interest, and my desire to get in the trenches and get my hands dirty.

I would like Affirm Inc. to establish itself as a premier merchandiser for midsize retail establishments. This is what I have studied for and what I most enjoy. Your challenge is exciting to me, and I would commit to your goal with tremendous enthusiasm and hard work.

I look forward to hearing from you by the end of next week, when you return from Los Angeles. Please contact me at any time if there is additional information you need.

I appreciate your time and interest very much. Thank you.

Sincerely,
Alexander Wetsel

Clock in Overtime

After the interview, you have a small window of opportunity to clock in overtime minutes. Marshaling extra face time is a strategic move often overlooked by many candidates. HR managers freely admit that interviewees who are at the top of managers' minds (thanks to astute persistence) and are otherwise fairly similar to other viable candidates are often the ones getting the job.

Back-end PR efforts should be professional and relatively low-key; the marching band won't be necessary. It's wise to remember that it is often the details, the small things, that most get you noticed. As such, consider these simple, but effective, tail-end PR tips:

- **Forward relevant and interesting materials.** Providing information of value to a recruiter puts you in a very favorable light. In "Thank-You Letter 2" above, Barry indicates that he will send an outline of ideas to help the school. Other viable follow-up materials that new college grads have used to their hiring advantage include:
    Newspaper or magazine articles of relevance
    Completed works (such as designs, models, artwork, written pieces, and so on)

- **Provide your reference packet or an additional letter of recommendation.** If you haven't been asked for your reference materials yet, or if you have an additional letter singing your praises, you may want to get these into the right hands before any hiring decisions are made. Assuming your recommendations are golden, this information is an attention getter and should be advantageous.

- **Use your KISS.** Some candidates conveniently "forget" to provide their KISS document during the interview and later follow up with it as a PR ploy.

- **Make a plug through the phone.** Any phone contact should include mention of your enthusiasm for the opportunity. This is especially true if you get voicemail, where waxing poetic is somewhat easier. As an example, if you are returning a call or following up as was earlier agreed upon, consider adding, "I want to emphasize again how much I am interested in the position, and I hope that I can move to the next step," or "I know that I've said how excited I am about the possibility of working for you, but I want to say it again; this job is one that I want. I would very much enjoy being a part of your team, and you would be able to count on me to be committed to your goals."

- **Consider timing.** You have a decision to make regarding when you will forward any of the above materials. You can include information with your thank-you letter, or you can create an additional opportunity that gets you noticed, as Barry did, by sending another packet at a later, strategic date. Use your instincts to guide you. You don't want to be annoying, but you also want to keep your name floating around the office, in a positive way, for as long as you can. This is especially important if hiring decisions won't be made for a while following your interview.

- **Explain yourself.** A brief mention in your thank-you letter or a separate note should succinctly spell out what you are forwarding and why. Any correspondence, even if it's more casual, is still better typed than handwritten and goes along the lines of the examples below.

Examples of Brief Follow-up Notes with a Big Message

Barry Thomas Gleason
42 Riverside Lane
Denver, Colorado 80204
barrygl3@gotomail.com   303-555-3456

Today's Date

Dear Mr. Pecham,

    As I mentioned in my letter last week, I am forwarding an outline regarding my ideas for expanding use of the fitness center at Denver Country Day School. I realize that my thoughts are only an outsider's viewpoint without an all-important insider perspective, but I am willing to go back to the drawing board countless times to get it right.

    I look forward to hearing from you in a few days. I remain very interested in the opportunity and sincerely hope that we can proceed forward together.

Regards,
Barry T. Gleason

Alexander Wetsel
96 Ashburton   41824 Sharon Road
Boston, Massachusetts 02108   Charlotte, North Carolina 28206
alexw@suffolk.edu   617-555-8889

Today's Date

Dear Ms. Berger:

    I came across two photos from my work experiences at Wannabes. One is a before shot, and the second is taken at the exact same location on the floor, after our merchandising plan was put into place. Store personnel were actually responsible for creating the look based on our guidelines.

    I thought you might find this information and the obvious transformation interesting. I look forward to talking with you by February 9 and hope that I have made my interest in joining the Affirm Inc. team known to you. I would approach my work enthusiastically and with great conviction.

Sincerely,
Alexander Wetsel

CHLOE HATHAWAY

10277 WESTSHORE DRIVE	1025 ASHLAND AVENUE
DALLAS, TEXAS 75275	EVANSTON, ILLINOIS 60202
chhath@smu.edu	847-555-3232

Today's Date

Dear Ms. Merrill:

I am enclosing a document that highlights my key attributes and those that best represent my fit with Over the Rainbow Foundation. While I hesitate to supply you with more paperwork on my behalf, I believe that unlike my more comprehensive résumé, this one- pager quickly spells out why I am the best candidate to help you realize your development goals.

I look forward to touching base at your earliest convenience. I know that I've missed you a few times by phone and hope that we can connect very soon.

Sincerely,
Chloe Hathaway

Chapter 13

Pull Out Plan B

"I don't get it; they said they'd call me back within a week.
It's been three, and I haven't heard anything. I even phoned twice
these last few days and left messages.
"I'm guessing this is the handwriting on the wall. But when I think
back to my interview, I really can't figure out why this happened.
"This is weird."
—*Senior, Secondary Education Major, DePaul University*

Her goal: "Teach; attend graduate school; become a principal or
superintendent; travel nonstop during the summers."

SNAFU: **"A CONFUSED OR** chaotic state." This about sums up the situation when you've crossed all the *t*s and dotted the *i*s and you end up with what looks like a dead end. You either get, "Thanks, but no," or you don't hear back after the interview. How can something so right go so wrong?

You clearly didn't bargain for this crossroads when you signed on for that heavily mortgaged college degree or this handy three-step program. But it might be helpful to know that disappointing interviews, or those with seemingly no visible light at the end of the tunnel, are bound to happen. To anyone and everyone.

Fortunately, this isn't the end of the line. There is a way to get to the bottom of the situation, regroup, and focus on making old and new opportunities happen. By following the advice below, you *will* be stronger and better positioned to face the job-clinching days ahead.

Do a Reality Check

As you figure out how to proceed, it's important to dissect your far-from-perfect interview status. While it may not be crystal clear why your straight shot to a paycheck got temporarily waylaid, a consideration of the possibilities is helpful and generally leads to the best rebound strategy.

Interviews typically plummet away from job opportunities and fizzle into oblivion for one of four reasons:

1. Bum luck
2. Interviewers with issues
3. Timing
4. Failure to make the grade

Bum Luck

It happens. Misfortune can occur at the hands of the recruiter or squarely in your corner. Sometimes your résumé gets misplaced or deleted, or your interviewing moment slips through the cracks and you're lost in a system pressed for time. While this circumstance isn't typical, it is a distinct possibility. HR managers have been known to forget or to scramble, furtively digging for your contact information embedded in a mile-high inbox, only to come up empty-handed.

Or perhaps you had a one-in-a-million brain freeze moment and pulled a doozy. You unfortunately did something wacky during your interview that unsealed the deal. While an unintentional tumble is usually forgivable, there are blunders that will burn some recruiter's bridges. No, you didn't mean it, and it was just an accident and an honest mistake, but the gaffe was enough to cause Lady Luck to turn her back.

Interviewers with Issues

As is true in any walk of life, some recruiters are simply ineffective employees. Unfortunately, this is a situation you may bump into more than you believe is possible; poor communicators densely populate our businesses. As a result, you may wait endlessly to hear back from a recruiter when you were promised otherwise. Since this circumstance is far too often the norm rather than the exception in many organizations, consequences aren't levied, and the problem perpetuates.

There is also the distinct possibility (as spelled out in chapter 9) that the interviewer takes ineffectiveness to another level, being a bozo or loser of the first order. In other words, you may end up hearing "no" simply because this yo-yo didn't like your tie or the fact that you have a brain in your head.

Timing

While you are in an intensely focused bubble during interviews, the rest of the world moves along fast and furiously. Markets tank or shoot through the roof, employees get promoted and fired, divisions are sold and reorganized, Mother Nature has a thing or two to say about profit and loss, and so on. And any of this might happen the minute you walk out the door from your "nailed it" face-to-face interview. For one of a variety of timing reasons, the rug was pulled out from under you in a nanosecond, and you couldn't possibly have seen it coming.

Failure to Make the Grade

You aren't going to be right for every job opportunity you've set your sights on. There are a variety of legitimate reasons why you didn't fit the bill. Anything from your skill set and lack of experience to your personality can be at odds with what the prospective boss needs right now.

Make a Date

Pity party? You bet; it's well deserved. Your buddies—in particular, your trustworthy confidant—can help you let off steam, find humor in the situation, and ultimately refocus. Not only will your misery love the company, but getting together with the gang is a meaningful way to understand more about what you're up against. Included in this section are believe-it-or-nots from interview hell that best teach the lessons you need to learn right now.

Your Pity Party

Clarity may be the last thing on your mind, but good friends can usually send the fog packing. Use this opportunity with your closest chums to accomplish the following:

- **Dish.** Tell your pals what's going on, laying out the details and emotions to the best of your most objective ability.
- **Learn.** Now listen to their insights, personal experiences, and heartfelt advice.
- **Probe.** Question what they're saying, so you wrap your mind around their input and make it personally meaningful and useful.
- **Dust yourself off.** Accept that roadblocks happen to everyone and knock back a new shot of confidence as a logical next step.
- **Party on.** Give yourself permission to have fun; you'll end up feeling refreshed and revitalized (if you enjoy yourself as opposed to drowning your sorrows, that is: shots of confidence are one thing, and shots of tequila are quite another).

Believe-It-or-Nots from Interview Hell

If you think you're the first person to get waylaid by a recruiter, circumstance, or personal blunder, read on. And remember that these true stories are only a minute representation of what goes on each and every day in the rough-and-tumble world of interviewing. Online message boards dedicated to your recruiting efforts further underscore this reality. You're clearly not alone.

Believe-It-or-Not 1

Sara swore she returned the interviewer's phone call. But she got a second message asking her to please get in touch. If she wasn't mistaken, it distinctly sounded as if her prospective boss were slightly exasperated.

Sara promptly phoned and left her second voicemail message. This game of telephone tag went on for three more rounds until the recruiter left a harsh message indicating that the offer was being rescinded, because Sara had never bothered to get in touch.

Perplexed and frantic, Sara finally took a step back. She realized that she had been leaving messages on another voicemail system (of a company where Sara had also interviewed—for the job she really wanted) and had done so all along. Two birds were killed with one ill-thrown stone.

Believe-It-or-Not 2

Diane had so far made it through college using her uncle's nine-year-old Buick. While Old Mavis was usually troublefree, only requiring the occasional oil change, she failed one morning on the expressway. Unfortunately, Diane happened to be flooring it to the job interview of her dreams ... with a dead cell phone battery. This was an inopportune time to be faced with such a double whammy.

In a smart winter white suit on the shoulder of I-294 in Lincolnshire, Illinois, Diane did what she had been advised never to do: she stuck out her thumb. In a matter of minutes—during which the promised snowstorm arrived with a vengeance—a semi pulled over, and the driver invited Diane to hop up and into the cab.

Heels, stockings, and all, Diane took a deep breath, said a prayer, gingerly hiked up her skirt, and climbed in. After she briefly explained the situation to the driver, he rammed on the clutch, got the rig in gear, and delivered Diane to her interview on time ...

And in style. Understanding more of what was at stake now, the driver jumped out of the truck after winding his way up the long, secluded drive to the corporate headquarters tucked away in a forested area. He swung open Diane's door and gallantly swooped her up into his arms, carrying her into the lobby so winter white might escape polka-dot slush. The two were greeted by Diane's first interviewer of the day—who happened to be briefing the receptionist at the time.

Believe-It-or-Not 3

Erik was usually an easygoing guy. He had endured a roommate who snored, redefined messy, and had a torrid relationship with the same girl all through college. Still, the two were good buddies; Erik hung in there and made the best of this and most other situations.

So it was no surprise when Erik interviewed for a trust-department trainee position and didn't worry when he hadn't heard back three weeks later. The bank's HR manager had said she would get in touch after a week, but Erik was ... Erik.

Another three weeks went by, however, and Erik finally felt uneasy. After all, he wanted this job, and he thought he had done well in the interviews. When Erik placed a call to his HR contact, he was solemnly informed that she had passed away several weeks earlier.

To Erik's credit, he took the high road and expressed his condolences before hanging up the phone. However, he waited another month before getting in touch with one of the bank's trust-department managers to inquire about the status of his candidacy. With apologies, Erik was informed that the position had been filled two weeks earlier.

Believe-It-or-Not 4

"CIS Program, PC/LAN Support Specialist, A+ Certification Program, Novell Certification" … Highpoint's ad indicated that completing one or more was important in order to be considered a viable candidate within IT Services.

Never one to be easily discouraged, Charlie was an econ major who knew about business and had grown up being the man when it came to anything technological. Charlie targeted Highpoint and specifically zeroed in on their IT consulting positions. His day was made when he realized Highpoint would be recruiting on campus.

Unfortunately, Charlie was asked to leave the campus interview approximately sixty seconds into the meeting when it was clear he didn't have the requisite background. As if this weren't enough, the recruiter announced to all assembled in the career-counseling office that Charlie was a virtual bonehead, and he hoped no one else was there to waste his precious time.

Believe-It-or-Not 5

Accounting may not be exciting to everyone, but Bill passionately hoped to make a profession of it. He methodically mapped out a career path and immediately focused on finding a job with a company that would help him launch his dream.

Early in January, Locust Partners advertised in the Sunday classifieds, and Bill drove in from Ohio one Friday for a day of interviews with the midsize firm. It looked as if all systems were go. Bill was even told they would get back to him with a firm offer the following week. He made his triumphant exit amid lots of backslapping and handshakes. Could anyone ask for a better way to finish out senior year?

Except that Bill never did hear back. He phoned several people. He e-mailed. He wrote. And he never heard another word from Locust Partners.

Work It Smart

Regardless of whether the interviewer is missing in action (MIA) or has just dished out a big, fat no, either scenario requires quick, intelligent, and slick action. Or, as one recent grad summed it up: you need to "work it like a cross-dressing rocket scientist and used-car salesman."

Even for those who normally talk fast and have a lot on the ball, this is a tough call to action. The ticking of the clock is insistent, panic is seeping into the equation, and you're at the mercy of people who rarely prioritize you. Despite the dynamics, you should jump into the fray rather than waiting it out. At the end of the day, you must be satisfied that you hung in there and fought the good fight. Otherwise, it's tough to face the future, no matter what it might hold.

First and foremost, make sure you identify your primary contact. Which of the individuals you just met is responsible for getting back to you? Moving forward is contingent upon being in touch with the right person.

Though the go-to guy usually sticks out like a sore thumb, this isn't always the case. Take some time to think it through. Often, the HR manager, an HR associate, or your prospective boss is the key contact. Or it might be another employee who set up the interview, organized the meeting, and then wrapped up the exchange. If you fortuitously asked this question before you exited from your interview, then you know who's been assigned to communicate with you about your fate. "Who will I hear from regarding next steps?"

MIA

Lacking a timely response from a recruiter frequently comes down to interviewers with issues. True, an impending corporate merger or a less than stellar face-to-face meeting might unconsciously push you down on someone's priority list for the day, but the recruiter should be in touch, no matter what.

As best you can, pinpoint the glitch and figure out why you have this MIA predicament in your lap. Then, devise a thoughtful action plan and follow through using all cylinders.

Pinpoint the Glitch

This isn't an exact science, by any means. Consider using these methods to unearth the gory details about why you aren't hearing back from a recruiter:

1. **Reflect on what you just learned from your friends.** Do their war stories or your recounting of the details surrounding your interview lead you to believe that you might be a victim of bum luck, or was it that you didn't make the grade? Replay your interview and evaluate your performance. You generally know when and why you shine, and the same applies when you blow it.

2. **Think back to the meeting and every point of contact there.** Did anyone specifically mention that the person responsible for getting back to you is sometimes unreliable, or that a circumstance within the organization is currently taking up a lot of time and focus? Was something said that could lead you to believe the date given was not firm? "I'll be in touch by the end of next week for sure," is a thoughtful and sincere indication, but "You'll hear back soon" was likely spouted off without much thought. "We're heading into inventory season right now, so it's tough to say, but … I'd guess … next week … maybe?" was pulled directly from recruiter heinie.

3. **Check out the Internet for circumstances that might impact business dealings right now.** Consider the economy, Mother Nature, industry updates, financial news and circumstances within the organization itself. Also search the Web using the names of the top executives and your interviewers (Erik might have found out about his deceased recruiter in this way).

4. **Touch base with your campus career center.** Remember these professionals who are always on your side? They may have heard some scuttlebutt about the company, or they may have history with the organization or interviewer that puts the situation into perspective.

You might be wondering, again, why in the world any of this is relevant when all you want is a straightforward and simple response—especially since you can probably only hazard a guess regarding the circumstances.

Basically, thinking it through impacts how you handle yourself in the days ahead. You might decide that you should be more or less aggressive based on what you pinpoint. Or you might respond far more calmly and prosaically when a recruiter ultimately gets in touch and zaps you with what otherwise might be a zinger. And finally, you might uncover another tidbit that will be useful to your overall interviewing strategy. Thoughtfulness and information haven't steered you wrong so far in this process, and you're unlikely to be tripped up by this duo now.

Use All Cylinders

You have to decide when the timing is right to make another move. When can you forge ahead to revive the process? Strike an important balance between aggressiveness and patience. You can't push the envelope so far that you are accused of being overly anxious or of not paying attention. But you also can't fade into the woodwork and let this opportunity slip out of your grasp. Professionalism is the underpinning, no matter what.

Below are general guidelines regarding timing that are useful, as long as you trust your instincts and all that you've recently learned. Because you have to start somewhere, start with the person who conducted your interview and/or who gave an indication regarding follow-up.

If the recruiter said you'd hear back …	You might follow-up …
"This week"	Early Monday morning of next week
"Next week"	Early Friday afternoon of next week
"Tomorrow"	One to two business days after tomorrow
"Soon"	About ten to fifteen business days after the meeting

"Within the week"   Early Monday morning of
                                     next week

"Within a week"   Early in the afternoon, the
                                     day the week is up

"Within the month"   Early in the morning, the
                                     last day of the month

"Within a month"   Early in the morning,
                                     about three to three and
                                     a half weeks later

"By [specific date]"   The day after the specified
                                     date

Timing was never discussed   About ten to fifteen
                                     business days after the
                                     meeting (and this point of
                                     contact should either
                                     provide an answer or define
                                     timing for next steps)

When to Make the Next Move

OK, you took the initiative, but got nowhere. Assuming that you are contacting the right person within the organization, when do you make your next move? And the move after that? While there isn't a hard-and-fast rule, use your level, professional head as you have up until this point. Once a week or once every two weeks seems reasonable in most instances. You can also mix it up in the way you make contact as time marches on (see below). This serves to make your approach less tedious and irksome for everyone concerned, yourself included.

You might be indignant about having to consider the feelings of the "other guy"—the corporate titan who is putting you through your paces for whatever reason. But this is the way it is. No matter what, maintain your composure and always take the high road, never accusing anyone or complaining about the state of affairs.

The Moves to Make

While the strategies aren't complicated, most candidates agree that nudging is awkward. You are often yanked in opposite directions by concerns that you're too brash or desperate, and worries that you're missing out by not pushing harder.

If you listened well, kept decent notes, considered the situation, and used your gut instinct, chances are you won't get trapped in a faux pas. And remember that your actions here are fairly mundane from a recruiter's standpoint. You're hardly in controversial waters with most of the tactics noted below, and you usually accomplish your primary objective: moving the interview process along.

Until you're forced to resort to guerilla tactics (see further below), continue contacting the person responsible for communicating with you about your interview process. To make sure you are always putting your best foot forward, briefly review chapter 9 so that your phone, e-mail, and letter communication skills are in top form. And keep track of the contacts you are making, recording the information in your files (chapter 6).

Phone

Put some sunshine in your voice and dial your primary contact's number. It's as simple as this. The advantage of a phone call is that you might actually connect and resolve the matter within a few moments.

When dealing with MIA issues, you might launch a conversation and/or voicemail message along the following lines:

Conversation Starter

"Hello, Ms. Banks. This is Liz Arronet calling. When we last spoke you hoped we might talk again by the fifteenth. I'm following up to let you know that my interest is as high as ever in Cudahy Industries and I'm happy to answer any additional questions you might have."

Voicemail Message

"Hello. This is Liz Arronet, Ms. Banks. When we last spoke you indicated that I might hear back from you by the fifteenth. I'm just touching base and hope that you will call with information or any questions. I am very interested in the research-assistant job and sincerely hope that I have the opportunity to work for Cudahy. I can be reached at 302-555-6604. Thank you, and I hope you have a very nice day."

A week later, your voicemail message to Ms. Banks, who remains MIA, might proceed along these lines (note that while you are not complaining, you are prodding—and politely highlighting your past diligence):

"Hi, Ms. Banks, this is Liz Arronet again. I'm calling as a follow-up to our meeting on the eighth and my phone message last week. I'm just touching base and hope that you will call with information or any questions. I remain very interested in the research-assistant position and sincerely hope that I have the opportunity to work for Cudahy. I've thought a lot about the challenge and I know that I'm up to it and welcome it in every way. I can be reached at 302-555-6604. Thank you, and I hope that all goes well with you."

E-mail

If you feel that e-mail communication makes sense, use this as a means to stir up the pot. Many new college grads readily admit that cyberspace is their inclination when a recruiter is MIA. It's the voiceless, faceless dimension that appeals in this new high-stakes game. And if your strategy entails alternating between phone and online communication, this is acceptable as long as you adhere to the protocol for when to make your moves.

Your e-mail communication is almost identical to the voice message above. However, "Dear" and "Sincerely" are required. The examples below indicate what your online communications should look like when you are trying to turn MIA into action.

Your Initial E-mail Message

Dear Ms. Banks:

When we last spoke, you indicated that I might hear back from you by May 15. I'm touching base and hope that you will call with information or any questions.

I am very interested in the research-assistant job and sincerely hope that I have the opportunity to work for Cudahy. You would be able to count on me as an enthusiastic contributor.

I can be reached at elizarronet@udel.edu or 302-555-6604.
Thank you.
Sincerely,
Liz Arronet

Subsequent E-mail Message(s)
Dear Ms. Banks:

I'm contacting you as a follow-up to our meeting on May 8 and the voice message I left last week. I'm touching base and hope that you will call with information or any questions.

I remain very interested in the research-assistant position and sincerely hope that I have the opportunity to work for Cudahy. I've thought a lot about the challenge, and I know that I'm up to it in every way.

I can be reached at elizarronet@udel.edu or 302-555-6604.
Thank you.
Sincerely,
Liz Arronet

Letter

You don't usually lead with a letter when you're working on MIA issues. Traditional written correspondence is more formal and definitely makes a statement (kind of like a "final notice" invoice). Basically, pristine stationery at this stage sends a loud- and-clear message.

If, however, you've left a number of voicemail and/or e-mail messages, and are still high and dry, consider writing a letter. Craft your communication so that you leave an out for the recruiter—some way to keep the door open. This is often accomplished by being a tad smarmy. While allowing the recruiter to save face undoubtedly causes you to recoil and cringe at the injustice, remember that sucking up is to your advantage.

ELIZABETH T. ARRONET
5 COURTNEY STREET, RUSSELL, #456
NEWARK, DELAWARE 19716
elizarronet@udel.edu   302-555-6604

Today's Date

Ms. Linda Banks
Lead Associate
Cudahy Research Affiliates
29 Hastings, Suite 310
New York, NY 10023

Dear Ms. Banks:
I'm contacting you as a follow-up to our meeting on the eighth and my other communications between the sixteenth and the thirtieth. I apologize if my persistence is bothersome in any way, but I assure you that it only represents my great enthusiasm for Cudahy Research Affiliates and interest in the research-assistant position.

I know this is a busy time for you and Cudahy, and I am happy to sit tight until you have a chance to be in touch. If there is anything else I can do to convince you that I am the right person for the job, I would appreciate the information and am anxious to follow-up. I am confident I would excel at this job and be a valuable member of your team.

I sincerely hope that all goes well with you and I look forward to talking further at your convenience. Thank you very much for your time and consideration.

Sincerely,
Elizabeth T. Arronet

Guerilla Tactics

It's true: when the going gets tough, the tough get going. If you have adhered to the protocol outlined above, and time is resolutely marching on and away from your last meeting, you probably don't have much to lose by pumping up the aggressiveness. Hard-core strategies maintain your professionalism here but assuredly push the envelope. As a result, it's important to be absolutely sure that you are squarely in guerrilla territory and not wielding the big guns prematurely.

You might again question why it's worth the effort to keep elbowing your way in. Isn't the handwriting on the wall by now? Sometimes. There are instances where extenuating circumstances prevailed, and it was definitely worth going for broke. Unless you have a number of job offers lined up and can honestly say you don't care if this dangler doesn't materialize, then you should give it your all. If nothing else, closure is logical in the scheme of things for many people, and you may require this for your peace of mind.

Consider these guerilla tactics when the time is right:

Induce guilt. While doling out money for this circumstance is painful, it often works. Consider sending a new book, with a short note included, to your interviewer. The book should be fitting for the business and the person (bestselling nonfiction is usually a sure bet). Because you've gone to this length, and because it is exceedingly classy, the tactic has a way of creating enough guilt to eke out a reply from even the most recalcitrant recruiter. Just be sure that your choice is appropriate and doesn't delve into nonpolitically correct topics. Relate the subject matter of the book back to the organization.

Dear Ms. Parks:

I hope you are doing well. I remain interested in the field supervisor position we met about a month ago. While we have had a tough time touching base since then, I continue to strategize about ways to improve operations.

Toward this end, I came across a book I thought worth sharing. *Made to Stick* drives home the point about solidifying messages so they take root. I feel the authors have done a decent job applying the lesson to a variety of industries. I thought you might be interested in the approach based on our specific conversation about organizational change.

I look forward to hearing from you. Please know that I would very much like to be a part of your team.

Sincerely,

Rob Anstedt

Try another contact. If there is someone else you can approach within the organization, this might be the time to get in touch with that person (someone in HR, the boss, another associate, and so on). This tactic obviously deserves your extreme thoughtfulness, because no matter how politely you couch the inquiry, you are indicting the guy who left you holding the bag.

But since you're contemplating this strategy, you clearly believe that waiting it out will mean waiting forever, and you're usually right. Technically, you're sitting on a dead-end "no" and have only way to go at this point: up. So hopefully you didn't put away your smarmy side quite yet, because you'll need it as you call or e-mail your number-two contact at the organization.

E-mail is decidedly an easier way to "talk" about this situation, and also has the advantage of allowing you to very professionally frame your communication. This is a "speech" that should be heard in its entirety. In this way, you don't omit key points or words that can put your intentions into question. Someone who is particularly confident and smooth, however, can certainly accomplish this mission over the phone.

Before proceeding, double-check the contact details you have used all along and verify they are indeed correct (even though claiming the opposite is a good ruse, as you will see below). This information will be helpful if you use e-mail to get in touch with others in the organization. Businesses, like colleges, use a formula for their online communications. You can typically figure out someone's electronic address when you have the correct spelling of their name.

Additionally, as you try another contact, remember to:

- Go easy and be nice (even though this is the last thing you want to do)
- Be specific, but avoid listing your trials and tribulations (this can feel like a pointed finger)
- Have handy a detailed record of how and when you attempted to get in touch (you might be asked)

Consider these examples:

Dear Mr. Drasso,

We briefly met when I interviewed with Linda Banks about six weeks ago. I apologize for involving you, but I haven't heard back from Ms. Banks, and I am wondering if I possibly have the wrong contact information for her. I've tried to get in touch and haven't had any luck; we were originally supposed to talk by October 15.

Again, I'm sorry to trouble you, but I am very interested in working for Cudahy and want to make sure that I'm doing what is necessary to keep my name in the running for the job.

Thank you very much for any help you might be able to provide. I can be reached at elizarronet@udel.edu or 302-555-6604.

Sincerely,

Liz Arronet

Dear Mr. Karzen,

I haven't had the chance to meet you yet, but I understand you are the Human Resources Manager and possibly the person who might be able to help me. I interviewed with Linda Banks about six weeks ago; I enjoyed the meeting and opportunity to learn more about your organization.

I haven't heard back from Ms. Banks. I've tried to get in touch, but haven't had any luck; we were originally supposed to talk by October 15. I'm wondering if I possibly have the wrong contact information for her.

I'm sorry to trouble you, but I am very interested in working for Cudahy and want to make sure that I'm doing what is necessary to keep my name in the running for the job.

Thank you very much for any help you might be able to provide. I can be reached at elizarronet@udel.edu or 302-555-6604.

Sincerely,

Liz Arronet

Show up. It is usually very poor form to arrive unannounced at a place of business. However, a few recent grads suggest that this circumstance is a valid exception to that rule, since you are a victim through no fault of your own. All is now fair game, they claim.

While pressing the flesh at this stage isn't a widely advocated tactic, it is reviewed here so you understand how to proceed if you are someone who simply can't turn the page any other way. You can target the person who has been dodging you for the past three months. Or, consider seeking out the number-two contact you may have identified above. In either case, use discretion and keep your tone of voice and overall approach measured and full of confidence, respect, and energy.

You proceed in one of two ways. In both instances you justify your presence by mentioning that you were "in the neighborhood." The first option is to use your phone to call from around the corner (literally) and ask if it's all right to drop by in a few minutes. "I recently met with Linda Banks. Since I'm in the neighborhood, I thought I'd stop by to say hello. Can you please see if she's available? I'm willing to wait. My name is Liz Arronet."

Or, as the second tactic, get right into the thick of it. Walk up to the receptionist and explain what's going on. "My name is Liz Arronet. We haven't met yet, but I wonder if you can help me, please. Several weeks ago, I interviewed with Linda Banks, who I understand isn't in right now. I haven't heard back from Ms. Banks, and I've tried to get in touch, but without luck; we were originally supposed to talk by October 15. I'm wondering if I possibly have the wrong contact information for her. Since I'm in the neighborhood, I'm stopping by to see if I can get more particulars."

If the organization is small enough, you might be able to walk right up to the person whose head shot is likely glued to the center of your dartboard—and has been for the past month. "Hi, I'm sorry to barge in. My name is Liz Arronet and we met several weeks ago. I've been having a hard time reaching you. Since I was in the neighborhood, and I understand that this is a busy time in general for Cudahy, I thought I'd stop by to see if we might connect this way. I continue to be very interested and hope the research-assistant position is still available."

A Flat-Out No

After all the work you just did to get a response, you might end up with, "We sincerely wish you luck elsewhere in your future endeavors." Or you might get the same flat-out no on a timely basis and in a professional manner from your recruiters. Either way, it can make you feel like putting your résumé into the shredder ... because at least the shredder doesn't require a stamp.

While it's difficult to not take this outcome personally, you can't beat yourself up over something that wasn't meant to be. You're better off dedicating your energies to learning more and regrouping for the next round of interviews. At this point, consider this conclusion as an opportunity to gain constructive insights for the future.

Before becoming so magnanimous and clearheaded, however, you might be tempted to believe that you can change minds and reverse decisions. Surely they made a mistake, right? Wrong. While miracles do happen, you're better off to not waste time on one here. You've got more robust possibilities, which you will uncover as you move forward.

Once you're ready to tackle the day with renewed vigor, you can get back in touch with the recruiter who just sent you packing. You want the skinny, and you should ask for it. Why didn't you get picked?

You may not always get the straight scoop, but it's worth a try. "I appreciate the opportunity I had to interview with you. To help me as I move forward, I'm wondering if you wouldn't mind telling me why I wasn't extended an offer." You generally have more luck over the phone, as opposed to asking for details through e-mail.

HR departments are hypervigilant about rationalizing their actions, so they cannot be accused of discrimination or breaking employment law. In our litigious society, this is a very potent consideration. As a result, you might get a very noncommittal, general reply suggesting that, "You have many outstanding qualifications, and it was a difficult decision, but we selected a candidate who very specifically meets the requirements of the job description."

If you ask, "Which specific requirements didn't I meet?" you might not get much more than, "As I said, this was a difficult and complicated decision, and we wish you all the best in your career endeavors." Or you might strike it rich and get someone who is chatty and will tell you more, possibly along the lines of these actual insights shared with new college grads who didn't get the job:

- "Others within the organization didn't sense a fire in your belly."
- "Your background wasn't as strong as a few of the other candidates and we wanted the experience, as long as we could get it."
- "You didn't stand out from the other candidates, while two other recent grads did."
- "Your GPA doesn't cut it."
- "Nothing about your background suggests that you are comfortable in a team-focused environment; our culture revolves around a community of collaborators, and we are very particular about honing in on this tendency when hiring."
- "The big guy just didn't warm up to you."
- "We like you but feel that we'll be a better fit once you get your feet wet in a bigger arena, at an organization with more formal training. We're open to talking with you again in the future."

Your response to this type of input is always, "Thank you for giving me these insights." You can next ask for more clarification if you feel there is an opening, but the conversation shouldn't go on much longer. This is a particularly wriggly can of worms, complicated by the fact that you are likely emotional, somewhat fragile, and ultradefensive, thinking along these lines: "You knew what my GPA was before I walked in the door. Why the heck did you even bring me in if this is the reason I didn't get an offer?"

Rather, accept the counsel graciously and exit relatively quickly, venturing no more than something like this: "I've been up-front about my GPA and always hoped that I demonstrated how my other experiences made me a very well-rounded candidate—one that brings a unique set of skills to the table. I'm disappointed, but I understand your position. I will use this information as I move forward with my interviews. Thank you again for the opportunity, and I hope our paths cross again in the future."

Use the information that was just shared with you to improve your interviewing skills. Consider what was revealed, and adjust your approach if you believe the insight has validity—but don't go so far overboard in one direction, compensating for what you've just been told, that you ignore other critical factors important to your next meeting. In regard to the specific examples noted above, you might make the following adjustments:

- **"Others within the organization didn't sense a fire in your belly."** You know if your nerves got in the way of your enthusiasm or if you just fizzled too early in the game. That someone else noticed is an insight you should use as you head into your next interview. No question about it: you're going to have to convey a spark the next time around.
- **"Your background wasn't as strong as a few of the other candidates, and we wanted the experience, as long as we could get it."** In this instance, getting more information from the recruiter would be helpful. What about the background of the other candidates was so appealing? Perhaps you have a similar base of experiences but haven't communicated it strongly enough through your résumé or your interviews. A simple tweak here or there (or simply a change in wording) might add the compelling dimension you need in future interviews.
- **"You didn't stand out from the other candidates, while two other recent grads did."** Just as with the background issue above, you should try to get more information here. How did the other two grads distinguish themselves? This might yield one of those invaluable tips that makes sense for you to incorporate into your upcoming interviews.
- **"Your GPA doesn't cut it."** If you have less than a 3.0, you need to take the time to figure out how to sell yourself on other attributes. Have you done this well enough? You're far better to take an offensive posture, than a defensive one, with something as highly scrutinized as your GPA.
- **"Nothing about your background suggests that you are comfortable in a team-focused environment; our culture revolves around a community of collaborators, and we are very particular about honing in on this tendency when hiring."** Count on the fact that just about any job is a highly dynamic matrix of people (customers and employees). Make sure you always emphasize your fit with the total

organization and the respect you have for the team.

- **"The big guy just didn't warm up to you."** This insight really hits below the belt, because it intimates that you weren't likable. Once you get past the poor phrasing of this remark, take it to mean that you may have missed some opportunities to establish a connection with the boss. Even if this guy was particularly disagreeable, and you wouldn't work for him in a million years, most of us benefit from a refresher course in relationship building (see chapters 8, 9, 10, and 11).
- **"We like you but feel that we'll be a better fit once you get your feet wet in a bigger arena, at an organization with more formal training. We're open to talking with you again in the future."** Assiduously record this type of a comment in your notes and get back to the person in writing, confirming what you were just told.

Look Ahead, Chin Up

You suck it up, act professionally, and ingratiate to the point of vomiting because it matters—to you and to your future. Conducting yourself like a pro and doing everything within your power to get the job bears dividends. The payback isn't always immediate or tangible, but there is truth to the fact that those who go down swinging rarely stay down for long. Integrity and fortitude instill you with confidence and present you with new opportunities far more often than doing it on the cheap or bailing out.

And the professional arena isn't really as big as it might seem right now. You will run into the same people down the road, even in other cities and states. The person who just met with you might be at the company where you interview five years from now. Not burning any bridges is to your advantage, because memories are long when you use your middle finger to assuage your disappointment. But you are also well remembered when you handle yourself with dignity and poise. Your maturity and composure are always noteworthy.

Keeping this in mind, close the door by taking the high road, even if the recruiter doesn't end on a professional note, or if you are advised to have a nice life elsewhere, Write a polite letter (formal, snail mail), always remembering that the best revenge is success.

ELIZABETH T. ARRONET
elizarronet@udel.edu
302-555-6604
5 COURTNEY STREET, RUSSELL, #456
NEWARK, DELAWARE 19716

Today's Date

Ms. Linda Banks
Lead Associate
Cudahy Research Affiliates
29 Hastings, Suite 310
New York, NY 10023

Dear Ms. Banks:

Thank you very much for the opportunity to interview for the research-assistant position. While I am disappointed that there isn't a spot for me right now, I hope you keep me in mind if another opportunity becomes available. I will certainly stay abreast of the industry and continue to sharpen my research skills.

I wish you all the best, and I hope that Cudahy Research Affiliates maintains its strong market presence and dynamic growth.

Sincerely,
Liz Arronet

ELIZABETH T. ARRONET
elizarronet@udel.edu
302-555-6604
5 COURTNEY STREET, RUSSELL, #456
NEWARK, DELAWARE 19716

Today's Date

Ms. Linda Banks
Lead Associate
Cudahy Research Affiliates
29 Hastings, Suite 310
New York, NY 10023

Dear Ms. Banks:

Thank you very much for the opportunity to interview for the research-assistant position. While I am disappointed that we never touched base after my initial interview, I hope you will keep me in mind if the job is still available or if another opportunity presents itself. I will certainly stay abreast of the industry and continue to sharpen my research skills.

I wish you all the best and hope that Cudahy Research Affiliates maintains its strong market presence and dynamic growth.

Sincerely,
Liz Arronet

Chapter 14

Strike Pay Dirt!

"It's similar to finishing up organic chem with a passing grade. Battle weary ... yet, what a high. A toss up between Coldplay's lament, 'Nobody said it was easy,' and James Brown's simple testimony, 'Whoa-oa-aa! I feel good, I knew that I would, now. I feel good, I knew that I would, now. So good, so good, I got you.'"
—*Graduate, Health and Sport Studies Major,*
University of Iowa

His goal: "Courtside seats."

WITH A JOB OFFER to your name and a paycheck on the horizon, you greatly deserve both the glory and chance to tell the war stories that come from your hard-fought battle. Hallelujah and congratulations!

Before settling in to captivate admiring audiences, however, you should take care of a few particulars. Whether you have one or more offers at this point, it's important to proceed with a tactful and very sincere game plan that isn't overshadowed by your new status as a job magnet. Additionally, there are behind-the-scenes details that helped carry the day. All of these particulars should be appropriately addressed and managed for your short- and long-range benefit.

Basically, before you have the wrap party, wrap it up—thoroughly and thoughtfully. And then, keep in mind that your present is always a part of your future. What you have learned throughout the interview process, along with the innumerable ways in which you have grown and triumphed, is meaningful now and in the years to come.

Steer a Steady Course

Considering that your reputation, long-range career strategy, immediate needs, and personal happiness are on the line, you should adhere to a careful, step-by-step strategy for managing a job offer, from the point it is made to the time you respond back to an interested employer. Whether you take the plunge comes down to how you feel about the organization, other details of the position, and your additional prospects. A methodical approach ensures that none of the critical details are neglected at this all-important juncture.

Receiving an Offer

An offer of employment is made in a variety of ways. You might receive it in person, over the phone, via e-mail, or in a letter. In-person, over-the-phone, and e-mail communications are often followed up with a hard-copy summary of the specifics. First, always express your thanks. Either say or write, "Thank you very much. I'm excited to get this offer."

Second, don't accept or reject right away. Ascertain how long you have before a response is needed. Even though your inclination is to take the money and run, there's no need to be hasty. This is true even if the offer represents your one and only opportunity at the moment and even if you want this specific job more than anything. Within a reasonable time frame, the offer is yours and won't be withdrawn. If the employer doesn't indicate a specific deadline, or probes for an answer on the spot, address the issue by posing a question along these lines: "Is it all right if I get back to you after I've had some time to think about your offer?"

Since clarity often comes when a job is more than a dream, you gain meaningful ground by taking a deep breath and stepping back to think through all the particulars. Whether you return in a few days with a yes or a no, momentarily easing off the gas pedal is only to your advantage now.

You might want to ask questions that are very appropriate for someone suddenly in a shopper's, versus a seller's, position. This is an opportunity to get the lowdown on the details that matter to you. "I'm very interested in your offer. Would it be all right if I took a few days to think about this important opportunity you just spelled out, and then get back to you with questions about specifics?"

Or you might need time because you're waiting to hear back after a few other interviews. Rather than trying to be coy, you're far better off to be up-front. "I'm very interested in this opportunity, but I'd like more time to carefully consider your offer and to weigh all my alternatives, if possible." If asked for clarification, reply as follows, without hesitation: "I'm waiting to hear back from another organization, and I would like to take the time to very thoughtfully make a decision, so it is the right one for both of us. I hope this is agreeable."

Chances are, you'll get their blessing. Your request is not unusual, nor is the fact that you are interviewing elsewhere a major news flash. Besides, employers want employees who are fully committed. If the occasional employer plays aggressively, launching a more demanding full-court press like, "No, I'm sorry, we need to know by the end of the month," you don't have the option of crying foul: "I understand. I'll get back to you within the month."

Weighing an Offer

Once you've bought some time, use it judiciously. You're a different person than you were before you started the interview process. You've come down a steep learning curve and you've garnered insight into what life after college is going to be like. Use the journey and the lessons learned as you take this next step. And since your first job out of school often sets you on a course that defines your future path in many ways, this breather is opportune, affording you space before you sign on any dotted lines.

No matter how many tempting offers you have to your name or anticipate entertaining over the next few weeks, carefully study each job to ascertain its fit. Then, if you have additional options, thoughtfully compare the opportunities and let the cream rise to the top.

One by One

Each offer should be evaluated as a standalone opportunity. This is the best way to determine whether a specific chapter belongs in your life story. As you consider the job offer on the table, scrutinize the following:

1. **The particulars outlined in chapter 11's "Hot and Heavy Inquisition" section.** This information covers everything from job responsibilities and salary to health insurance and

vacation days. Ask yourself these questions:
- Is the pay enough to cover my bills and then some?
- Are the benefits decent, and do they meet my realistic needs and desires?
- Can I do the job?
- Am I satisfied with my prospects for growth and upward mobility?
- Am I comfortable with my immediate boss and the reporting relationships?
- Do I have any deal-breaking concerns about the organization and/or other stipulations of employment?
- Is this an organization I would be proud to be a part of?

2. **The connections you made during the interview process.** As you recall your meetings and look through your notes from the past several weeks and months, gauge your comfort level with the individuals you met. Was there anything said or done that requires further clarification, now that you think more about it?

3. **Market/industry dynamics.** Pose these questions to better understand the larger viability of this career move:
   - Is the market strong and/or showing signs of stability and growth?
   - Is the organization well positioned and viable?
   - Are there any worrisome extraneous factors (economy, climate, trade relationships, weather patterns, and so on) potentially impacting business?
   - Is this an industry I am comfortable staking a claim in over the long term? (If not, is it feasible to apply your experiences here to move in other directions down the road? Which directions are feasible?)

4. **Your gut.** What is your overall, most honest sense about this job, and how have you felt about it all along?

5. **Your trustworthy confidant.** What is your confidant's assessment of the opportunity?

The Cream of the Crop

Choosing which offer to go with, if you have the luxury, should be complicated.

Very little in life is absolutely perfect, and most jobs are no exception. Your goal is to find an opportunity that feels right and looks good on paper. As you have seen, the considerations are multifaceted; it doesn't only boil down to perks. The company with the best vacation policy might not make the grade when it comes to your overall career goals.

To figure it all out, slightly massage that old reliable exercise of listing pluses and minuses. Decide which five aspects of any job represent your most critical needs and desires (refer to chapter 1 if you need a reminder regarding your A-to-Z reality). Then, using the specific information you just analyzed about each offer, draw explicit comparisons between the opportunities.

Additionally, always consider two more variables. First, define your overall sense regarding the people, the organization, and the industry—is there an essence of solidness? And second, let your gut and your trustworthy confidant weigh in on the comparison.

You might realize that you need more input in order to make an informed decision; definitely pursue the necessary research or seek out answers from HR for clarification. Once the facts are in, you can clearly analyze the various offers across parameters that are important. While the choice isn't always crystal clear, a winner will slowly but surely emerge.

For example, your evaluation might proceed as follows:

I. Top Five Job Requirements, Plus Two

1. Gross annual salary of at least $39,800
2. Major medical health insurance, at least 50 percent of premium paid
3. Opportunity for promotion within the first eighteen months of employment
4. Location in the Midwest
5. Tuition reimbursement
6. Solidness quotient
7. Gut and trustworthy confidant weigh-in

II. Comparison Between Job Offers

	Job Offer 1	Job Offer 2
1. Gross salary	$42,500	$49,600
2. Health coverage	80% paid	100% paid
3. Promotion opps	Solid	Questionable
4. Midwest	Yes	Yes
5. Tuition	50% and 2 years	No commitment
6. Solidness quotient		
People?	Yes	Yes
Organization?	Yes	Unsure
Industry?	Yes	Unsure
7. Additional Input		
Gut?	Excellent	Fair
Confidant?	Excellent	Poor

III. Analysis

In this particular example, the salary differential is significant and meaningful. However, Job Offer 2 raises concerns that must be considered. The longer term shouldn't be sold for an immediate deposit to the new car fund.

Each of the five parameters might hold a different weight in terms of importance to the person evaluating these two job offers. The points of persuasion are very unique and personal, leading to different decisions for different people. There are no right or wrong answers here; it all boils down to what you want out of the opportunity, now and in your future.

Negotiating an Offer

First-round draft picks and rainmaker executives get to call the shots when it comes to employment deals. And even though a small percentage of college grads makes news headlines with signing bonuses, most new degree holders aren't quite so lucky. Still, there is a sliver of hope for the masses when it comes to asking for a teeny, tiny bit more than what the job offer provides.

True, many HR managers tell recent diploma holders to be satisfied with any offer that comes their way. Their advice is to say thank you and nothing more. These professionals point to the fact that the market keeps businesses honest, so that salaries and perks are largely competitive, especially for entry-level positions.

But a number of HR managers urge that it never hurts to try for more. They confirm that your offer certainly won't be rescinded, and you only have upside potential (albeit miniscule). They caution, however, that it behooves you to continue in a painstakingly professional vein as you make your request in person, over the phone, or in writing.

As you navigate these arbitration waters, keep in mind some decisions are simply nonnegotiable; the verdict is impersonal because of long-standing internal policy or even laws. Paid insurance premiums are a companywide, dyed-in-the-wool benefit that you cannot expect to alter.

Requests that tap into areas where organizations have more wiggle room regarding individual employees will be more readily considered when you indicate the pain you are willing to go through for the gain you are proposing. This helps to take your request out of the "opening the floodgates and setting a dangerous precedent" zone.

> "I wonder if it's possible to increase my tuition reimbursement to 75 percent of the total cost once I have worked here at least a year and receive a performance review with a rating of excellent or above."

> "Because I am very interested in upward mobility, I wonder if I could have a performance and salary review after nine months instead of one year. I'm willing to make this contingent on my ability to secure at least one national account by the end of eight months on the job."

Fair-game negotiating possibilities for new college grads with an offer in hand are outlined below. Definitely arbitrate any one of these before accepting the offer. Choose only one major goody, and don't assume you have agentlike rights to keep going for the jugular. You usually have a single shot, and that's it. Any agreements reached should be confirmed in writing. "I'd like to confirm our recent discussion in which you agreed to _____. I hope you will let me know if I misunderstood the specifics in any way. Thank you very much."

- **Salary.** The most negotiating takes place regarding salary, where there is some latitude to improve for new college grads. You must stay within the humble realm of reason, however. And don't lie about an offer from another organization, but by all means use this if it is a reality.
  "I appreciate your offer and am very interested. However, I was hoping that the salary would be approximately ten percent higher to meet my needs. Is it possible to consider this request, please?"
  "I appreciate your offer and I'd like to accept … however, I've been offered five thousand dollars more annually from another organization. This is a meaningful amount, given my school loans. I'm wondering if you are able to similarly increase my starting salary."
- **Time off (this will be without pay) for a trip already on the books.** Your paid vacation might not be available until you've clocked in several months of employment. If you have plans to attend a family reunion and would very much like to see your Aunt Mae, you can ask for this time off without pay.
- **Start date.** If possible, enjoy yourself; this is about as footloose as you will ever be in your life. You can't postpone for a year, but a month or two longer is often doable.
- **Relocation to another office in a more desirable location.** If relocation isn't an option now, perhaps it is available down the road.
  "I'm committed to this job and excited about starting in Atlanta. But my longer-term goal is to return to Boston. Is it possible to be considered for relocation to the Boston office after a year?"
- **Length of time until your first performance/salary review.** The goal is to increase your responsibilities and/or pay on a faster schedule.
- **Tuition reimbursement (amount and/or timing regarding eligibility).**
- **Increased responsibility.** "I would really like a shot at repping two territories simultaneously and believe I can handle the challenge."

Responding to an Offer

It's time to let the employer know whether you're on board. At this point, you are either wanting to pull a fast one, feeling totally confused, walking away, or preparing to commit.

Pulling a Fast One

You'd like to keep interviewing *and* you want to hang onto this one offer until you're sure all others are exhausted. As a matter of fact, you're thinking about yielding to pressure and saying yes, only to bid a very hasty retreat if the A-list advertising world opens up its arms to you sometime over the next month. After all, no one need be the wiser, since this will never show up on your résumé.

While it's tough to condone disreputable behavior, posturing and manipulation are tempting when the pieces don't fall into place. You're dealing with deadlines and other people's agendas, and you have a lot riding on this decision. It's easy to see how these ingredients combine to encourage a less-than-honorable approach.

Still, be as up-front with prospective employers as possible. If you need more time—and even though you may have pushed way too hard already—ask. Such requests are far better than shady tactics. You might believe that what happens here stays here, but remember that we live in a small world after all—especially when corporations operate in the same town and within like industries. Looking over your shoulder at the ripe old age of twenty-two isn't the way to start your career.

If you get caught in a bind and are made to face up to a mess you created, be appropriately chagrined and indicate that you've learned your lesson. "I apologize. I got caught in a bind. Instead of managing the situation by being up-front, I thought I could quietly handle this on my own without bothering anyone else. I realize this was a bad decision, and I understand that it is far better to approach those involved for support and advice."

Totally Confused

Despite all your efforts, you still can't decide. You're definitely sitting on the fence, worrying about falling down hard on one or both sides. While some of this simply goes with the territory, it might also be an indication that this wasn't meant to be. To sort out where your head is at, try the following.

- **Revisit your analysis.** Even though you've gone over it ad nauseam, give it one last review, tweaking the way you look at the opportunity. If you're comparing offers, expand your list of key requirements from five to eight and see if clarity bubbles forth. Or ask to meet with another employee (or travel with a sales rep) for additional insights.
- **Consult with your trustworthy confidant.** You've come full circle together and this isn't a time to cut the apron strings. Use this rock to enhance your perspective yet again.
- **Be honest with the employer.** While baring your soul is dicey, it has been done—to everyone's advantage. Obviously, this approach must be handled professionally, and you can't use a prospective employer as your daily sounding board or as a close gal pal.

"I'm sorry to be so indecisive; I rarely operate this way, and you certainly won't see it from me on the job. I'd like you to know that I am torn between two very attractive offers. My main concern boils down to working in Seattle for at least three years before being considered for an East Coast transfer."

Walking Away

While it's usually hard to let any job offer go, it's especially difficult when you don't have another opportunity waiting in the wings. Unless there is something that absolutely repulses you about the one and only job offer you hold right now, it's important for you to realize that you shouldn't say no easily.

As you go through life (choosing a college, buying and selling houses, and so on), you'll realize that your best offer is often made at the onset. Many new college grads admit they made a mistake when they turned down their first job offer. These individuals admit to believing that opportunities were a dime a dozen, and they were a hot enough commodity that they could afford to wait for the ideal position and salary. A majority of these candidates further confess how wrong they were. Many had to scramble for months and ultimately ended up with work that was even less desirable.

And sometimes it's worth giving the underdog a chance. If you start with both feet in, and a will-do attitude, you often make luscious lemonade out of a crop that might seem a bit sour. Many grads who ended up with a job several notches down from perfection have found satisfaction and career bliss.

Still, you have to be excited enough about the job and the opportunity ahead. If you simply can't muster the enthusiasm and commitment to give it a fair shot, or you clearly prefer one job over another, you must tell the employer you are turning down their offer.

Phone the person who extended you the offer and explain your decision. A direct conversation is more professional than leaving a voice message or e-mail (unless directed otherwise by the organization). "Thank you very much for your offer. I'm very impressed with the people I've met and the organization as a whole. I've thought a great deal about the opportunity you presented, and while it was a difficult decision to make, I'm not accepting the offer."

If asked for the reason behind your decision, you are not obligated to share specifics ... and actually, it's sometimes a cheap shot to do so: "Well, for starters, I got five grand more a year from Pelham Industries." Rather, you politely indicate where you're headed. "I'm accepting an offer from Pelham Industries in their inventory management and purchasing department." Or, "I'm continuing to investigate opportunities available in the market."

If you end up with a nosy associate who wants to know why, your response shouldn't place blame. You're better off to isolate one somewhat personal factor on which to hinge your explanation. "I realize it makes sense for me to pursue my interests in hospital administration; I will now dedicate my efforts exclusively to opportunities in this field." Or, "While I originally believed that relocating to another part of the country was agreeable, I now realize that it is very important to me that I remain on the West Coast."

If you end up being treated poorly or receiving a snide comment (it happens, but rarely), be a bigger and better person and exit on the highest of notes. "Thank you again for the opportunity. Good-bye."

Committing

This is about as good as it gets: smiles all the way around, and everyone's future looks bold and bright. Accepting a job requires that you shout it from the rooftops by picking up the phone and making direct contact with the person who extended the offer. "Thank you very much for the offer. I've thought a lot about it, and I'm very excited about the opportunity you presented. I would like to accept, and I look forward to coming on board."

If you haven't negotiated your start date or additional time off for your great grandma's birthday bash in Poughkeepsie later this year, now is the time to throw out these curveballs in request form. "I'd like to make a request, please."

Following Up

Basically, this is akin to an Academy Awards acceptance speech. You have a great number of thank-yous to deliver. Start by expressing gratitude to all of the organizations that extended you a job offer. Finish up with the mothership—the people in your personal camp.

Thanks for the Offer

You should always send a hard-copy letter expressing thanks to the person who extended you the job offer (if you got particularly close to others during the interview process, you can't go wrong by also sending these individuals their own letters). This is true even if you are declining an offer.

There are two reasons to go to this length. One, these organizations have gone to a lot of trouble and time to meet with you—often on several occasions. They have also expressed enough interest to extend you a coveted job, usually to the exclusion of other candidates. Two, you're still dancing to the same old song: you will likely bump into these people again not too far down the road. It would be unwise to break rhythm now.

Your letter should be brief and very direct. Use the same professional format and presentation you have since you penned your first cover letter way back when. When there are "off the beaten path" negotiation specifics that you have agreed to, this is a good time to reiterate these. It's also smart to mention your start date, so this is very clear.

Les Colton McCarthy
7 Spire Drive
Little Rock, Arkansas 72223
lesmac@spool.com   501-555-9533

Today's Date

Mr. Scott McCallister
Regional Sales Manager
Ahearn Pharmaceuticals Inc.
One Ahearn Parkway
Aberdeen, Arkansas 72134

Dear Mr. McCallister:

Thank you very much for the offer of employment you extended last week. I'm glad we had a chance to talk further on the phone a few days ago. As we discussed, I am very excited to accept the sales-associate job and I look forward to starting on July 7. You were kind enough to understand plans I have with my family for the week of August 12, when I will be absent from work for five days.

I appreciate the time you and other individuals at Ahearn Pharmaceuticals Inc. took to meet with me over these past several weeks. I learned a lot and certainly understand why the organization is so successful. The new-product introductions will undoubtedly be well received at the sales meeting this month.

I will see you in a few weeks, and I am anxious to hit the ground running. Thank you again.

Sincerely,
Les Colton McCarthy

Thanks for Everything

There are a lot of people who helped and pulled hard for you. While you personally brought it on home, there is no question that your job offer was a team effort. It's appropriate to let these individuals know the outcome of your trials and tribulations.

Most of these supporters aren't looking for flowers or extravagant dinners in a fancy restaurant (although a small, special token for those who went above and beyond is fitting). Rather, the people in your camp want to know that you landed on your feet, and what the next chapter of your life holds. They want to celebrate your success.

As you go down this long list of champions, be considerate and thorough. These backers deserve your heartfelt, sincere gratitude. And since you and your team clearly form a winning combination, this is a peanut gallery you want on your side into the future.

Give a call, send an e-mail, or write a letter. The following are among the people who deserve a great big "thank you for everything":

- Parents
- College career-center office staff
- Professors, coaches and other college staff
- Individuals who wrote your letters of recommendation
- Previous employers
- Other relatives
- Friends of the family
- Good buddies
- Confidant

Take Note

Record keeping is meant to be a lifelong responsibility. The sooner you accept "the right stuff" mentality (chapter 6) as a routine proposition, the more benefits you will derive. A list of tail-end interview and job-start details to document is included here.

Update Old Files

Reexamine your interviews for noteworthy information. Think about details you received involving movers and shakers; potential contacts; any general, pertinent tips; and personal feedback. Update your Interview Lineup, Market Stats, and Personal Bytes files. These particulars are food for thought today and beneficial for future reference as you go forward and make a name and place for yourself in the world after college.

Create New Employment Files

Each time you begin a new job, start a new folder (Current Employment—[Organization Name]) on your computer. Record personal information and stipulations pertaining to your employment, action plans regarding your new position, and strategies for furthering your career. Rename this folder (Previous Employment—[Organization Name]) when you leave for another opportunity at a different organization. Rather than dragging yesterday's news into the trash, you'll want to keep your history accessible for reference purposes.

Also, keep track of general data about individuals within the organization, contacts you make, and relevant details you encounter about the market and industry. Keep this information focused on the professional aspects of your job and relationships, rather than making this a "dish and bitch at will" diary. In this way, you will always have critical details (of which there are many on most jobs) at your fingertips.

Organize these specifics by creating three files within the current-employment folder: Personal, Company, and Industry. Make it a habit to update these documents at least every few months (every change of season is a logical benchmark)—and possibly monthly. Include the following information in these files:

Personal File
1. General Details
    Person who extended the offer (name, title, date)
    Start date
    Title
    Reporting relationships
    Compensation
    Benefits
            Insurance
            Vacation policy
            Personal days/sick pay
            Other
    Company property issued
    Company credit card issued
            Type
            Number
            CID
            Phone number in case of loss or theft
    Other

2. Insurance Particulars
Major medical coverage
       Carrier
       Group number
       Identification number
       Address and phone
Dental coverage
       Carrier
       Group number
       Identification number
       Address and phone
Prescription benefits
       Carrier
       Group number
       Identification number
       Address and phone
Other

3. Days Off
Vacation days taken (note when and what you did)
Other days taken (note when and what you did)

4. Performance-Review Information
Reviewer name and date
Brief summary
       Strengths
       Weaknesses
       Explicit recommendations
       Other
General feeling about the review
Other

5. Career Movement
Date of promotion or lateral move
Title
New responsibilities
Update General Details (above in number 1) regarding compensation, reporting relationships, and so on after a promotion or lateral move.

Update Company (below) file, if necessary, after a promotion or lateral move.

6. Three Reasons I'm Satisfied Working Here

7. Three Changes I'll Undertake to Improve My Job Over the Next Six Months

8. Other

Company File

1. Details About the Boss
    Name
    Title
    Brief background
    Hot buttons
    Known likes/dislikes
    Other

2. Department/Division Specifics
    Overall structure
    Key players
    Teamwork dynamics
    Immediate goals
    Recent major changes
    Other

3. Organization Specifics
    Overall structure
    Key players
    Overall culture
    Financial health
    Top three challenges
    Recent major changes
    Other

4. Other

Industry File
1. Economic Climate
   Key factors impacting our organization
   Major recent shifts or changes
   Forecast
   Other

2. Competitive Overview
   Key competitors
   Comparison
   Noteworthy news
   Other

3. Career-Furthering Opportunities
   What
   Why or why not
   Timing considerations
   Other

4. Other

Routinely collecting and cataloging information ensures that you are organized, perpetually informed, and more reasonable than knee-jerk. With archived facts and figures, you can periodically take a step back to thoughtfully examine particulars that define you in so many ways. Consequently, you have a chance to leverage opportunities at the right time. This is healthy and strategic.

Stay Hungry. Stay Foolish.

Purpose and effectiveness: they got you here and will assuredly serve you well into the future. As you start this new chapter in your life, use what you learned from your interview process to help you capitalize, from day one, on all you bring to the job. After all, you haven't just crossed a finish line—you've started a robust new journey.

You are clearly capable of seizing big opportunities. This came from within and from your willingness to accept the offer of time-honored advice. The tried-and-true, along with your distinct skill set, trustworthy instincts, and hard work put you squarely on the road to success.

So sit back, slide on those flip-flops for a glorious, celebratory moment, and reflect on what you now better understand about yourself and the importance of plugging in, connecting, and powering up. Then floor it toward your very bright future, staying hungry and foolish all the while.

- Maintain a positive attitude.
- Embrace your financial obligations as your reality and personal responsibility.
- Continuously recognize and leverage all that you bring to the table.
- Count on your friends and family and let them count on you.
- Be confident, but humble.
- Understand that your reputation can, and generally will, be used against you or for you.
- Prepare well.
- Prepare even more, recognizing that it's hard to find fault with earnest effort.
- Thoughtfully and proactively step outside the box sometimes.
- Remember that your head-to-toe appearance counts every single day.
- Stay organized and on top of record keeping.
- Maintain a balanced, focused approach.
- Strive to be interesting, interested, likable, and valuable.
- Be respectful, honorable and polite to a fault.
- Be punctual and always follow-up on a timely basis. Ten minutes early is on time.
- When in doubt (or when emotions threaten to get the better of you), default to a professional demeanor.
- Keep plan B in your hip pocket.
- When the going gets tough, get going.
- Take the time to routinely and strategically look ahead.
- Cut yourself some slack every so often.
- Routinely express your heartfelt thanks.
- Celebrate the good times.
- Own your endeavors and the path they take.
- Smile often.

Conclusion

The plot of *The Devil Wears Prada* comes to mind; the details suddenly hit close to home. Andy Sachs, newly graduated from Northwestern University, showed up for her job interview with onion breath, fully intent on "writing her own ticket" after sticking it out for a mere year at *Runway* magazine. After fumbling her way up the elevator, she admitted to being clueless about her potential boss, the editor in chief. As a matter of fact, Andy had never even thumbed through the fashion bible she planned to write for. We won't even talk about the frumpy interview outfit Ms. Sachs proudly wore to this meeting. Suffice it to say that "painful" aptly describes Andy's job interview and her launch into the working world.

It can be argued that Andy ultimately triumphed and perhaps needed to learn the important lessons the hard way. But most successful professionals confirm that clinching a rewarding first job doesn't have to be as gut-wrenching as it was for Andy. She paid a far too exorbitant price simply because she didn't subscribe to a fundamental formula centered on purpose and effectiveness. True, these come with their own set of responsibilities and sacrifices, but not at the expense of your integrity, relationships, and self-respect. Andy almost lost it all.

You're no longer this vulnerable, nor so naive. As you turn the last page of this book, you will hopefully realize that the formula isn't complicated once you accept ownership. If you approach your job interviews, and this next phase of your life, with the conviction to plug in through A-to-Z preparation; forge meaningful connections via an honest, tuned-in effort; and power up with initiative and perseverance, you will accomplish much and achieve your dreams. You'll do this over and over again.

I wouldn't steer you wrong; I owe you as much.

Sources

In order to provide the best information about interviewing for soon-to-be degree holders and recent college grads, I drew from a number of resources. Most notable are the hundreds of interviews and conversations I have had with young career professionals over the past two decades. Their unique experiences, with all the inherent challenges and triumphs, form the basis for the most valuable insights found on these pages.

Additional Key Sources

Armour, Stephanie. "Generation Y: They've Arrived at Work With a New Attitude." *USA Today.* November 6, 2005.

Basic Quotations. http://www.basicquotations.com

Covey, Steven R. *The 7 Habits of Highly Effective People.* New York: Simon and Schuster, 1989.

"Generations at Work." *HR Matters.* Temple University Department of Human Resources. Fall 2002.

The Last Whole Earth Catalog: Access to Tools. New York: Random House, 1971.

McGinn, Daniel. "Helping Get That First Job." *Newsweek.* December 5, 2005.

NACE (National Association of Colleges and Employers). "One in 10 Employers Will Use Social Networking Sites to Review Job Candidate Information." *NACEWeb.* September 2, 2006. http://www.naceweb.org

NACE (National Association of Colleges and Employers) Principles for Professional Conduct Committee. "Principles for Professional Conduct for Career Services and Employment Professionals." *NACEWeb.* http://www.naceweb.org

NACE (National Association of Colleges and Employers) Technology Committee. "Bridging the Gap Between Student Expectations and Employer Reality: Electronic Tools and College Recruiting." *NACEWeb.* http://www.naceweb.org

Scott, Mary E. "Can High Tech Coexist with High Touch? Online Application Processes and Career Fairs." *NACEWeb.* Summer 2004. http://www.naceweb.org

Smith, Lee. "How Nexters Behave in the Workplace." *Fortune.* November 14, 2005.

Warren, Rick. *The Purpose Driven Life.* Michigan: Zondervan Publishing Company, 2002.

Weisberger, Lauren. *The Devil Wears Prada.* New York: Doubeleday/Random House, 2003.

Index

While luck is never a strategy,
I hope it's a bonus you occasionally enjoy.

Michael, Andy, Jamie, Maggie, Marshall, Nicholas, Laura, Mark, David, Lisa, Justin, Jade, Kristina, Katherine, Alexandra, Cassie, Maggie, Brennan, Chelsea, Duncan, Matt, Catherine, Lisa, Gordon, Goose, Andrew, Brielle, Molly, Stephan, Daniel, John, Adam, Chris, Greg, Brad, Lani, Matt, Lisa, Amy, Michelle, Jon, Matt, Peter, Andy, Walker, Anna, Adam, Max, Jack, Joe, Megan, Paul, Caroline, C.C., Neal, Dirk, Emily, Kim, Erik, Ariana, Kate, John, Brian, Bonnie, Phil, Katherine, Laura, Erik, Jimmy, Doug, Robert, Ryan, Caitlin, Melissa, and Maddi.